*Proceeds to Benefit*

*San Francisco Sunnydale*

*Boys and Girls Club*

*www.kidsclub.org/sunnydale*

# A Song For
# MS HENRIETTA

A Community Matriarch's Bedside Story
About The Community and The People She Loved and
HER UNSHAKEABLE FAITH FOR HER BELOVED COMMUNITY
San Francisco's "Sunnydale Housing Projects"

And The Mayor's Office of Housing and
Community Development

## DARRO JEFFERSON

**To order additional copies of this book, contact:**
Xlibris
844-714-8691
www.Xlibris.com
Orders@Xlibris.com
855273

# What is Sunnydale Hope SF?

*VISIONS DREAMS HOPE*
*TO REVITALIZE THE PHYSICAL IMAGE*
*AND NEIGHBORHOOD FABRIC*
*In San Francisco's Sunnydale Housing Projects*

# A Song for Ms Henrietta

**OUR STORY
OF
COMMUNITYSHIP RESISTANCE
TOGETHERNESS COMMUNITY PRIDE
AND THE PEOPLE IN SAN FRANCISCO'S
SUNNYDALE HOUSING PROJECTS WHO MADE
OUR PLACE ON THE PLANET MAGICAL**

**Gloria Ann Pitre**

*A Quest of Two Communities From The Same Neighborhood
One Revisiting its Rich History
The Other Struggling to Shed its Negative Image
In San Francisco's Sunnydale Public
Housing Projects Community*

**Mother Hopkins and the Roberts Family
Every Kid In Sunnydale Played Outside The Recreation
Center Sitting Atop Benny "The Bear" Bufano**

### In the Sunnydale Projects

*Not a day went by that I didn't spend time riding on the Bear in front of the Recreation Center. I think I still have a few of the bumps and bruises to remind me"* **Kathy Stewart**

# A Song for Ms Henrieta

*By Darro Van Jefferson*

*A Community Matriarch's Bedside-Story*
*About The Community and The People She Loved*
*HER*
*UNSHAKEABLE FAITH FOR HER BELOVED COMMUNITY*
*San Francisco's "Sunnydale Housing Project*

# CONTENTS

# Our Story

*When you come from a struggling Community, from a Family that struggles day to day to provide and place food on the table, then I have no doubt you will embrace our story. Should you not come from such a place, then you will not understand what it is like to carry a crinkled, wrinkled up recycled greasy brown paper bag to school for lunch containing if you were lucky, Government Cheese, SPAM, Butter, Sugar, Mayonnaise, Gravy with three day old Meatloaf and "Wish Me Sandwiches" if you don't know anything about "Wish Me Sandwiches" they are two pieces of bread and you make a wish you had some meat. Only someone from a struggling family would know about these nourishing Sandwiches*

*Randy Roc Minix*

# Dedication

*To my mother Victoria Manning Jefferson and Theresa Etoy Jefferson who encouraged me to read, write and recite the literature that inspired me.*

*To the countless unsung Mothers Women of Sunnydale who raised us while carrying the weight of an entire community on their tiny but powerful and caring shoulders.*

*To my Brother Victor Doran Jefferson, RIP for bringing home those Black Scholar Magazines with contributing articles by James Baldwin, Nikki Giavonni, Lorraine Hansberry and countless other prolific Black Writers,*

*To Dr Carlton B Goodlett, Publisher of the legendary Metro Sun Reporter Newspaper and his Editor in Charge Thomas Fleming who took me under their literary wings and taught me how to fly.*

*To the Sons and Sisters of Sunnydale, Forever grateful am I.*

# A Song for Ms Henrietta

## With The

# Sons n Sista's of Sunnydale

*From the Desk of Neal Hatten*
*Director of Administration*
*Bayview Senior Services*

*Dear Reader:*

*I sometimes think I've been in the community service arena too long. Five decades is undoubtedly a long time to have worked in youth development, workforce development, sheltering unhoused (mostly Black San Franciscans), and (currently) serving my fellow seniors.*

*However, when I consider the accomplishments of Ms. Henrietta and the many colorful characters Darro Jefferson portrays in this book, I realize that I still have work to do to rise to their level of commitment and caring about a neighborhood.*

*I'm one of those now increasingly rare San Francisco natives. I spent my infancy in the Crocker Amazon projects adjacent to the Sunnydale neighborhood that Darro recalls herein. From about 3 years of age.*

*I grew up in the Bayview (later dubbed Bayview Hunters Point) community. And, though I infrequently visited the Sunnydale neighborhood in my younger years, I met Jefferson, aka "Mack Jeff" (just one of close to a dozen nicknames) around 16. I was introduced to him by "Big Doug," whom I met at school in the third grade and whose family moved to the Sunnydale projects a few years later, making him one of that community's "Sons."*

*Darro and I formed an odd friendship that I initially didn't understand.*

*He was tall, athletic, and very much the lady's man, and I not so much any of that.*

*However, I later realized our love for literature and laughter forged a friendship. We were and still are fascinated by the possibilities of the written and spoken word. Darro's internship with KALW allowed me and Barry Shabaka Henley to produce a radio program for several years.*

*We also performed poetry at venues throughout the Bay Area in the mid to late '70s before "spoken word" became a thing.*

*More importantly, Darro's connection to a fledgling non-profit organization put me on the community service path I continue to walk down.*

*Generously woven with the remembrances that the "Sons and Sistas of Sunnydale" have about Henrietta "Momma" Harris, this book captures the indomitable resilience of a community of people who, while barely holding on financially, were enriched by an undying love and support of each other.*

*One teller remembers Momma Harris as a community first responder, "...it seems every time someone was going through something, she was there like First Alert. With her there was no need to call 911, she was already and always there to help in the nick of time."*

*Her service to others persisted even during her final days in the hospital as Jefferson recalls a nurse told the many visitors that "...*

*they were having a hard time keeping up with her because most of the time she was not in her room but paying visits to other patients in the hospital, many of them not even on her same floor."*

*With his own multiple decades-long commitment to community service, my friend Darro uses his professional background to inform his colorful prose, mixed deftly with the stories shared by Sunnydale's youth of yesteryear, those "Sons and Sisters" who have all worked hard at building a legacy of their own. While not ignoring Sunnydale's tremendous challenges, like other of San Francisco's poorest communities, the people in this book uplift the essential ingredient to overcoming adversity—a caring person who takes direct action to help others.*

*Occasionally, some people depicted in this book strayed off course; fortunately, the "Song of Ms. Henrietta" and the songs of others like her continue to get most of us past the hard times.*

*In closing, I need to express my gratitude to Darro for putting this work together.*

*Stories like the ones shared in this book always touch me deeply; they keep me inspired and ever-interested in living up to the example of all the Momma Henrietta's of the world.*

*Neal Hatten,*
*Community Servant*

# Introduction

*A Song for Ms Henrietta*
*With The*
*Sons n Sista's of Sunnydale*
*Tribute to the Mothers of Sunnydale*

*A Song for Ms Henrietta, is more than a story about two long time friends Georgia Hughes and Henrietta Harris two Sunnydale community matriarchs who both knew their blessed time on this precious earth was nearing and the promise made between them to sing a Song at the Homegoing services of whoever between them would leave this earth ahead of the other.*

*Our hope is that the following offering will serve as a constructive instrument to help restore and revitalize economically challenged communities.*

*At **Henrietta's HomeGoing** service before a small gathering who came to pay their final respects at the San Francisco Christian Center, **Georgia Hughes** more than delivered on her promise to pay **Tribute and Remembrance to her longtime friend.***

*Henrietta Harris left this ole earth well into her <u>90's</u>.*

*Ida Pitre of Sunnydale went to the heavens <u>1 month short of her 100 Birthday</u>*

*Izola Cudjo Frierson Sunnydale's Unsung Community Leader passed at the youthful age of 101*

*Sunnydale of their past no longer exists but their legacy will not be forgotten.*

***Georgia Hughes'*** *rendition of one of gospel's greats, legendary singer **Shirley Ceasar's Precious Lord**, brought the SFCC audience to their knees.*

*A fitting tribute to a Sunnydale community matriarch **Ms Henrietta**.*

*Unfortunately what was not a fitting send off for her to the **Pearly Gates wearing a long white robe and golden slippers,** was there were less than **100** people in attendance to say farewell to the woman who had given so much of herself to the Sunnydale community, and the families and the people she loved unconditionally without reservation or hesitation.*

*How could Sunnydale, her beloved community, forget her?*

*Many of those from back in the day had moved, some too proud to look back and remember the woman who had paved the way in the making and development of their community way before **Sunnydale** began to decline and become known as the **"Swamp"** a neglected, isolated prideless community of violence, desperation and hopelessness*

*Less than 100 people! A cryn' shame, a piss poor representation and no excuse for those who knew of her passing and did not attend her funeral. 100 people! A cryn' shame! A piss poor representation! For a Ceremony that should have been Meant For A Queen*

**The Writer and Contributors Of**
***A Song for Ms Henrietta***
**Dedicate Our Then and Now Story To The People**
**Of The**
**"The Sunnydale Housing Projects"**

The Sons and Sistas of Sunnydale invite you to join us on this wonderful journey *as we travel back through time, through the 1950's, the 60's, the early days of the 70's.an experience the brotherhood, communityship, the happiness, the sorrow, hardships and cherished memories we never left behind.*

*We hope that you will share that this composition serves as an instrument to unite communities throughout.*

**Alvin Burleson. The Dale helped make us who we are today**

**Randy 'Roc" Minix, Communities like Sunnydale are rich with history**

**Skip Roberts, My hope is that this story will enhance people's lives**

**Glen GT Taylor, Good things now are happening in Sunnydale**

**Thomas Warren, The community changes appear to be more than just fresh paint**

**Eric Peters, Every community and the people who live there should have a sense of pride**

*James Nelson, It was through adversity and reliance of some truly remarkable women who struggled and endured the tough times is what kept our community together. Single mothers raising one another's children through Prayer and Sacrifice*

*Kermit Burleson, Time has stood still much too long in Sunnydale. Today I am proud that the future of our community is bright*

*Annette Hughes, The people there now are deserving of new changes*

*TC Caracter, Sunnydale is making progress. The future there is bright*

*Harold Williams, A high five to the people in the neighborhood*

*Sunday Go To Meeting Day*
*The Bishops, Ms Bishop, {L to R} Sista's, Ruth and Juanita, Maxine Hughes GT Bishop and Bubba Hughes*

*"Where we lived and the people we grew up with Darro more than captures the intricate lifestyles of our treasured past by going through the neighborhood, at times almost going door to door and bringing to Life the priceless day to day Life experiences and true total essence of the people in the Sunnydale Housing Projects. I am so proud, extremely grateful to join Darro and the Sons and Sisters of Sunnydale on this most remarkable journey back to a Place So Magical Indeed" Gloria Ann Pitre*

*"Little Jeff, he was known in the Sunnydale Community as, and I grew up together. It's not surprising at all to me that he has authored A Song for Ms Henrietta. I can vividly remember even though we were kids playing football in the park, Darro had a pen and paper in his back pocket. No doubt my brother must have had this story, our story in his visions way back then. He in my honest opinion has truly captured in our story many of the times we all shared together" Al Burleson*

*We all used to ride the 15 Third city bus from Sunnydale to wherever then return back to the neighborhood. DJ's composition is almost as if he gathered up a busload of us from Sunnydale. With that said I personally would like to thank him for letting me ride along with the people from our community and share in this magnificent sometimes painful journey back home. Like we would tell my Mother after she cooked one of her delicious meals, "Momma you put your foot in it" Brother DJ you did just that, put your foot, heart and soul into A Song for Ms Henrietta" Skip Roberts*

*"I would come to the Jefferson house and grub on Ms Jefferson's screaming sandwiches. I couldn't count the many books the family had on the living room coffee table. Reading and writing was in the Families DNA" Randy Roc Minix*

*"My brother, you have dug deep into the rich history of the Sunnydale Housing Projects. Your reflections of the people in our community*

*are vivid reminders of where I grew up yet what I love is how you have not ignored some of the dreadful things that brought our community down to its knees while all the time writing with hope and promise for a better day in the neighborhood" Maxine Hughes*

*"My younger brother has enjoyed a storied career in broadcasting and journalism. Not only do I have several of his Stage Plays but Darro writes with a contagious sensitivity, a style that draws the reader or audience into his creative spaces of originality. His Stage Play Daffodil, the story of a young inner city woman trying to escape the pitfalls and generational dependency of our Public Welfare System he wrote sitting inside the County Public Assistance Offices in San Francisco". I can only offer my younger brother the utmost support and thanks for recreating our story of the Sunnydale Housing Projects" Respectfully, Coyle Jefferson*

# The Creation of This Composition

### *A Song for Ms Henrietta*

*Our hope is that the following offering will serve as a constructive instrument to help restore faith and trust in economically challenged communities that once were.*

*Life in San Francisco's Sunnydale Housing Projects was far different then in 2012 when San Francisco based KCBS news reporter Doug Sovern's Cover Story broadcast "The Dangers of Living in SF's Sunnydale Housing Projects" a compelling hard hitting account of lifelessness, drugs and violence in Sunnydale.*

*"The community was a cultural acceptance of violence" said former San Francisco District Supervisor Malia Cohen, who represented the community. "People become so desensitized to it"*

*The airing of KCBS broadcasts placed Sunnydale on the map as one of the most dangerous and notorious housing projects in the nation.*

*The story painted a vivid portrait of what day-by-day life challenges the community faced at the time the story was broadcast.*

*However like most news breaking stories the events, although timely, landed miles short of capturing Sunnydale's rich history and sense of community making this composition most significant and necessary.*

*I made a vow to myself that one day I would revisit Sunnydale and help share its treasured past.*

***Sunnydale*** *was once a prideful self resilient community governed by its love and humanity.*

*In creating this composition I discovered several significant journalistic revelations of my own career path that coincide with a number of economic, political and social events that are timeless and necessary to share with you.*

*In 1984 as a young roving street news reporter for Oakland based KDIA Radio News.*

*I was encouraged by* **Clarence Johnson** *News Director and local city alumnus who had family ties in the neighborhood to produce a series of similar reports on Sunnydale that I declined instead taking an assignment with black radio pioneers Vince Sanders and Ed Castleberry of the National Black Network {NBN} covering the Democratic National Convention at San Francisco's Moscone Center. The same year Jesse Jackson ran for President.*

*The opportunity to be a part of a legendary broadcast team providing live gavel-to-gavel coverage was a tremendous opportunity but left me with empty feelings of regret.*

***This*** *is more than a story, or trip down the author's memory lane but an honest depiction and reflection through the eyes and lives of the people who lived in the Sunnydale Community and what life was about growing up in the* ***Sunnydale Housing Projects.***

***The writer and contributors*** *invite you to join us on this rewarding journey of discovery, introducing you to the people and families in the community going door-to-door to meet with them and share with you the reader intricate details of their lives and challenges, a collaboration of individuals dedicated to preserving that memory.*

xxx

*"We didn't have much but we had each other. There were some tough times, some families struggled more than others but none of them were looked down upon. An extra biscuit, some leftover food went a mighty long way and was shared. People were welcome in each others home" Dwayne Robins*

*"We were young and we did some silly things but there were those dudes who far exceeded what Ghetto calamity was about. We had a few characters "dumber than a box of rocks" as my Father would say. I mean the idea of sniffing model airplane glue in a brown paper bag or siffling gas from cars to get high ain't my idea of having fun. In fact it was suicidal, them cats sadly I am sure some of them are no longer with us probably as a result of graduating to more hardcore drugs" Eric Peters*

*"There was a Thrift Store on Hahn Street where folks could buy used clothes real cheap and if our mothers couldn't afford to buy a jacket or something for the house the people at the store would give it away to the person in need. All of the stores in the neighborhood were like that. The business owners were as much apart of the community as the people who lived there" Kermit Burleson*

*"When we came home from school there was always a Mother outside looking out for us especially the young girls in the community" Lisa Burleson*

*"I was as much of a tomboy as any of the girls, jumping off the washhouses playing dodgeball, a day never passed when young girls like me growing up in Sunnydale were outside playing street project games with the boys and some of us could out run and jump them knuckleheads to" Kathy Friierson*

*"We as a community were always there for one another. That's not to say the people who live there now cannot enjoy the same kind of communityship, but it's going to take people pulling together for*

*one another. I think the right people can make that happen if the community is willing to trust them and what they stand for" Leon Booker*

*"Sunnydale was rich with pride and people who cared for one another. That's not to say we didn't experience our share of suffering, bad times and the loss of young innocent lives from drugs and violence. But during the difficult times families were there for one another" Robert Taylor*

*"I was part of the old Sunnydale and lived in Sunnydale when things began to decline. It don't take no rocket scientist to figure out what way of living the folks from the Swampe D would choose between the two" Dennis Pettway*

*"We moved to Sunnydale in the early 1950's quite a contrast to what the neighborhood has experienced but a tremendous joy it brings to knowing that there are new things on the horizon for the people who live there now" Melvin Pitre*

*"The women mothers in Sunnydale carried themselves with dignity and grace, they served as positive role models for young girls growing up in the community" Debra Lablanc*

*"Life may have dealt us not the best of hands but because people cared for each other hard times were made easier. Sunnydale was a place where troubles and trying times were shared among the people" TC Caracter*

*"Outside our world may have been closed to us but that didn't and doesn't really matter now and especially back then. To me the people who wrote us off and left us alone to survive are the unfortunate ones because they were not apart of something so true and beautiful, a community rich with pride and more importantly a community with genuine concern for their brothers and sisters" Gloria Ann Pitre*

*"I thought Sunnydale was a utopia, a land far away, another world from the hustle and bustle of other well known San Francisco communities. We were on the outskirts of town, isolated but on the inside strong were we"* Rafiki Webster

# A Song for Ms Henrietta

*With The*

# Sons n Sista's of Sunnydale

Randy Roc Minix, Walter Harris, Glen
Chop Porter and Royce Lloyd

*Invite You On This Wonderful Journey
Back To Our Neighborhood
San Francisco's Sunnydale Housing Projects*

# A Song for Ms Henrietta

## *With Personal Testimonies From*

Michael Harris, LaFrance Graves, Coyle Jefferson, Otis "Bubba" Hughes, Melvin Pitre, Eric Peters, Leon Booker, Glen "Chop" Porter, Kermit and Al Burleson, Randy 'Roc" Minix, *Rafiki Webster,* Levi Bryant, Dennis Pettway, Robert Taylor, Stephen Skip Roberts, Dewayne "Tyrone Robins, James Nelson, Ken Harris, Darnell Hughes, Willie Francis, Tyrone Ferguson, Robert "Buchie" Freeman, Berle Grant, Dennis Billups, Thomas Warren, Glen GT Taylor, Randy C, Harold Williams and the Sista's of Sunnydale, Gloria Ann Pitre, Annette Hughes, Maxine Hughes, Val and Lisa Burleson, Patricia Willis, Kathy Stewart, Kathy Frierson Eddrena Peters and Lexie TC Caracter

**Glen Chop Porter, Darro Van Jefferson,**
**Al Burleson and Ken Harris**
THE SONS SHARING A TREASURED MOMENT
AT THE SUNNYDALE REUNION

*"OUR SUNNYDALE HAD ITS SHARE OF PROBLEMS AND CONFLICTS THAT ENDED IN TOO MANY UNFORTUNATES, TOO MANY SAD DAYS WITH FAR TOO MUCH GRIEFING. WE WERE NO DIFFERENT NOR IMMUNE TO THE ECONOMIC AND SOCIAL SYSTEMATIC HARDSHIPS THAT PLAGUE OUR BLACK COMMUNITIES.*

*HOWEVER IN OUR SUNNYDALE, WE DIDN'T TRY TO SWEEP THE UNFORTUNATE UNDER THE RUG. THERE WAS NO SUGAR COATING THE TRIALS, THE CHALLENGES WE FACED AS A COMMUNITY. HOWEVER BAD, THE UNFORTUNATE BECAME OUR RALLYING CRY OF TOGETHERNESS. WHEN PEOPLE WERE DOWN ON THEIR LUCK, IN PAIN AND SORROW, DOORS OF COMPASSION AND SUPPORT WOULD OPEN. OUR SUNNYDALE WAS A PLACE THAT PULLED ITS PEOPLE UP FROM THE GROUND"* COYLE JEFFERSON

# The Sons n Sista's of Sunnydale

### *Our Story*

*"Our story is most significant. It seems to me that the only time people from Sunnydale get together are at funerals for those who are Going Home. We need to do more than just pay homage to them"* Randy Campbell said in a quiet private moment with me at the Home Going Services of Ola Mae Minix at Duggan's Funeral Home in San Francisco, California.

*"This story means everything to me. I was born and raised in Sunnydale"* Harold Williams

*"Sunnydale was our magical place on the planet"* Ann Pitre

*"We hope that our story finds a place in the hearts of struggling communities and individuals seeking to empower themselves learning to rely on a Higher Power much greater than their will to survive and change their ways of living"* Coyle Jefferson

*"Henrietta's got all of Sunnydale's Angels smiling down on all of us"* K Burleson

*"Most of us were too young to understand so many of the things happening around us, but what we did learn growing up was to face up to the good and the bad"* Glen "Chop" Porter

*"From the first day we moved to Sunnydale there was nothing but good times and good people living there"* M Pitre

*"Brother I am so grateful you are writing a story about the times and place where we grew up, brings back hella memories"* D Martinez

*"DJ my brother you have like an archaeologist unearthed our priceless heritage buried over time by despair and decline"* Skip Roberts

*"I would like to thank brother Darro Jefferson for allowing me to share the memories and include my testimony to A Song for Ms. Henrietta Harris with the Sons n Sistas of Sunnydale"* Rafiki Webster

*"I remember we played outside together then went to each other's house to eat. B Grant*

*"Our journey revisiting our past is well worth the trip back in time"* A Hughes

*"Everything we did, everytime we went outside is a treasured moment, Sunnydale was our legendary Playland at the beach"* A Burleson

*"When you grow up in a community where every parent is your parent and they can beat your behind, for sure you are growing up in a community that cares"* R Taylor

*"During the 60's when the riots broke out Sunnydale showed our solidarity for the cause. It didn't take much for us to come together for one another. Our problems were everybody's problems"* Darnell Hughes

*"Thanks for joining us on this journey to empowerment"* L Graves

***"Back n the Dayz when the sounds of children playing brought laughter and joy and manicure lawns were Crayola colored green and families stuck together like Ten Toes In A Sock"***

***Glen Chop Porter***

*"Every household was a food pantry to those in need" Randy Roc Minix*

**Elmira, Delores, Diane, Norine and Randy Ray Minix**
*Henrietta "Momma" Harris*

*Sunrise*
*December 11,1918*
*Sunset*
*July 5 2016*
*A Nurturing Gift Giving Caretaker and Peace Maker*

*Henrietta was born in Arcadia Louisiana in 1918, the oldest of three children in her early 20's she moved to San Francisco, CA in 1941 studied nursing and worked in the Hunter's Point Naval Shipyard.*

*She and her husband Whitehead moved to Sunnydale in the early 1950's raising five children, three boys Napoleon, Danny Ray and Michael along with daughters Sharon and Loretta.*

*At a very young age Henrietta developed a compassion for helping others and it was her kind heartedness that transcended into a nursing career where she received her nursing credential.*

*The commitment to help and comfort others in time of need was adopted by those she helped ton nicked named her Momma Harris*

*Henrietta attended public schools in Arcadia and spent considerable time attending church services where she was baptized at a very young age.*

*In 2007 she renewed her Baptism and Commitment to the Lord and became an active member of the St. Phillips Baptist Church.*

*In Sunnydale she was a "Nurturing Gift Giving CareTaker and Peace Maker"*

*Henrietta leaves to cherish her memory 18 grandchildren,32 great grandchildren and three great great grandchildren*

*"Henrietta was a sit down share your burdens with me and the Lord Prayer Partner" Lisa Burleson Next Door Neighbor*

*"Women like Momma Harris and their community commitments won't be found in any scrapbooks" Ann Pitre Community Organizer*

*"She was an unsung advocate for safer streets and the well being of the families in her community. She was not a civil rights advocate but a community advocate. A Soldier in God's Army who put the needs of her community first and foremost" Eddrenna Peters Sistas of Sunnydale*

*"The warm meals she shared with those without food were as warm as her God Given Heart"* Maxine Hughes Sistas of Sunnydale

*"I am sure before Henrietta took her last breath her thoughts were on the children and families of her beloved community"* Annette Hughes Sistas of Sunnydale

*"She was like Star Trek, always showing up in places we never expected her to, like the time when she busted us shooting dice in the washhouse. She just shook her head and told us to be careful"* Levi Bryant Sons of Sunnydale

*"There were lots of women in our community like Ms Harris. We grew up in a community where women helped raise each other's children. As a young girl I would watch them leave the house, go to work and then come home hoping and praying that bad news didn't greet them at the front door. Ms Henrietta was an unofficial den mother who looked out for the children in the neighborhood"* TC Caracter Sistas of Sunnydale

*"My mother sometimes I felt because of her compassion had as much concern for the people of Sunnydale than for us children, but her commitment to others I learned was a true testament of the community work she so dearly loved"* Kathy Frierson

*"We lived in the very first building on Hahn Street. We had a family business there so all the time during the day I could see either Ms Frierson, Ms Henrietta, George Davis engaged in conversation with people hanging out on Hahn Street"* Patricia Willis

*"The women in Sunnydale helped keep the community together. They made us proud of who we were and where we lived"* Kathy Stewart

# Before The Homegoing
# At St. Mary's Hospital

**Bedside at St Mary's**

## _The Telephone Rang It Was Randy Roc Minix Calling From Leland Mississippi "Ms Henrietta Is In The Hospital"_

*Placing the telephone down, Instantly by concern I wondered "How does one comfort the comforter? How does one help heal the healer?*

*Everyone she had touched knew her time was drawing near. But how could the news of her health reach Leland Mississippi and bypass those closer to home?*

*It was one of Sunnydale's harsh realities that was destined to leave our community powerless, pondering, thinking of only the worse, many in total denial, others afraid of what their lives would be without her and all the time forgetting Ms Henrietta was Sunnydale's Calm in The Storm*

With Ms Henrietta there's no real way to describe her, the role she took on in the community.

The term **Matriarch** can mean so many things to so many people.

*"Henrietta brought the neighborhood a sense of compassion some people were hard to embrace, times were good back then growing up but by no means was Sunnydale immune to hard times. What Henrietta did was make life growing up in the community simply put was she made life for alot of people a little more easier to bare"* Randy Roc Minix

*"All I can say is that she meant the world to all of us"* A Burleson

*"Momma Harris was Sunnydale's leading lady, even in her last days I was told from her hospital bed she spoke only about the wellbeing of the people in her beloved community"* A Hughes

*"She didn't live this long and care for so many people to have her legacy placed in a cupboard for safekeeping"* Otis Bubba Hughes

*"Ms Henrietta had the same stuff, performed the unsung duties, embraced and shared relentless commitments to the people in Sunnydale that others throughout the lands, if you asked me have been awarded a Nobel Prize"* Glen GT Taylor

There are those esteem authorities who suggest loosely and will argue the term **Matriarch** in the black community is a reflection of the black man's lack of leadership, inability to provide for his family and therefore they are dependent on the strength of black woman to lead the family.

However, no matter the philosophical differences and opinions in our inner cities, a family, white or black without a strong fatherly influence for whatever reasons, the emergence of **strong resilient women does exist and everyone in our community are beneficiaries of women like Ms Henrietta for one reason or another.**

**It was a role without title, women in our communities take on without hesitation in spite of their own personal family hardships.**

**Ms Henrieta always had time to give of herself without asking for anything in return.**

*She was* from the old school of long-term Sunnydale residents, a Sunnydale icon.

*"I am not sure Henrietta ever slept through the night, I mean that's not to say Sunnydale didn't have its share of drama, but it seems every time someone was going through something she was there like First Alert. With her there was no need to call 911, she was already and always there to help in the nick of time" K Burleson*

*"She raised three boys and two beautiful daughters and was respected by all. A real life fairy Godmother" L Burleson*

*Ms Henrietta* knew more about the people of Sunnydale than some of our very own kinfolk.

The community was not above infidelity. She could have hosted *Paternity Court because she knew "who was the father"* the neighborhood's *DNA...*

The calm in the storm. Her door was open 24/7 A real dose of Southern Sunnydale Comfort, like Folgers Coffee, *"good to the very last drop"*

She was Sunnydale's *Mother Theresa, Harriet Tubman and Sojourner Truth.*

*The community epitome of* grandmothers and mothers who kept their families and their communities woven together with pure unconditional love.

She was truly an ambassador of goodwill dressed in an evening gown, house slippers, a wrap-around headscarf and granny-like eyeglasses.

She epitomized *Bill Withers*, classic songs, *Grandma's Hands or the Spinners Sadie and Shirley Caesar I Remember Mama.*

Everyone in the hood came to her for one reason or another in spite of her own personal family hardships and their dysfunctionality.

She always had time to give of herself, and like so many others in our neighborhood she was not immune to the challenges and tragedies of ghetto life.

*Black mothers will always be strong, responsible, compassionate women within the black family structure and their roles extend far beyond their own households and the entire community.*

*Women like her are exclusive members only of single mothers who pledge an oath of allegiance to provide for their children.*

*It was a role Ms Henrietta cherished and never took for granted.*

# Visiting Momma Harris

I arrived at St Mary's Hospital well after the others. The Burleson's were already there waiting in the lobby upstairs.

I had stopped at a flower shop and pondered what plant to buy for her, remembering her front window was always filled with succulents so I bought her a nice turquoise colored cactus with sandy colored stones that I was sure she would enjoy.

Strangely, the Burleson's were waiting because Ms Henrietta was not in her room, nowhere to be found.

Even the floor duty nurse did not know her whereabouts.

We all thought perhaps she was receiving treatment elsewhere and there may have been a minor slipup between staff of where she was.

But as time passed by I thought to myself, how the hell could an *80 old woman in the hospital be unaccounted for?*

Then to our amazement there she was coming off the elevator, Bible in hand lightly humming *"If Ya Wanna Help Me Jesus It's Alright"*

Immediately all of us knew, like always, she was making her rounds especially with her faithful Bible in her hand, turning from page to page, doing her ministry caring about others, putting her own needs on hold for the sake of others.

It didn't take a doctor's diagnosis to figure out what she was doing.

We followed her to her room. She discarded her slippers, got in bed, smiled and started holding court.

Inside her fourth story room were **Napoleon**, her oldest son, his wife who upon introduction to us was not too social to Al, his wife Valerie, Lisa and especially me.

*"Henrietta looked like one of those people you visit in the hospital and they look more healthy and more vibrant than you. She was as alert as ever" V Burleson*

There in the room was Lisa, the youngest of the Burleson family who I personally had not seen in years.

We used to call Lisa **Channel 5** because around her we could never get away with anything.

Their mother should have named her 411, but she was the sweetest thing we knew other than her private eye mentality and need to be in our business.

Lisa was quite a character in her own way.

Ms Henrietta sat on the edge of her bed, jubilant and looking quite healthy as I hugged and kissed her soft cheeks.

She responded by making me take off my Warrior's ball cap, rubbing my head, shaking her head and saying **"boy what happened to all that curly hair"** the others especially **Al** broke out in laughter because he knew the routine, growing up, that woman must have rubbed my head a million times or more.

That exchange sparked some comments from *Val and Lisa* as well.

*Napoleon* introduced me to his wife as the younger brother of *Theresa,* my sister who he had told his wife the two of them used to date.

That introduction did not go over well, no fault of mine but it obviously put a dagger in the room.

I to this day don't have a clue what he said to that woman about his former lovelife.

To tell you the truth I was too young to know anything about their relationship.

But *Ms Henrietta* picked up on it right away and began to tell stories about *Theresa and Napoleon,* boy! That didn't help me at all.

That woman gave me a look that could stop a Bart Train, but there was *Ms Henrietta* right there on cue to save the day.

She asked about **Chop** and said "I thought the two of you were coming together that's what Alvin told me" Payback time as *Al* looked to his wife and *Lisa* to bail him out. *"Well y'all make sure you tell Glen", Chop's real name to call Ms Henrietta",*

*"Sitting near her in the hospital was like being in her living room, She knew her time was coming near but we really couldn't tell, that's just the way she was, always putting others first" L Burleson*

*Henrietta,* was a master of defusing situations and this was yet another sample size of her unique motherly ability to listen, intervene and take control, telling Lisa how proud of her she was and telling Val if she had any problems with Al to call her.

Ironically during our past visit to her Hahn Street apartment a few weeks before, she bestowed the nickname of Stout on Val, because

Val we always teased her about being a Six Footer, but Valerie who wasn't quite pleased with Henrietta calling her that, at that time but to this day both Al and I teased Val about that nickname.

Being in Henrietta's presence all of us were completely mesmerized by her charm, warmth and storytelling as she skillfully guided us through The Dales landscape stopping at each intersection holding our hands then allowing us to cross the street safely with her down memory lane.

She talked about how the neighborhood was once like and more importantly how the community was changing by the day.

Not once did she complain of feeling ill, she was upbeat and coherent.

Her conversation was focussed on the people in Sunnydale.

*"If there is someone in the community there now to help our people God Bless Them, there is no need for people to remember me, Give them the chance to do God's Work. I am counting on all of you," She said.*

She was articulate and not caught up in the past but emphasized the need to change her beloved community on all levels but especially the need to save the children of Sunnydale.

*"Young people dying everywhere in our communities for no reason at all".*

I remember her pointing at each of us and saying, ***"everyone in this room has lost someone, a brother, a sister, a love one, a friend to violence"*** *and that* ***"none of us should lose sight of our losses"*** *but try and do* ***"God's Will to make a difference, Sunnydale cannot be forgotten"*** *those were her exact words.*

She was a loving mother to all who sadly had to experience the deaths of three of her own children.

# Her Children Were Her Pride and Joy

*Danny Ray, Loretta and Sharon Harris*

*Ms Henrietta* was a resilient woman but her pains had to run deep.

A parent's nightmare is the loss of their own child, but as far back as I can remember she was the first one out the door when others experienced hardship and crisis.

She said what she yearned for more than anything was *sitting at her front window watching us growing up playing outside on grassy lawns and not having to dodge bullets or witness drug dealing* that times in Sunnydale could be like they once were.

*"These old eyes of mine have seen a lot in my lifetime"* She said

*Ms Henrietta talked about the need for more pe*ople *"doing street ministry"* *community organizing and "loving one another"*

Not once did she display an ounce of discomfort but we could all see that our visit and her testimony was wearing on her but like the trooper she was she continued to put it out there *religiously, relentlessly* until the medical staff suggested we cut our visit short and visit with her again.

*One of the nurses pulled us aside and said they were having a hard time keeping up with her because most of the time she was not in her room but paying visits to other patients in the hospital, many of them not even on her same floor.*

We could only smile and shake our heads in approval because this is who she truly was **An Angel of Mercy**

Us having to leave didn't go over well with her, and she gave those nurses a piece of her mind.

Before we left each of us took our own very special moment with her and I noticed a stream of soft tears running down her cheeks and giving me that look to do the right thing and therefore we are all proud to share with you *A Song for Ms Henrietta.*

*"Don't any of y'all weep for me"* *was the last thing I remember her telling us before we left the hospital.*

# Homegoing Services

## {*A Ceremony To Honor Our Queen*}

*Henrietta's Homegoing Services should have began with the Heavenly Majestic Voices of Rance Allen and Mahalia Jackson singing down from Heavens Way, Standing On The Banks Of Jordan, The Lord's Prayer and How I Got Over*

*Without question Community Matriarchs across this nation deserve a proper sendoff to the Pearly Gates. A Worthwhile Unforgettable Tribute Is What They Deserve.*

*Homegoing Services are much more than just funerals.*

*A Homegoing, like its name implies, is the symbolic return of the human spirit back to its heavenly home, invoking the Christian idea of God as Father and so therefore going back home/to heaven to be with one's Father/Creator of life.*

*It is a culturally distinct end-of-life ceremony within the Black American community that is steeped in the religious culture of the Black church.*

*During slavery, Black people weren't allowed to have formal ceremonies or rituals to mourn the dead, as slave masters viewed their gatherings as a sign that they were conspiring against them.*

*When African people were taken to America and enslaved, they believed that death meant their soul would return to their homelands in Africa. For them, death was freedom from a life of suffering and a pathway home to be with their ancestors. Thus, the Black community adopted our own form of Homecoming.*

*The relief provides the necessary steps toward healing for which the songs and the eulogy, which doubles as a sermon, both play a very important part.*

*The syncopated sounds and rhythm can provide balm to a hurting soul while the eulogy reaffirms the importance of the decedent's life and the notion that they are in a better place.*

*Sunnydale's Noblewomen will forever be immortalized by The Sons n Sista's of Sunnydale.*

*They will serve as honor guards and honorary pallbearers for a celebratory service where there will be no caskets.*

*At high noon Bells of Peace will ring out, traffic will come to a standstill.*

*This day there will be no parking or vehicles allowed to drive on the Streets of Sunnydale.*

*On each street corner throughout the community School Crossing Guards will stand in salute formations.*

*In every household in the neighborhood residents will stand arm in arm door to door wearing colorful arm bands, symbols of peace.*

*The ceremonies will start at the top of Sunnydale Avenue in front of John McLaren Elementary School.*

*Choirs members in long white robes will start down the John McLaren Hill singing Going Up Yonder followed by a procession of jazz musicians and the Children of Sunnydale gracefully praise dancing, wearing beautiful multi colored bright royal, metallic gold, scarlet, deep purple, black and white celebration of life dancewear with matching streamers marching to lively jazz playing happy music.*

*A high stepping HBCU marching band and a Drum Major will High Step parading down Sunnydale Avenue.*

*Colorful balloons will be released to soar high in the skies above.*

*Brotha's and Sista's from the Black Panther Party will line the streets wearing revolutionary Black Berets march[ng in military fashion down the hill stopping in unisom between each building saluting and paying homage to the Mothers and People*

*The Jackson Southernaires and the Mississippi Mass Choir will follow singing Sam Cooke's A Change Is Gonna Come*

*Preachers of all denominations will then walk arm in arm to show their religious solidarity.*

*City Water trucks will spray mist of Heavenly sweet vanilla floral citrus fragrances on the street to represent A Cleansing in the Community.*

*The Royal Ceremony will be held at the Sunnydale Rec Center.*

*Inside the Rec center the stage will be decorated with beautiful bouquets of flowers.*

*Birds of Paradise will be placed on the stage, and white doves and song birds will be released freely to fly, an Acappella singing group will sing Negro Sprituals of the past.*

*Portraits of Harriett, Sojourner, Maya, Mary, Rosa, Corretta, Angela, Shirley and Michelle will line the walls of the center.*

*An enormous silver sterling water flowing fountain with rose colorful rose petals will stand center stage*

*Saxophone player Sonny Rollins will serenade the audience with a soulful rendition of Curtis Mayfield's People Get Ready.*

*The personal testimonies of Only the Brotha's, Sista's, Sons and Daughters of Sunnydale will be allowed to grace the podium.*

*Spoken Words poets will deliver uplifting poems and Black ballet dancers will perform freedom dances and ceremonial offerings.*

*Childhood preaching prodigies will deliver heartfelt eulogies.*

*At the conclusion of the ceremony everyone will know and cherish that Henrietta's Homegoing Service was "Just A Rehearsal" because when Ms Henrietta Gets To Heaven She's Going To Really Sing. "Willie Neal Johnson and the Gospel Keynotes"*

# Henrietta's Unshakeable Faith for Her Beloved Community

*A young grandchild once asked her aging great grandmother why her hands were so rough, wrinkly and hard to the bonelike.*

*The great grandmother simply told the child she had picked cotton every single day of her life and her worn wrinkled hands told the story of Life in the cotton fields in the Deep South.*

*Those who came north brought with them more than dreams of a new way of life.*

*It's a valuable history that Ms Henrietta often spoke about, a rich history that cannot be ignored or swept under a rug by generations who don't know about the rich exterior of Grandma's Hands.*

*"Henrietta was as much of an historian as that of a community advocate. She talked about the need for people to remember our history. It wasn't what she preached but by no means was she one of those bible thumping holier than thou kind of people" Randy Roc Minix*

*Henrietta and women like her never wavered on their will, their desire to help others, but Life's demands on them were enormous.*

"The mothers of the Sunnydale Housing Projects had to be a unifying force with Ms Henrietta leading the way" Rafiki Webster

"Her Life Tank may have been running on half a tank but her Heart was overflowing with compassion. Henrietta was a Spiritual Woman with God Given abilities that put the needs of her community first and foremost" Kermit Burleson

Each day Henrietta was confronted by insurmountable odds, carrying the woes and needs of the people on her feeble shoulders, aching knees barely having the strength to rise up each morning but knowing that so many lives were dependent on her.

"In the early hours, or late in the afternoon sometimes at night, she would be outside doing God's will. The candle in the night may have not been seen shining from her front window but people found their way to her front door when they needed her help. She was always helping those in need" Al Burleson

Few in the community knew their constant calls for Help were taking an enormous toll on Ms Henrietta's health when she without hesitation responded to their pleas for Help.

The compassion and commitment she had for others was her Achilles Heel.

"Life wasn't all that kind to her on some days, but she carried herself with Grace and Dignity" Maxine Hughes

Her family life was no walk in the park by any means, nor did she try to suffocate or sugarcoat her emotional distress.

Having to raise five children on her own was a tremendous task, there wasn't always good news waiting for when she returned home from helping others in the neighborhood.

Henrietta knew the neighborhood was a close knit community and there was no need for her to conceal herself from the frustration, pain and hardships that challenged every family in Sunnydale.

"That's the sad thing I remember about her. She gave Sunnydale much more than she had to give. She put the weight of the community on her frail shoulders morning noon and night" Leon Booker

"I admired the women in Sunnydale, they were my true heroes and Henrietta was at the top of the list right after my Mother" TC Caracter

It was not in her DNA nor apart of her character, she like the others in Sunnydale had been knocked down time and time again but it was undoubtedly Henrietta's UNSHAKEABLE FAITH FOR HER BELOVED COMMUNITY that awakened her every time there was a need for her to put on her house slippers, robe, granny glasses and respond to the needs of others.

She was a trusted servant in God's Army doing God's Work and God's Will for the people in her community.

Many knew of her physical limitations but she kept her emotional vulnerability hidden relying on strong Faith to provide the strength to Lend a Helping Hand to others.

"Henrietta felt her purpose in her life was to serve others, do God's Will, in spite of her own traumatic experiences" Coyle Jefferson

Henrietta's deep rooted community advocacy commitment to others is part of our southern heritage shared by Henrietta and the people throughout our communities

In our Northern communities the passageways to the North are filled with scars, hardship and sacrifices of endearment.

Sunnydale's southern families migrating north could not put the brutality, the suffering, the rapes, lynchings and unspeakable horrors of the South behind them.

They had no choice but to rally among themselves.

"I never experienced Jim Crow, heard more than my share about it, but racism I know for sure is not limited to the deep south. It is a painful experience wherever you are" Melvin Pitre

It was the Gospel that Henrietta preached relying on her Spritual upbringing, memories, southern roots going to backwoods churches riding on the back of a hay wagon guided by the family mule singing Negro Sprituals providing our families the fortitude to continue Northward Bound

"I'll let you in on a remarkable truth most West Coast Black people don't know. Greyhound had express routes from New Orleans to San Francisco. That was our main route of travel out of the south. Our people fried chicken, baked tea cakes and pound cake for the 3 day ride. Some rode the train but most rode Greyhound. In those days we could not drive. It was too dangerous' '. **Gloria Ann Pitre**

Upon our ancestors' arrival in the North hoping for a new way of life they were greeted with no rainbows, only the dreaded **Ism's** in the North, Racism, Social and Economic Disparity the very same things they thought they had left behind.

It's a valuable history that Ms Henrietta often spoke about, our rich history. The rich exterior of Grandma's Hands. But more importantly it was Henrietta's UNSHAKEABLE FAITH FOR HER BELOVED COMMUNITY that got her people, the families in Sunnydale through the difficult times without asking for anything in exchange.

# Remembering Ms Henrietta

*Eric Peters, Henrietta was out there everyday a lot of times in her bathrobe and house slippers, spreading joy throughout the community. Her feet from walking through the neighborhood must of been tired but her heart was filled with so much compassion she never seemed to be tired at all*

Rafiki Webster, Henrietta Harris was the foundation, a staple within the community and many parents looked to her for advice. Our mothers were an extension of Ms. Harris, like branches of an oak tree

*Kathy Stewart, Loretta Harris and I were childhood friends. Tragically she left us all too soon but I can remember her like it was yesterday*

*Glen "Chop" Porter, When we lost my mom Henrietta was there to comfort our family showing up everyday making sure we were okay*

*Al Burleson, The Harris Family lived a few doors from us. She experienced so many heartaches in her life but she never uttered one word about her own hardships*

*Kermit Burleson, Danny Ray and I ran the streets but Ms Henrietta didn't give up on either of us. She was there for everyone in the community*

*Dewayne Robins, The women in Sunnydale had their hands full just looking out for their own children, raising families by themselves and then having to watch out for other kids in the neighborhood was a mighty big task but without them who knows where some of us would be today*

*Harold Williams, A wonderful woman who gave everything she had to the people in Sunnydale. She was one of a kind. There wasn't a miserable bone in her body*

*Kathy Frierson, My brother Kermit hung out with Danny Ray and Michael Harris and I have no doubt the three of them by no means were Cub Scouts*

*Coyle Jefferson, She never wavered once on her commitment to her community*

*Dennis Pettway, I was fortunate to be apart of the old Sunnydale and lived in the neighborhood when things began to change, but had not it been for strong women in our community more of our young people could have taken a wrong turn going down the wrong roads in life*

*Skip Roberts, My mother and the other women in Sunnydale had great respect for her. She taught us all about being there for someone else*

*Thomas Warren, She only knew one way. God's way. I remember many a conversation with Ms Henrietta and my mother*

*Melvin Pitre, Don't know how these remarkable women in our community got up each to deal with everybody's situations in the community, but I thank God they did. Ms Harris' community's well being was her business*

*Annette Hughes, May she Rest in Peace. Henrietta your work down here is done*

*Otis "Bubba" Hughes, It wasn't the things she did for people but the love she shared for them. There's no real way to explain but one thing for sure, Henrietta was loved by all of Sunnydale*

*Randy "Roc" Minix Her's was a journey few have traveled*

*Rafiki Webster, She reminded me of those courageous Black women the history books don't talk about but were a part of conversations around the dinner table when we sat down listening to stories about our past over plates of greens, gumbo, rice and beans and every now and then a Sunday roast*

*Leon Booker, It seems like it was only yesterday when I saw her walking through the neighborhood on her way to help some family out. I say this because she was out there everyday, never took a day off, never asked for anything in return. Wasn't any holidays in her life, helping people in need was her full time job*

# Ghetto Glorification

*There has to be something mentally wrong with the mental state of Black People in our communities across this nation who come out in droves standing in lines three rolls deep to **GLORIFY** community drug lords, king pins, street hustlers and gang bangers laid out lavishly in silver and gold plated personalized coffins, laid to rest decked out in thousand dollar suits resting in peace with diamond studded earrings, blinding stick pens and pallbearers dressed to the max.*

*No doubt, there has to be something mentally wrong with this strange form of **Ghetto Glorification that ignores the Courageous efforts of Community Advocates Peace Makers and in particular the Women Street Soldiers of Our Communities.***

**TRACY WILKINSON AND STEPHANIE CHAVEZ OF THE LOS ANGELES TIMES WROTE In MARCH 2, 1992 THE FOLLOWING: "The young man was eulogized by 500 relatives, friends and fellow gangsters. His deluxe funeral included a silver hearse and four stretch limousines, six floral sprays and other trappings befitting a veteran of more than a decade of gangsterism".**

**But if that kind of Ghetto Glorification and Patranism seems alarming there can be no greater form of extreme Gorification than that of drug cartel bosses in Sinaloa known to bury their**

*comrades in lavish tombs with jacuzzis, air conditioning, bedrooms with scenic views for family visitation, Cable TV and elaborate security systems.*

**Graveyards house the corpses of Mexico's most feared drug lords in tombs that can range in cost from $340,000 to $1,200,000 dollars, in a poor community plagued with violence.**

*In our inner city communities Ghetto Glorification services include ghetto gangsters being carted off in Bay horse drawn carriages followed by entourages of stretch limousines vintage Bentleys and Cadillac Escalades through the very streets of the same neighborhoods where they caused havoc, destruction and violence.*

*Their passing doesn't go unnoticed. Media outlets provide up to the minute coverage of this strange form of **Ghetto Glorification.***

*Our neighborhood churches are filled to capacity with people who show up to bid their farewells decked out in Armani suits, lavish Cartier watches, diamond studded sunglasses and custom made "phatt" ropes of gold chains draped around their necks. Bling Bling is everywhere for services you would think are meant for a king.*

*This strange form of Ghetto Glorification has been met with strong opposition from some inner city churches and their Pastors who have taken a strong stance to not allow gang member and drug lord funeral services to take place in their House of Worship*

*Charles Brevitt, Pastor of two Seventh Day Adventist churches said "We are not going to have funerals for anybody who has brought devastation and death to our community. Our churches are going to move to impose new protocol to regulate the type of funerals that will be allowed at our churches"*

*The graveyards are full of these societal hoodrat heroes idolized for living large at the expense of their own brothers and sisters.*

*Too many people these ghetto pests are no more than notorious street gangsters responsible for mayhem and fear and loss of human lives and family devastation.*

***Therefore Ms Henrietta's, Mrs Pitre the Mothers and Women of Sunnydale*** *contributions cannot be ignored and memories of them shall not be forgotten, nor can the contributions of countless neighborhood den mothers, community ambassadors, organizers and street soldiers like her throughout our inner city communities who have taken to the streets to save their beloved communities with only* ***Broomsticks and Bibles Love and Compassion****...their contributions will be acknowledged throughout this composition.*

*These Women were Torch Bearers who placed their Unshakeable Faith in the Hands of our young Sista's in Sunnydale, many who became community organizers and peacemakers in the Sunnydale Community.*

*In addition the creators of the composition will revisit some historical events in San Francisco that will highlight the contributions of* ***Women of Courage*** *who stepped forward traveling down the same pathways of courageous women helping to restore humanity and communityship in their Communities.*

# The Communities Tribute

To The Women of Sunnydale Who Made Our Community Magical
Sunnydale's Humble Servant

IZOLA CUDJO FRIERSON

***BORN FEBRUARY 2, 1922 RECEIVED
UNTO THE LORD MAY 2, 2023***
*"Whoever Wants To Be My Disciple Must Deny Themselves
And Take Up The Cross Daily And Follow Me" Luke 9:23
REST IN PEACE*

*"Ms Frierson was Sunnydale's Bread and Water"*
***Al Burleson***

*"The things she did for people were from her heart"*
**Annette Hughes**

*"She made a big difference in people's lives"*
**Coyle Jefferson**

*"Her heart was as big as all of Sunnydale"*
**Ann Pitre**

Being Chosen Is An Opportunity To Participate

To Do God's Will In Our Own Lives And Others
"For Many Are Called And Few Are Chosen
Matthew 22:14

Sunnydale's Humble Servant

*"My mother refused to give up on serving her community. She found joy in her work and never complained about her workload, nor did she tire of doing the work she so dearly loved"* Kathy Frierson

*"Ms Frierson was outside on the Front everyday dealing with everything that came her way. A powerful caring Black Woman"* Levi Bryant

*"Her and my mother worked together at the EOC. I know the job didn't pay all that much but the work they did was priceless"* Skip Roberts

*"I didn't know who Ms Frierson was until one day walking through the neighborhood, this woman came up to me asked my name and*

*signed me up for the Summer Jobs Program, that's how I first met Ms Frierson" Dewayne Robins*

*"She had an office on Hahn Street but her home was also open 24/7 she never took a day off from helping people in the neighborhood" Kermit Burleson*

*"The community service work she did, Ms Frierson would have done for free. The people she touched need to be forever grateful" Maxine Hughes*

*"Man her and Geogre Davis, the EOC staff were one helluva tag team" Thomas Warren*

*"We had community values and we attended various churches, many of us shared the same values as our families originated from the South and those southern values were felt throughout the Sunnydale Housing Projects. Ms Frierson made sure of that" Rafiki Webster*

The CUDJO FRIERSON Family came out in droves to pay Homage and Respect to Izola, their Mother, Grandmother and Great Grandmother at Her Homegoing Services in Daly City California.

Her Homegoing Celebration was reminiscent of those southern Black families so large in representation the churches had little room to accommodate all in attendance.

There were people there representing Izola's impact on their lives and her 40 years of community service work with the EOC Organization.

She was part of Sunnydale's old guard and there were also those in attendance from the early days in the neighborhood.

Her services were a touching tribute, an uplifting education of the tiny slender frame woman who put the weight of the community on her shoulders.

Family member after family member from the CUDJO FRIERSON Family stood before the audience with tears in their eyes, laughter and joy in their hearts expressing revealing intricate details of the Woman many knew of, many who had been touched by her, but few in the audience paying their respect had little insight to the personal life of Sunnydale's Humble Servant

## Reflections of Izola's Life

Izola Maxine "Cudjo" Frierson was born February 2, 1922 on Little River in Sasakwa, Oklahoma to the union of Mictchel Cudjo and Mable Dennis.

Izola accepted Christ at an early age and was baptized at Middle Creek Baptist Church.

The oldest of five children, she graduated from Langston University. A HBCU Black University in Langston, Oklahoma.

Langston University produced many pioneers and distinguished athletes.

Bessie Coleman, was an early American civil aviator, the first African American woman to hold a pilot license. Marques Haynes of the Harlem Globetrotters.

Thomas Hollywood Henderson, who played professional football in the NFL playing in Super Bowl X11 with the Dallas Cowboys.

Michael C Henderson, was a Major General in the United States Army National Guard and member of the Oklahooma Governor's Cabinet and Nathan Hare, a noted African American sociologist and activist. Mr Hare was the first person hired to coordinate a Black Studies Program at San Francisco State College.

What a beautiful Homegoing Ceremony Izola's Celebration of Life would have been if Jennifer Kate Hudson another of Langton's notable alumni could have been there to Serenade the Life of Izola Maxine "Cudjo" Frierson at Duggan's Chapel on May 19th in Daly City California.

Izola's loved gardening but her passion was helping people. For more than 40 years she worked for the Economic Opportunity Council {EOC} as Executive Director developing uplifting personal discovery programs for youth and people in the Sunnydale and Bayview Hunters Point Community.

Those who knew her closely affectionately called her "Bernie" her Family was her Life. Her commitment to Life was serving others. She was truly a giver. A Humble Servant.

Izola touched many lives, there were no strangers in her Life, her Heart was a welcoming mat to those in need, she was a Southern Comfort, a Life Preserver, a Woman who put the needs of the Community, and Her people first and foremost.

She is Blessed to leave and share in Her memory, a loving daughter Kathy, twenty one great grandchildren and eight great great grandchildren, a host of dear family and many friends and countless Lives touched by an Angel.

Izola stood underneath a Halo of God's Grace, without reservation. She was Sunnydale's Humble Servant.

"For Many Are Called And Few Are Chosen
Matthew 22:14

REST IN PEACE
**IZOLA**

# I'll Always Love My Momma

*Kathy Frierson*

*My mom was a helper of all. At times we thought she had more concern for the people of Sunnydale she helped, then for us children but helping others was in her DNA.*

*Where she got the energy to manage our family while helping the people she cared so dearly for was simply amazing.*

*My mom was just that, an amazing woman. There are people today who often tell me she got them their first summer jobs or she got them out of some tough situations or came to visit them in Juvenile Hall.*

*That in itself makes me proud that she touched so many lives.*

As a young girl I couldn't help but feel a little jealous. But Momma had enough love and care in her heart to spread around the community and that's just who she was. A Soldier in God's Army doing good in the neighborhood.

It seemed she was always busy tending to the needs of others in the community.

When she wasn't in her office or doing street work the doors to our house were always open. In fact that's what made Sunnydale a special place. You couldn't find someone who would turn their backs on their neighbors. I can truthfully say that being there for your neighbor, in a lot of ways, is a thing of the past. Times are far too different now. Far too different.

Momma took pride in her community work and we were never left out and none of us, my brothers and sister felt we were not loved. Her service commitments came with the territory.

Sunnydale had its share of problems. Some more than others. My brother Kermit was a handful but Momma never wavered on helping him and his hangout crew.

The group Kermit ran with would give any parent a migraine BC Headache Powder Super Dose of Tylenol migraine, twice a day and maybe even more.

It's funny looking back, thinking of Sunnydale, I remember if a kid got into trouble some of us would be better off dealing with someone else's mother than our own and Kermit was no exception to the rule. In fact there were many times my brother tested her last nerves.

My brothers and sister didn't realize how much the community relied on her but as we grew older her community compassion was something we began to accept and for me admire.

*Sometimes Sandra, my sister, took on the role of Momma because my mom's work often kept her out of the house for long periods of time. I have to tip my hat to her for helping raise me too.*

*Devaughn was loved and respected throughout the neighborhood. My big brother was the unofficial head of the household and a strong influence over his peers and a big support to all of us.*

*It felt good when I started hearing Ms Frierson do this, Ms Frierson did that for me.*

*Hearing the people in the community call out her name gave us reassurance that everything no matter what was going to be alright.*

*Even when we moved out of Sunnydale over the hill to the Excelsior neighborhood we spent everyday in Sunnydale. It was because my mother continued to work at the EOC and all of our friends were there.*

*Today I have life term friendships with people from Sunnydale, friends we went to school with and played with, jumping off the washhouses, climbing trees, playing dodgeball, going to the talent shows doing everything with each other, all the fun and games good safe things we kids did in Sunnydale.*

*Knowing that my Mother played a huge part in what our community was like back then makes me eternally grateful, proud and so thankful to be a part of this wonderful journey back home to Sunnydale. Just a short time ago I ran into someone who spoke so very highly of what Ms Frierson had done for them. Pride gleamed across my face.*

*Loretta Ms Harris' youngest and I were childhood friends. From time to time her brother Michael and I still cross paths.*

*I am also grateful that my mother was still very much alive when the Revitalization began in Sunnydale.*

*Knowing she is smiling down from the Heavens Above hoping the best for all the people in Bayview Hunters Point and the Sunnydale communities is truly a Blessing.*

*My hope is that the new changes in the neighborhood will bring with them social services and programs that will inspire people to take pride in their community. Without community enhancement programs our young people will be headed towards fast tracks and bad outcomes. I can't help but tell you how proud I am of my mother and the work she embraced and the people she stood for.*

*People need someone like Momma, Geogre Davis and the EOC. Our communities today are especially in need of people like my Mother and strong Black men like Mr Davis.*

*Without reservation I'll Always Love My Momma.*
*Ida Frank Pitre*

## Ms Ida

*June 14th 1923-May 12th 2022*
*Honoring*
*The Life and Times of Ida Frank Pitre*
*99 Years*
*One Month Shy of Her One Hundred Birthday*

# The Pitre Family

*The Pitre Family were among the few families in Sunnydale with a mother and father but to me they were not unique because a lot of us kids were without both parents, the Pitre's unofficially adopted us, sharing what they had and gave us kids as much love and guidance as they did to their very own children.*

*Their door was always open and those of us in Sunnydale in some way were very much apart of the Pitre Family" Lafrance Graves*

*Graves' comments are significant, supporting statistical data and research that two parent households are more likely to raise children who are goal oriented and likely to pursue higher education and career paths.*

*In Sunnydale and communities alike there is minimal data available that reveals the influence of surrogate families like the Pitre's who helped many of our young brothers and sisters pursue long term educational and career goals.*

*Sunnydale has produced more than its share of successful men and women. "We looked up to the Pitre brothers they mentored a lot of us youngstas" Al Burleson*

*"Sunnydale didn't have many two parent households in Sunnydale, but those that were there didn't look down on us like they were better than us, that's just the way it was, the Pitre's and the other households who had both parents were supportive of those of us without a mother or father. I think that's what made Sunnydale a care for your neighbor community" Skip Roberts*

*Substantial family structure data supports the success of black children raised in two-parent homes located in low economic communities compared to black children raised by single-parents or in stepfamilies.*

*"If your family didn't have those basic essentials there was always a door to knock on and your neighbor was willing to share. It was that way with the Pitre's to" Robert Taylor*

*"It's amazing that the youth today wear designer jeans with holes in them, but when we grew up, holes in our jeans were all too common but the Mothers in Sunnydale like Ms Ida knew how to sew, this was way before they had iron on patches. Their sewing skills helped weave the neighborhood fabric in the community. None of us were ashamed of wearing hand me downs or jeans with holes in them" Robert Butchie Freeman*

## Ida's Story

*Ida "Darlin" Frank was born in Ville Platte, Louisiana on June 14th 1923, she retired from this earth on May 12th 2022.*

*She lived a long beautiful life that the contributors of this composition are proud to acknowledge.*

*In 1941 she married Onezime Pitre, and gave birth to four children.*

*The Pitre's were one of the rare families in the community, a two parent home of loving supportive Black parents who many of those in the community gravitated to.*

*By no means were the Pitre's the Cosby's, they were the real deal doing the very best to raise their own children but not ignoring those children who needed love and support.*

*The family moved to San Francisco in 1950 settling in her beloved Sunnydale Community like a number of Sunnydale families who lived in the Crocker Amazon housing development over the hill.*

*She loved to sew, loved to cook, skills she learned from her mother back home.*

*Mrs Pitre made some of the best gumbo, dirty rice and pineapple cakes this side of Lousianna, she was adamant on making hungry folks wash their hands and Say Grace before sitting down to eat.*

*She was a Woman who believed in the Power of Prayer.*

*If I were a betting man I'd put my money on Ms Ida winning any community cooking contest. The woman knew her way around the kitchen and could Burn.*

*Ida had a longtime career working as a seamstress and shared that artistic skill with her grandchildren and those in the community willing to learn the craft.*

*It was with a kind Heart and Love for sewing she weaved a connection of Life giving thread through the neighborhood*

*She brought to the community an unconditional spirit of compassion, a go above and beyond humanitarian commitment to help those in need.*

*Ms Ida was one of the rare individuals who put the welfare of the community and others first.*

*Many of her free days were spent canvassing the community from her front or back yard windows, always with an encouraging smile and waving hands to help people get through the days or times of grief. She was always there for others.*

*The Pitre household was a home away from home for many in the community.*

*She "kept it real" as only a mother can do. She was a bright light in a community that had its share of dark moments.*

*Ms Pitre lived by a merciful motto of helping others during troublesome times, her internal strength and fortitude are immeasurable qualities many of us yearn for but are unwilling to listen to our Hearts, and the Word of the Almighty which Ms Ida embraced.*

*Her house was always meticulously cleaned but not nearly as cleansing as her Heart of Purity.*

*Ms Ida was blessed to leave a legacy of 10 grandchildren, 23 great grandchildren and 7 great great grandchildren.*

*At her Homegoing services at St. John's Baptist Church, there was a significant representation of those in attendance who came to pay their final respects, these were the people she touched and her send off was a wonderful celebration.*

*Her contributions to the people of Sunnydale shall not be left behind and the Community will forever remember Ida Frank Pitre.*

# The Mothers and Women
# of Sunnydale

*Neighborhood Den Mothers - Community Ambassadors*
***Their Legacy Shall Not Be Forgotten***
*Nor Of Those Who Came Before Them*

*Sojourner Truth*
***A Song for Ms Henrietta***
***Pays Tribute To***
***The Women and Mothers of Sunnydale***
***Women Who Made A Way Outa Noway***
***Those Who've Went Above And Beyond***
***Those Who Kneeled And Prayed - Giving***
***Thanks To The Lord For Another Day***

*"We were raised by some strong Black women. I remember seeing so many of them shopping at the thrift shop, making a dollar out of fifteen cents saving coupons, S&W Stamps, sewing patches on our clothes, doing without for themselves doing anything, whatever it took to put food on the table and clothes on our backs. None of our families had a lot and not one of us went without. Life in Sunnydale was good. Our mothers did the best they could, there was always bread on the table" Robert Taylor*

*"I must give a lot of credit to the mothers who raised kids on their own in the projects, they had to be very stern, protective, and they did it on their own" Rafiki Webster*

*SUNNYDALE'S GROUND TRAFFIC CONTROLLER*
*Mae Burleson*
*GRANDMOTHER Of CBS MORNING SHOW HOST*
*NATE BURLESON*

*"Man, my mother could make 50 meals outta a pound of ground beef" Al Burleson*

*If Ms Henrietta was the neighborhood's door to door Street Soldier Ambassador then Mae Burleson, her next door neighbor was the Broomstick Brigade's **"Ground Traffic Controller"***

*There was no more difficult of a job within the Brigade than that of the **GROUND TRAFFIC CONTROLLER.***

*It was a hands on **"stare you in the face, navigate, see through all your jive and bullshit, tell it like it is, try and help ya' ass from taking off down a flight of dark stairs without a planned destination and do everything in my power not to call ya momma again" Ugly Ugly Ugly Job!** which fell on the tiny mighty shoulders of Mae Burleson*

*"Mae was young at heart. That more or less may have been the biggest difference about her, and why people gravitated to her. She knew what the young people in the community were up to, but really all the mothers knew and they had their own ways of sharing the low down on us good and bad. Mae just had her own way of relating to people but she was as old school as they came. She had her responsibilities to the Mothers in the Community, she just handled situations a little differently, but Mae was a straight up down to the bone old school parent." Randy Roc Minix*

*The Burleson household was a reception and recovery center, a stop by and chat landing strip, a crisis intervention sanctuary for all of Sunnydale wayward souls.*

*"Our house was a safety net for all of Sunnydale, I guess because Mom was from the old school and could somewhat relate to the younger crowd. All we know was that there was always someone knocking at the front door, back door and I damn sure know they whatnall trying' to borrow a cup of sugar" Kermit Burleson*

"Wasn't nobody sitting down on Momma's couch in dirty clothes! She'd feed you. But she made sure people wiped their shoes before they came into the house, especially my hard headed brothers. My mother was PineSol clean and Neat! She must have cleaned the house two three times a day" Lisa Burleson

"Dude 78 Blythedale, the Burleson crib was always open for business. But Mae ran a tight ship. She wasn't about jive and could relate to everyone. If you got out of line, she'd be the first one to check your ass and put you in your place, that's on the real tip". Glen Chop Porter

"Ms Mae was a frequent rider on the Teardrop Express. Another one of the women I admired, she had to deal with a lot being a single parent, Kermit! Wow! Was more than any parent could handle. He must of been majoring in "getting in trouble" on the days he went to school" TC Caracter

"It was better going, telling on yourself to Mae than your own Momma finding out. She sort of broke the ice for us but we still got whuppin. Mae was old school but she could relate to us youngstas" Glen GT Taylor

"With Lisa, her daughter, Wanting to be an FBI Agent or an Investigative News Reporter we were better off telling on ourselves. Somehow Mae always had the goods on everybody in the neighborhood. I'm thinking Lisa and Uncle Ike had something to do with that" Glen Chop Porter

"Anyway we looked at things we got into trouble with. it was in our best interest not to squirm out of what we did. It was just best to come clean with Mae, cause she was gonna tell your mother anyway what we did. She was a Card Carrying Member, an official with Captain's Bars Street Soldier in Ms Henrietta' Broomstick Brigade" Thomas Warren

*"She was my unofficial Probation Officer. I ask my mother could I go down to the Burlesons, she'd smile, give me an extra nickel cause Moms knew I was in good hands"* Glen GT Taylor

*"Pick your poison when it comes down to getting in trouble. Wasn't no getting out of trouble with any of the Sunnydale Moms. Yeah Ms Burleson was cool, but many times I saw the other side of that coolness. Ask Big Kermit and Alvin, about those beatdowns, butt whuppn's Hahaha"* Harold Williams

*"Ms Burleson was some kind of woman, some kind of mother, some kind of neighbor who never turned her back on anyone. She was always there for everyone in the community"* Maxine Hughes

*"She was a stickler for making you wash your hands, say Grace before you ate, make you sit at her table with a napkin in your lap but when you got up from her table you were full well fed and learned a thing or two about manners"* Randy Roc Minix

# Miss Cleo Nelson

*Homemaker Community Advocate Community Gardener*

*"My mom endured many tragedies yet managed to start a community garden and feed the people of Sunnydale" James Nelson*

*The tragic loss of her daughter Norma, the victim of a serial killer. The killings of a son Leotis "Toastie" on Hahn Street and a daughter Erma the victim of a sick prank, someone pouring acid in a drink at a Friday Night Dance that left her deranged, weighed heavy on Ms Cleo.*

*But through the Power of Prayer, a group of mothers there to pray and support her, the Mothers help lift her up and endure.*

*She found salvation and support and a passion for gardening.*

*The forming of the Community Garden was her refuge during difficult times, not only for herself but for others having emotional difficulties during troubling times.*

*Miss Cleo Nelson came to California from Shreveport, Louisiana in the early 1950's.*

*Briefly her young family lived first in Oakland, CA, then moved to San Francisco's highly Black populated Fillmore District.*

*Ms Nelson moved to the Sunnydale projects in the mid fifties and like most families that lived in the Sunnydale Housing Projects Cleo was a single mother with four children.*

*She raised twins Irma, and Norma, James, and the oldest of the Nelson children, older brother Leottis 'Toastie'' Nelson.*

*Cleo had a great relationship with all the children in the neighborhood because of her "my door is always open" policy.*

*Her Southern roots in spite of the deeply rooted prejudices, the separation and segregation she endured were not road blocks to her commitment to serve in her community.*

*But the many families who came to Sunnydale could not initially separate themselves and their experiences from the South.*

*Ms Cleo was the exception to the rule. She painted a vivid picture of irrational unequal conditions in the South and was not hesitant to use her upbringing as an instrumental tool of discussion to those who crossed her path.*

*"Ms Nelson let the cobblestones of her past be the reason of her firm belief, Sunnydale should be like "One Big Ole Family" Coyle Jefferson*

*"She was the reason as a family basically we did everything together. When most of our parents were at work, one of the neighbors watched after us. That's the thing I think most my mother loved about Sunnydale" James Nelson*

*'I am not surprised at all that it was Ms Cleo who started a community garden hungry kids use to come by her house and she, would share everything including the leftovers" Levi Bryant*

### Ms Cleo in Her Garden
*Sweet Mothers of Mine*

*The contributions of Sunnydale Mothers cannot be ignored, just the thought of dealing with the struggles and hardships facing insurmountable obstacles, providing essentials and safety for their children was a day-to-day struggle for survival and God's Miracles.*

There are many who performed various roles and duties in the community like **Ms Henrietta, Ms Frierson, Ms Webster, Mae Burleson, Ms Taylor, Mrs Porter, Mrs Pitre, Ola Mae Minix, Mrs**

**Hughes, Ms Warren, Ms Billups, who raised two blind children, Ms Ruiz, Ms Caracter, Mrs Peters, Ms Battie, Ms Graves, Ms Latham, Mercy D Williams, Ms Nelson, Vivian Williams, Ms Rose, who ran the community center, Ms Nelson, Mrs Phillips, Sherman's grandmother, Ms Ellenwood a Native American single mother, Ms Mollison, Ms Baker, Ms Agnew and my mom Victoria Jefferson,** these women and many many others will forever be Surrogate Moms to all of Sunnydale

**Ms Nelson,** *from Santos to the top of the hill going up Sunnydale Avenue there should be chrome plated benches for resting seniors with Ms Nelson's name enshrined on each and every bench*

**Mrs Pitre,** *always a confort, was always sharing with others, noone who came to her door was turned away*

**Ms Burleson,** *her Heart was wide as all outdoors, open to all of Sunnydale.*

**Ms Ellenwood,** *simply amazing organizing retreats to Native American historical sites, while raising five young children*

**Ms Baker,** *wonderful white woman who raised three children and was heavily involved in community developments*

**Ms Guzman,** *Hispanic mother with three boys help start and organized the Sunnydale Boys Scouts*

**Ms Mollison,** *Polish woman with young boys who help organize events at the Rec Center, worked closely with Ms Frierson at the EOC Center*

**Ms Hughes,** *Ms Henrietta's shoulder to lean on, always a comfort in the storm*

**Mrs Pitre,** *Baby Ray and Ann's mother, cordial and compassionate*

**Ms Graves** was well respected, Loved by all of Sunnydale, God's goodness. His Grace was in her Heart

**Ms Taylor, "GT's"** mom with the bright sunshiny smile and the epitome of politeness

**Mercy D Williams,** a mom's mom, spoke her mind was always right on time

**Ms Warren,** Sunnydale's go to Mom for whatever you need

**Ms Martinez,** Danny Boy's mother never missed a community meeting, her energy and commitment and contributions were most significant

**Ms Agnew,** Larry's mom, a white woman who lived on the Front and was a friend to all. Walk through a group of brotha's hang'n on the corner like it was the thing to do

**Vivian Williams,** beautiful mother of Sunnydale's Native Sons

**Ms McClain,** the Park and Rec Director knew every kid and their momma in Sunnydale

"Every child who attended John McLaren Elementary School is eternally grateful to **Ms Wooten,** this education first no nonsense, All About The Books Black Woman and Schoolteacher" Glen GT Taylor

# Sunnydale Mothers

### *Ola Mae Minix*

*"Not a soul in Sunnydale would go hungry as long as Ola Mae was cooking" Al Burleson*

*"The Minix household was always full of people good food, playing cards and dominoes sometimes there was just standing room only with brothers outside waiting their turn to try and charm get their Mac' on Ola Mae's fine young daughters Sista's Diane, Delores, Elmira and Norine faking like they was coming by the house to see if "Roc" could come outside and play. Where else could a brother get a free meal and a chance to fulfill his fantasy? Man! We could smell Ola Mae's cooking all over the neighborhood" Glen "Chop" Porter*

*"Ola Mae had an infectious smile. We would see her waiting at the bus stop on Santoes going downtown to work, from across the street we would wait on the very last school bus and she would wave to us. It was her way of telling a bus stop of Jr High School kids to have a good day. For some of the kids from troubled homes Ola Mae's smiles and waves may have been the only signs of encouragement they may have received for the entire day" Eric Peters*

*"She was truly a southern bell charming, cordial, sharing, hospitable and most importantly a caring and loving soul" Kermit Burleson*

*"Funny my friends never saw the other side of Momma. Believe me Ola Mae could be tough as nails. She didn't have to tell us twice, my sisters and me. Believe me growing up we got the message" Randy Roc Mininx*

## Forever Sunnydale Surrogate Moms To All

**Ms Granderson,** *raised two children and wasn't afraid to share the Word of the Good Book*

**Ms LaBlanc,** *raised three wonderful children with her husband but was involved in many neighborhood activities.*

**Ms Hopkins,** raised six children while working as a community activist for EOC

**Mrs Peters,** held countless activities at her home for young kids to participate in

**Ms Mable and Ms Mary,** two beautiful southern sisters. *Ms Mary* became Roc's beautiful wife

These women and many many others will forever be Surrogate Moms to all of Sunnydale

# Inspirational Words

*Sunnydale had some strong awesome outstanding women and Super Mothers' back in the Day.*

*Let me take this moment to acknowledge them, Thank Them All for raising us, helping us and looking out for us.*

*May God Bless Them All. Sweet Mother of Mine*

Victoria Teresa in San Francisco, CA

*Victoria Jefferson*

*Every day of my Life, I wish the Mothers of Sunnydale, a Happy Mother's Day, they deserve and are worthy of All of His Praise and Blessings*

*Coyle Jefferson*

## Sunnydale's Humble Servant Izola Cudjo Frierson RIP

# Women Who Paved The Way

## Mother's of Sunnydale

*She had more concern for the welfare of our community than mosst social workers could ever dream of. TC Caracter*

*Ms Frierson was Sunnydale's Bread and Water Al Burleson*

C

# Berniece Donna Billups

All BY MYSELF
*"She raised four children. Two of them Blind"*
HER REMARKABLE JOURNEY

*Of* all *the* **Sunnydale Mothers** *who came to Sunnydale many with Southern Roots and traumatic life experiences, none typify the struggles of Bernice Donna Billups who contributed greatly to the development and welfare of the people in the Sunnydale Community while raising four young children two of them blind.*

*Today at 92 years of age, bright, vivid and alert she shared her remarkable life journey.*

*She was born in the 5th Ward in Houston Texas and dreamed of becoming a nurse.*

*When she reached the age of maturity she moved to Los Angeles, California to attend a nursing school after writing a letter of introduction to a nursing school facility.*

*Upon arrival at the school she was told her application for admission had been rejected because the school refused to admit Black Nursing Students.*

*Not being deterred and with family in San Francisco she headed north to the Bay Area with her dreams still intact.*

*Upon arrival to the city she met her husband, the two were married and their union would produce two young children and sadly cancel out her original career plans.*

*The nursing dream would never materialize because her first children were born premature, weighing slightly more than two pounds and both Dennis and Denise were born blind.*

*"It placed an enormous strain on my husband and me. We didn't get a lot of help from family and the medical staff and I found myself pregnant again with Anthony after their birth and a fourth child Madonna to follow shortly thereafter"*

*Her husband's family were not understanding of handicap children in the family but UCSF Hospital reached out to her offering care and resources that at the time were minimal.*

*The family lived in a flat on Harrison Street and for the time managed what little they had but the strain was wearing heavily on her husband but it was Ms Billups who wanted to take sole responsibility for her young children.*

*With their differences and isolation they ended up in court appearing before a judge who mandated the family remain intact.*

*"I wanted to be independent and didn't want to listen to anybody, my husband, a judge or family was going to tell me how to raise my children, but the judge ordered me to stay with my husband"*

*Ms Billups refused to comment on what eventually happened between her or to Mr Billups but she did comment, "then one day I was all by myself and all alone"*

The family was offered housekeeping and social services assistance before the Housing Authority became involved.

"The Housing Authority offered us an apartment on the fourth floor of the Pink Palace in the Fillmore District and a place on Potrero Hill. I told them I ain't moving taking my babies to no projects, My God! First they wanna put my kids in a place where they could fall out a window, then they offered me a place on a hill where my kids could roll down and kill themselves,"

Ms Billups came to Sunnydale in the early 1960's.

"The Housing Authority got us a place right next to the Recreation Center where my children could play outside in front of the house on the grass with the other children. It was a safe place and the kids in the neighborhood were receptive to my children and my kids were happy. It was then that I got involved with volunteering at the Center"

Over time the Billups Family became a mainstay in the community especially around the Sunnydale Recreation Center.

Ms Billups would become one of the most respected women, parents and community leaders in the neighborhood.

"I did the very best I could for my children who I am proud of and for the wellbeing of my community"

More of Ms Billups' contributions to the Sunnydale Community will continue in our story of George Davis Sunnydale's Anchor

I Ain't Always Been Blind<br>Dennis Billups

"Dennis may have been blind but that didn't stop him one bit from hanging out with the fellas. He ran the streets, drank his share of wine, played congas and could have been the next Stevie Wonder *the way dude played his harmonica. Dennis was a member of our singing group, sang a mean baritone and chased the girls just like the rest of us"* Levi Bryant

*"I never let my disability be a hindrance to me growing up in Sunnydale. The community had a warm sense of belonging, culture and ambience like when the winds blew through the trees or the sounds of the Ice Cream Man a few buildings away from our house. Hell I was always first in line when the truck parked in front of the center. It was times like this, my keen sense of my surroundings were most beneficial. Sure there were a few times some of the brothers teased me, my mom put a quick stop to that right away but I fired right back, held my ground. I can remember having a few scuffles but that was apart of growing up in Sunnydale"*

*Dennis is involved in the Obama Disability Rights Commission for the Disabled along with a number of community enhancement programs serving the handicap.*

*He attended Balboa High School where he acted in stage plays, played music and even worked at the Dugout Lunch Counter making and serving Frosties. Upon graduation he attended San Francisco State College and was part of the Black Students Union.*

*Today he is actively working with staff from the George Davis Senior Citizen Organization in Bayview Hunters Point.*

*"In spite of my disability I am the oldest child, I had to carry myself with an independent attitude and strength to look after my younger siblings"*

*"Dennis was all over the neighborhood. He slid down John McLaren Hill on cardboard boxes with us bumped his big head many a time and got right back up and slid down the hill, laughing from ear to ear time and time again"* Douglas Latham

*"My growing up was an advantage over the other children because my visualization of things was truly much more vivid and fun. I was twelve years ago before I even got a walking cane so I saw more than people ever expected that I could see. To tell you the truth I Ain't Always Been Blind"*

# CHAPTER 1

# BROOMSTICKS BATHROBES AND THE BIBLE

## The Broomstick Brigade

*Courageous Black Women Ambassadors of GoodWill*
***Following in the Footsteps of Harriet, Sojourner,***
***Maya and Mary***

*Marching through puddles in the pouring rain or weathering the heat of the blistering sun, these women Ambassadors of GoodWill are known throughout our communities-welcomed in every household-on every street corner, they understand better than anyone the need to help others in times of need are essential.*

*They take to the streets with **Broomsticks, Bathrobes and Bibles**, the only things they need to help those in their beloved communities.*

*In front of them each day stand the Mount Everest of Hardships, Desperation and Despair.*

*Without relentless training they rely solely on an intense community bond that fosters help and encouragement.*

*Their roles require a strong healthy relationship with the people in their community.*

*Throughout each day these women call on* **The Almighty** *for strength and guidance.*

*They sing in harmony before taking to the streets* **"If Ya Wanna Help Me Jesus, It's Alright"**

*Their* **Broomsticks** *are not for protection but for sweeping up-cleaning up the trash of hopelessness.*

*Wrapped with* **Bathrobes** *of warmth, heartfelt dedication to help those in need, their robes can be seen from street corner to streetcorner-a beautiful encouraging sign that help is on the way.*

*Their* **Bibles** *contain powerful scriptures of Inspiration, Words of Wisdom, Prayers of Solace and Forgiveness.*

*Their work is never done. They are not tall striking women but many are meek in stature, quiet and unassuming powerful through* **Truth and Prayer.**

*They are* **Courageous Black Women Ambassadors of GoodWill.**

# CHAPTER 2

# SUNNYDALE'S RESUSCITATOR

## Breathing Life Into Her Community

*Infused with Rich Humanitarian Spiritual
Compassionate Activism To Do The Right Thing*

*Raised in segregated Arcadia, Louisiana, Ms Henrietta came to
San Francisco California in 1941 with many southern families who
migrated north seeking employment and quality of life opportunities.*

*Arcadia means Beautiful Hills, and was the battle ground that ended
the reign of the notorious outlaws Bonnie and Clyde in 1934.*

*Ms Henrietta had an alert system of compassionate response to
help those in need, whether in crisis, in need of essentials, sharing
groceries with what little she had or providing a comforting shoulder
to lean on. Helping others was in her DNA.*

*Sunnydale owes Ms Henrietta a Gold Mine of Ghetto Gratitude.*

*She was a firm believer in Building Her Community from the
Ground Up.*

*"I ain't working for myself" she used to say, "I'm working for the community"*

*Ms Henrietta was Sunnydale's Resuscitator, a Breath of Fresh Air. Her presence was felt throughout the community day and night.*

*When the calls for her help came, she was minutes ahead of 911 and EMT.*

*Oftentimes she would make multiple visits to the same families on the same day over and over again.*

*She was Sunnydale's unofficial Ambassador of GoodWill, always on lookout for someone experiencing difficult or trying times.*

*Always was she the calm in the storm, the voice of reason, Sunnydale's Community Matriarch, responding without judgment without reservation.*

*Her understanding of people wasn't limited by hugs and well wishes. She was a diehard community street soldier who dealt with Life on Life's terms.*

*She had to be because being a single mother raising a family of five she was not immune to hardships and the survival needs to provide for a family, but she frowned on domestic situations where children were involved.*

*"I Do God's Work for every Family and every Child" she would say.*

*Ms Henrietta raised two beautiful daughters **Sharon and Loretta** who exemplified Henrietta's youthful beauty.*

*No doubt back in her day Ms Henrietta was a picture of sure beauty.*

*Her sons, **Napoleon, Danny Ray and Michael** were respectful of her, well mannered, cordial and ghetto inquisitive.*

*She, like all single mothers did her best but the school of life came calling early for Danny Ray and Michael.*

*She faced the same challenges as every single mother raising young boys alone.*

*Ms Henrietta was strong in her beliefs, streetwise, yet sweet as the home baked cookies and cupcakes she used to bake.*

*When the **Toe Tickler** put Sunnydale on alert for entering the houses of women through open windows and unlocked doors tickling their feet, then escaping in the darkness.*

*Ms Henrietta and women in the community walked through the neighborhood in the early morning hours and dark nights to locate the perpetrator, more likely to offer him help rather than confront his insane behavior.*

***Even the City's serial killers the Zodiac, Richard Ramierz or The Doddler would have been no match for the Broomstick Brigade.***

*Al and I would see Henrietta out before dawn when we were delivering the morning newspapers unafraid and without a candle or flashlight. She was tough as nails, soft as melting butter.*

*The Tickler caused so much havoc and paranoia in the neighborhood the police patrolled Sunnydale well after dark with Doberman Pinscher dogs and flashlights.*

*Eventually it was the community who urged the Housing Authority to install lamp lights on the buildings to deter the Tickler.*

*Sunnydale of old will never know The Notorious Tickler.*

*He was never identified but many residents believe it could have been a number of outrageous wayout brotha's in the hood.*

*Rumors have it that one of the dudes people thought may have been the Tickler, ironically lived a few apartments down from Ms Henrietta.*

*In her two bedroom apartment on Blythedale Street she was forced to take the reins while being a leader in the community.*

*She was a fulltime mother, a fulltime street soldier, a full time community activist under pressure to parent, under pressure to empower her community.*

*Ms Henrietta faced the challenges of trying to hold her family and community together at the same time, balancing parenthood with communityship.*

*For her there was no daydreaming, no time to pamper herself.*

*Her need to provide, her need to serve were far too great. Her plate was full.*

*Ms Henrietta wasn't trying to be a role model, she wanted nothing to do with being nobody's super hero.*

*Sacrifices and obstacles single women face raising families on their own are not visually apparent.*

*Their tears don't provide substantial nourishment for evening meals but they do provide substance for hidden relief.*

*Without hesitation, because of Unconditional Community Courageousness and Love for her Beloved community,* **the Sons of Sunnydale hope that one day the City and County of San Francisco commision an artist to construct a statue to honor the memory of Ms Henrietta Harris and the Mothers of Sunnydale in the front of the Rec Center at Sunnydale and Santoes Streets.**

# The Revitalization in Sunnydale

*"When I heard about the changes. I went out to Sunnydale and introduced myself to the people living in our old house" Harold Williams, born in Sunnydale 1959*

SAN FRANCISCO'S MAYOR'S OFFICE OF HOUSING AND COMMUNITY DEVELOPMENT, SF HOPE, MERCY HOUSING, COUNTLESS INVESTORS HAVE TAKEN ON THE ENORMOUS TASK OF HELPING TO CHANGE THE CONDITIONS IN SAN FRANCISCO'S SUNNYDALE PUBLIC HOUSING COMMUNITY.

*"Our story means everything to me. My brothers and I were born and raised in Sunnydale" Harold Williams*

**Sunnydale's Native Sons Anthony, Lonnie and Harold Williams**

## A COSMETIC APPROACH IS NOT WHAT THE DEVELOPERS HAVE PROPOSED. THE CONCERNS OF THE PEOPLE ARE VALUED

*"The Sunnydale where we grew up and the people who live there now deserve to see these changes become a worthwhile reality. It's a win-win situation for both the old and the new residents. There's a lot of excitement out there, good things are happening in Sunnydale" A Burleson*

*"Nothing at all is wrong with progress, those of us who lived there back in the day are proud to see the new developments but our memories are priceless. My sister still lives there" T Warren*

*"I drove through Sunnydale just a few days ago. Man there's alot going on but the old neighborhood for me will always be the same" B Hughes*

*"It's a long time coming rebuilding the community, too bad the people there who lived in the neighborhood when the community was not a nice place to live had to go through all of the drugs, crime, loss of life and gang violence before something like the new developments came along" L Booker*

*"It's a good thing tearing down the old and building the new" K Burleson*

*"The new changes in the community are not threatening for most. I think the changes are welcomed but it's going to take time. Our communities have heard false promises from developers before, but what's happening now in Sunnydale seems to be the real deal" E Peters*

*"I have no doubt that the changes will have an impact on the people who live there, but it's still up to them to make a difference in their neighborhood. A lot of mental changes need to take place if the community is to progress. It doesn't make sense wearing new clothes and not taking a bath. There's a lot of cleansing, healing and trust needed if the investors and the people expect significant results" T Warren*

*"Where we grew up and what the community is like now are quite different in terms of the physical appearances but the survival of the people struggling from day to day are one in the same still the same" M Pitre*

9

*"I know the changes are good for the people in Sunnydale. Everyone in those apartments reminds me of something and someone, the people who once lived there when I was growing up in the neighborhood. What they are doing in Sunnydale providing jobs and getting people involved in community activities is amazing. My only wish is that some part of our past history can be restored with a mural or something that reminds the people there now of what Sunnydale was like back when we grew up in the neighborhood"*
*Harold Williams*

*"Better recognize. Things are changing in the Swampe' D" Harold Williams*

# Sunnydale Lives Newspaper

## NEWS FOR TODAY FROM SAN FRANCISCO'S SUNNYDALE HOUSING PROJECTS

# BREAKING NEWS

**MEDIA OUTLETS CONVERGE ON NEW DEVELOPMENTS IN SUNNYDALE USA**

## THINGS ARE CHANGING IN THE SWAMPE D

*"Shedding the neighborhoods negative identification is a job in itself"* **Melvin Pitre** *"Now the Swampe' D' can represent a symbol of ethnic and community pride" Eric Peters.*

### The Praises have gone up The Blessings have come Down on Sunnydale

### Oh Happy Day

MLK said "Our basic mobility should not be from a smaller ghetto to a larger one"

**New Pride –New Opportunities–New Community**

*Harold Williams, "Sunnydale now has the chance going from last place to first place"*

11

# Fighting Back To Save The Neighborhood

## "Sunnydale's Swampe' D"

### *A Chance At The Title*

*To outsiders Sunnydale's decline became quite possibly the most dangerous depressed and decrepit areas of the city.*

**"Our Community's Been Down On The Deck Of Life Much Too Long"**

*"By the time our precious Sunnydale became notoriously known as The "Swampe D" most of us from the early days, our families had moved on. The people there deserve a chance to get up off the Deck Of Life, no doubt in my mind the community has earned a Second Chance At The Title" Melvin Pitre*

**"We were outside playing the congas.** *The almighty hawk, the wind was blowing hard, the wind was swirling around through Sunnydale and one of the brothers said the wind is blowing through Sunnydale like a desert Swamp. That's how the Sunnydale SwampeD got its name" Dennis Pettway*

Things Are Changing In The Swampe' D

*"I just hope the people in the community can wake up each morning, look outside their front windows and watch their children going to school, playing outside with smiles on their faces" Eric Peters*

*"Time and change has a way of mending broken communities" TC Caracter*

*"We will truly know when things are changing in Sunnydale when the children are outside playing without a care in the world" Eddrena Peters*

*"There was an imaginary demarcation line, separating the*

*single-family homes in Visitacion Valley from the projects, but you couldn't miss the pink and yellow buildings, 41 Brookdale Avenue was our home" Rafiki Webster*

*"Sunnydale was back then a different place than now, but people there in the community today have a right to know what it was like*

13

*for us kids growing up in a community that cared for one another"*
***Berle Grant***

*"We weren't ashamed of the people but ashamed of the things that were happening in the community. Some of us believe me tried to ignore the dreadful things people, the news media everyone who never lived there were saying about Sunnydale"* **Robert Butchie Freeman**

*"Sleepy eyed children in Sunnydale should not have to wake up fearing for their safety. The future of the community is with the children, that's the biggest investment that's needs to be shared with all the people involved in trying to change the community climate from top to bottom"* **Thomas Warren**

*"I give them developers credit but unless the project has some job training programs to offer the residents, nothing is going to change. Unemployment and lack of job training will only result in people doing whatever it takes to put food on the table"* **Dwayne Robins**

*"If anyone sat down with the children in the community and asked them what they want for the Swampe D, I am sure they'd want a neighborhood like ours where we grew up"* **Harold Williams**

*"I never really left Sunnydale, it's where I grew up, there are still some people out there from the old days that I visit from time to time"* **Robert Butchie Freeman**

*"A lot of what happened in Sunnydale is the blame of the City and the Housing Authority. They moved people from other declining housing projects to Sunnydale. It was a bad move; those from the other neighborhoods brought with them all sorts of drama and things began to clash. Those of us from Sunnydale weren't going to back down, be intimidated from those who came to the*

*neighborhood. The City and the Housing Authority didn't tell us anything about what was happening and then when it did they turned their backs on all of us" The relocation could and should have been handled differently, it only pitted one group against another and the people in the neighborhood were the ones who suffered" Dennis Pettway*

## Resistance to Revitalization

*"When you've been down so long sometimes it's hard to look up. There are mixed emotions among the folks there about the changes going on in Sunnydale, I know because my sister still lives there. Not everyone is welcome to the changes and that only makes good sense because change is challenging. Their resistance to revitalization is real. What the community service workers need to be doing is helping the residents realize that when a community is down there's no place to go but up. It's a difficult realization but a most necessary one" Thomas Warren*

*"I remember when the Housing Authority called themselves making improvements in the neighborhood. All they did was install some aluminum windows and towed away a few cars in the parking lots. I wouldn't call that neighborhood improvement at all" Dennis Pettway*

*"There are many ways to describe the heartaches and pains our communities struggle through but it almost seemed like a bat of an eye that yesterday, once a beautiful place was now a desert, a far cry from the oasis where we grew up" Melvin Pitre*

## Public Housing Communities Across This Nation

*Have long struggled to survive the hardships, disparity and oppressive hands of fate dealt to them.*

*The People in San Francisco's Sunnydale Public Housing Community are no exception confronted with insurmountable odds and obstacles living day-to-day on the edge of hopelessness and despair.*

*Revitalization has often been on the forefront of investment and political agendas often producing nothing more than false promises and deeds of mistrust.*

# Community Revitalization Has Had Its Share Of Failures

*Our communities have a long history of being the least and last beneficiaries of proposed revitalization.*

*However in the Sunnydale Projects the people of the community are seeing for themselves through the committed efforts of the Mayor's Office of Housing and Community Development the planned proposals for revitalization and community involvement are well underway and utilizing the input of neighborhood residents to transform their neighborhood and way of life.*

*There is no single formula for success and transformation in low income communities across this nation.*

*Successful revitalization projects put the interest and needs of the people first.*

*Therefore there must be infrastructure in place to help people in the community benefit.*

*Community leaders have expressed the need for Support Mechanisms, Social Services, Employment Opportunities, Income Enhancement Job and Skills Training Programs, Leadership and Mentorship Development, Parenting and Community Ambassador, Safety Awareness and Conflict Resolution Skills Training Programs.*

*No approach is better than the other for the process and struggle to change inevitably has its ups and downs. Yet nothing is impossible.*

*Revitalization of our communities is a difficult delicate balancing act of innovation, resident involvement, visionary sharing, courage and trust to encourage people to empower themselves and make it happen.*

*In San Francisco's Sunnydale Housing Projects the Mayor's Office of Community and Housing Development has taken on this enormous challenge to encourage residents to chase their dreams, become involved in their community and improve their way of living.*

*This is the story of a community, the people, an organization and some remarkable women who fostered hope, breathed life into the community and wanted something much more than they could've ever imagined to look down from Heaven Way and see the revitalization in their beloved Sunnydale Community Become a Reality*

# "Memorable Moments In Sunnydale History

*"A lot of the kids, teenagers and families migrated to Sunnydale from wherever, all we knew was that Sunnydale was our very own little magical place" Ann Pitre*

**Some of the Original People Who Lived in the Sunnydale Housing Projects were White Families**

*"I always thought why did I have to comb my hair, wash my face and do all those things, to get ready to go outside and play, because when I came home from playing I was so dirty my parents wouldn't let me in the house" Melvin Pitre*

*We could go outside and play and didn't have to worry about anything bad happening to us" Annette Hughes*

**Suunydale Crocker Amazon Park Children
At John McLaren Elementary**

"I remember when **Siro stole the Gallo Truck**. All of Sunnydale got drunk for weeks. People who didn't drink got wasted, even **Rin Tin Al** and Kermit's german shepherd dog got loaded" Levi Bryant

"There was a storefront church down on Hahn Street right next to the liquor store, we would watch through the window the Preacher preaching' the women fainting and the ushers fanning them with those popsicle fans with pictures of Mahalia Jackson on one side and a Bryant Mortuary advertisement on the other" Al Burleson

"There was always something good going on in the community at the Rec Center. Those talent shows were jam packed and people had a good time. There was a lot of talent in the community" Maxine Hughes

"Back in the day there wasn't much arguing, conflict or disputes. Family conflicts were taken care of behind closed doors in private. Personal conflicts were settled over a bottle of White Port and lemon juice, some Annie Greens Spring Wine or a half of pint of rot gut depending on who was buying" Glen "Chop" Porter

*"The ToeTickler, no one really **knew who he was,** maybe a few, but this dude tormented the community by climbing through bedroom windows and tickling women's feet. Rumors have it, it could have been" Kermit Burleson*

*"We would wait for the soda trucks to deliver soda's to Big Black's Store and the Little Village Market, stand guard watching the trucks and get free Nehi Grape Sodas" Al Burleson*

*"We lived at 1951 Sunnydale Avenue at the very top of the hill by John McLaren Elementary School. I had friends everywhere in Sunnydale. We played at the schoolyard in between the buildings up and down all of Sunnydale, morning noon and night" Dwayne Robbins*

*"Wasn't much different from playing outside at night then from going outside in the daytime. We was just as safe in the daytime as we were at night" Robert Taylor*

*"I remember the brothers down on Front at the bus stop playing the congos. We could hear them playing at the top of the hill where we lived" Eric Peters*

*"The brothers in Sunnydale with outstanding parking tickets on Friday night before midnight would get drunk catch the bus down to the Hall of Justice turn themselves in, then spend the weekend in jail and appear in traffic court on Monday morning, have their tickets dismissed for time served then come back to the neighborhood and get drunk as a skunk" Leon Booker*

### *"If You Ain't Been Chased Home By Those Ghetto Black Birds You Ain't From Sunnydale"*

**"Kids were afraid to go outside. Go to school. Those damn Black Birds up in the pine trees ruled Sunnydale protecting their nest. People didn't go to the store, they chased us home when we got off the bus, our dogs hid underneath cars, those damn ghetto birds**

*were everywhere. They even snatched wigs off of women and held Sunnydale hostage every year their eggs were hatching. Anyone tell you they don't know nothing about them ghetto Black Birds ain't from Sunnydale" Levi Bryant*

*"When those good samaritan white folks in Viz Valley couldn't find a volunteer Santa Claus to come to Sunnydale. Levi Bryant, all 160 pounds soak and wet and drunk as a skunk stepped up to the plate. The funny thing is that big and robust Vernon Caracter also dressed up as Santa. Now Sunnydale had not one but two Santa's, both Black and one reeking of alcohol, stumbling and stuttering barely able to say Ho! Ho! Ho!". Kermit Burleson*

*"They had a police squad car that patrolled the neighborhood. The number on top of the squad car was 054 almost like the name of that TV Show "Car 54 Where Are You". It was funny watching them police officers jump from their car chasing the brothers who only needed a dash around the corner building headstart to get away. Because everyone's doors were open back then, some of them fleeing brothers would run through the backdoor out the front door. I will never forget the look on those officers' faces. Tired and beaten red. The brothers who they were chasing would change clothes, come back down to the Front and pretend like nothing had ever happened. One time this brother on the run came back and offered to wash the officers car" Coyle Jefferson*

# CHAPTER 3

## CRUISIN' THROUGH THE DALE

### With

### Otis "Bubba" Hughes

*It was a bright March Saturday afternoon when the phone rang. It was **Otis "Bubba" Hughes,** calling to say he wanted to take a drive through the neighborhood and see if I was interested in **Cruisin' Through The Dale**.*

*Without hesitation I jumped at the opportunity because the two of us had shared countless stories of his growing up in the Dale, and were in discussions collaborating on **this composition** and I thought with some luck we'd be able to run down **Michael, Ms Henrietta's** youngest surviving son.*

***Bubba's** invitation was a no-brainer so I grabbed my recording and camera devices and met him a few blocks from my house and we were off to **Cruise' Through The Dale**.*

*Little did I know that this journey would take us through the city sharing comments and revisiting the **Mission District, The lower***

23

*Excelsior, the businesses and shops along legendary Geneva Avenue, Crocker Amazon Park, and many of our old school stomping grounds that have significant histories connected to our growing up in the city.*

*It was one of those symbolic trips connecting **each of us** to our early childhoods.*

*Since **Bubba** was a few years older than me, I felt that I should be more of a listener, soaking up his knowledge and information almost like a tourist in my hometown with my own **Sons of Sunnydale** personalized tour guide.*

*It was like riding one of those **double decker hop on and hop off sightseeing tour buses** complimented by **Bubba's** street by street, ghetto fabulous commentary.*

***The Big Bus and San Francisco SightSeeing Buses** casually cruise through the city without mention to the inner city communities in the Southeast Sector with traveling tourists listening to tour guides commenting about San Francisco's **Tenderloin District, a neighborhood of homelessness and illicit drug use.***

***Giavonni,** a black Big Bus ticket salesman told me the tour bus companies and the Tourist Bureau feel that the Southeast Sector communities and their histories are not where and what tourist want to see, yet throughout the prosperous tourist season these double decker buses **navigate** their way through the city's **eyesoar** the **Tenderloin District.***

*He and I both agree that upon their arrival home, tourists have no panoramic pictures in their photo galleries showcasing the beautiful hillsides of McLaren Park, nor glamorous views of the San Francisco Bay from Potrero Hill and Bayview Hunters Point.*

*Denying tourists the opportunity to visit the scenic sights in BVHP, PH or McLaren Park is worse than stringing barbed wire around a House of Worship.*

*Bubba skillfully navigated the landscape and eloquently shared stories of his younger days growing up, running the streets, chasing skirts and hanging out in San Francisco.*

*Memories clicked faster than my camera at each and every turn.*

*When we turned left on Geneva/Mission Avenue heading east toward the Dale he began to tell me about going to the Amazon/ Apollo Theatre and watching those real scary movies, like Blood Feast, the Wolfman, Dracula, the Mummy and staying well after dark knowing that the only way home meant having to walk down Geneva through Crocker Amazon Park, and over John McLaren Hill in the dark.*

*So badly did I yearn to go door-to-door, holla' at Tyrone and Bobby, buy some candy from the William's family candy store at the top of the hill ride on the merry go round or teeter totter at Hertz Playground, creep on a few of those pretty young gals that back then wouldn't even look my way or give a brotha' the time of day.*

*If only the two of us could turn back the hands of time and visit the households and families that Bubba and I had spent so much of my childhood with.*

*Tears of bitterness began to slowly weather our faces because this was the Sunnydale we knew and sadly now she was only a thing of our past.*

*Gone were the days of old, the beautiful McLaren Park and lush hillsides, the landscape was far different now.*

*Today **McLaren Park** is a beautiful hillside of bike trails with walking paths with a panoramic view of San Francisco Bay Visitacion Valley, but at the bottom of the hill quite apparent are harsh times and neglect and present throughout our beloved community.*

*The pine trees we climbed that lined the streets of Sunnydale withered helplessly in the notorious winds and the sounds of children playing were non existent.*

*Driving through the Dale I could still smell the mouth watering taste of **Ola Mae's, Ms Minix** hot water buttery **"melt in ya' mouth"** cornbread. Stop in and grub on Ms **Ida's** Sunnydale famous **gumbo, dirty rice and pineapple "tree cakes"**...*

*We drove by Santoes Street and could see **Mr. Porter polishing his Stacy Adams shoes, washing waxing then wiping the paint off his pride and joy vintage blue automobile,** swign' on his favorite drink' then telling' of us youngsta's his make up a war story in a minute about how he saved the **USA** from the **Koreans'.***

*I thought about **Papa Scales** chasing youngsta's away from his manicured front yard.*

*We always wondered why **Papa Scales** in the middle of our football game would come out of the house and start watering his lawn.*

*I remember **Papa Scales and Mr Pitre** having some **"put ya hands over yo' ears"** arguments about watering his back yard when the kids were trying to play outside.*

*It would have been nice to stop in and sit with **The Character** family eating red beans and rice from a gigantic ten gallon military pot that seemed to last forever.*

*Looking back scanning the hood I could visualize **Ms Cobb** sitting in her front window trying to get the **411** on everybody in the neighborhood.*

*She was Sunnydale's **curbside reporter**. That woman was in everybody's business. Ironically in spite of her shortcomings she really meant well.*

*Canvassing the neighborhood brought memories of the **Hot Tamale** man yelln' **"Hot Tamale! Hot Tamale"***

*I thought about the **Ice Cream** truck that came every day and buying one of those nasty slurpy sugary messy chocolate ice cream bars and the **Watkin's Reumatism** liniment man going door-to-door peddling back home remedies, and the **Argo Starch momma used to eat and then wash our clothes with and those smelly liniment oils meant for livestock that we had to take a bath in. It's a miracle that the kids from back in the day have any skin left, that liniment would rip the skin right off of you.***

*Man the **Amazon Theater brought** back some crazy, full of zoo zoos and wham whams candy from the Penny Store while overdosing on back-to-back scary movies that made for some incredible hide under the covers nightmares.*

*Bubba and I both laughed, reminiscing about those parental lectures **"Boy! you'll remember next time to bring ya' ass home on time"**...*

# CHAPTER 4

## "THE DALE"

### The Early Years With Melvin Pitre

*"Back n the Dayz when the sounds of children playing brought laughter and joy and manicure lawns were Crayola colored green and families stuck together like ten toes in a sock" Glen Chop Porter*

*"The Sunnydale we knew will never be the same*

*Sunnydale was easily a place where children of all colors could play freely without a care in the world" Robert Taylor*

*"As a young girl from my bedroom window I would watch our Mothers leave the house going to work bundled up from head to toe sometimes in the pouring down rain. It brought me joy and a sense of courage and pride to see them going to work in the early morning hours, but today as I look back on those early days I realize that their sacrifices meant that a lot of the children were left at home having to raise and fend for themselves. Our moms were the real heroes in my life" Lexie TC Caracter*

*"Families looked out for one another. Some of us were better off getting out of line with our own parents than having one of the neighborhood moms catching us up to no good doing something or being somewhere we had no business being. There may have not been a hella' lot of fathers around but we had more than our share of Mother's looking out for us" Maxine Hughes*

*"Man! Sunnydale back in the day was a model neighborhood, can't say that bad things didn't happen but we did stick together during the tough times, unfortunately what happened was over time when the early families moved out things began to decline for all the wrong reasons" Leon Booker*

*"I wasn't a saint, typical kid stuff, but the mothers of the neighborhood kept us in line and did not hesitate to discipline all of us if necessary" Rafiki Webster*

*"The older siblings who were born in the South and came to live in Sunnydale were quick to forget about their southern upbringings. Living in Sunnydale offered many of them a new sense of security and belonging. The hostility in the South was nothing compared to living in Sunnydale" Melvin Pitre*

*"A lot of the Black families like ours moved to Sunnydale in the early 1950's were two parent households. We were not the first Black family to move there, maybe the third or fourth but that doesn't really matter. All that mattered to my brothers and me was playing outside. We had a lot of fun, remember I was only about three years old when we moved there, too young to give a damn about the skin color of my playmates. The color of our playmates didn't make a damn bit of difference to me, in fact as a kid growing up in Sunnydale I never heard of Jim Crow laws in the deep south".* Melvin Pitre

*Located South of McLaren Park in Visitacion Valley. aka Viz Valley Sunnydale was first constructed in 1941 and at that time San Francisco's largest public housing project, a 50 acre site with 767 units originally developed barrack style housing for war workers and families transitioning from down south who came westward looking for jobs in San Francisco or opportunities in the shipyards.*

*Many escaped the oppression, segregation and hardships of the south. The dynamic of southern blacks and white war workers intermingled together in a spacious environment set the foundation*

*for Sunnydale's resident population being diversified, neighborly and supportive of one another.*

*"Man! There was nothing transparent between us kids playing together. Nothing at all" Melvin Pitre*

*"Racially mixed neighborhoods are not as rare as people think, in fact they are more stable" Ingrid Gould Ellen, Brookling EDU. 1997*

*Many of the families were already closely located near the neighborhood, having moved over the hill from the* **Crocker Amazon** *public housing projects a stone's throw away from Sunnydale.*

*"People just felt safe living in the neighborhood. That's how communities should be, a place where people can congregate and get along with one another" Melvin Pitre*

*The development included 1-to-4 bedroom garden apartments on Sunnydale Avenue, Brookdale and Blythedale streets south of McLaren Park.*

***There's*** *no denying Sunnydale, like a number of low income minority communities across this nation, experienced economic hardship and could not withstand the infiltration of guns, street gangs, drugs and violence.*

*"I just drove through Sunnydale a few days ago. People need to know Sunnydale has a treasured past rich with history worth sharing. Today the neighborhood doesn't look like public housing projects but downtown San Francisco doesn't look the same either. What I saw were changes all around but the memories will always be the same, that's something they cannot change" Melvin Pitre*

*Melvin's assessment of Sunnydale's past, its decline and promising future couldn't be more true because Sunnydale over time our Dale* had become a modern day west coast ghost town complete with tumbleweeds showcasing utter defeat.

Gone were the grassy manicured lawns run over time and time again now being used as makeshift parking lots.

The grassy lawns are now desert dirt lots with tire threads running from the street to the front of the houses, dumping grounds for sidewalk mechanics working on "hoopties" broken down vehicles and cars on milk crates.

There is no actual account of how many families from back in the day still live in Sunnydale today from the good ole days, but the **Little Village Market does** remain and even it is far different.

Traces of what once were a strong communityship are gone, vanished as if they never existed.

**Michael, Ms Henrietta's** youngest son and surviving child said the **Little Village Market was still open but not accessible.**

**The store was nothing like the quality market of Sunnydale and some folks from Viz Valley shopped for groceries at.**

*"In order to purchase something you have to give your money to a Chinese man behind some metal bars and he would have one of his workers pick out your order and return it to you with your change"* Michael Harris

*The store made its money selling single cigarettes, alcohol and outdated expiring goods* **Michael** *told me later.*

*To me it was like turning the pages in a book and the rest of the book contained nothing but blank pages.*

*An entire block of businesses was gone. Nothing but our treasured memories remained.*

*In the early days the families who migrated to Sunnydale were war workers, many living in* **single parent households led by women.**

*"The mothers in Sunnydale took on many roles without choice, that's just the way things were. There were Black father figures maybe not in every home but those Black men who were there pitched in where they could. That's what made Sunnydale a community, a special place, people helping people, there were a lot of Black men lending a helping hand to some youngsters on the verge of trouble. They were running to responsibility not from it"* Melvin Pitre

*"Mr Peters help me get my first job working as a custodian for the school district, in fact he helped a lot of brothers find jobs"* Leon Booker

*An unknown qualifying criteria for acceptance or entry into the complex was families headed by single, divorced or widowed women received preference and the presence of strong authoritative black father figures was in most households non-existent.*

*There were some families led by very strong black men, like* **Mr Porter, a veteran, Mr Hughes, Mr Qualls, Mr Pitre, Mr Odom, Mr**

*Peters*, *who started Sunnydale's Boys Scout troop along with* **Mae Guzman**, *a wonderful hispanic woman with three boys.*

*Stories have it that there were those black men who left their homes and families behind not by choice but for a number of reasons including sacrificing their homeship, sleeping in abandoned cars, staying away from home so that their family could maintain their housing.*

*"There are always situations not so pleasant that only a Black man can understand my brother. Life has many twists and turns, just because there were fathers maybe not in every home in the physical sense, but that does not mean the absence of a father does not exist nor not felt in the home. There were alot of bullpen relief pitchers weekend dads in our community" Melvin Pitre*

*It was a harsh reality especially if the bread winner's ability to obtain gainful employment was extremely challenging.*

*"It wasn't like we didn't see black men getting up and looking for work, some of the men sometimes found work in non traditional piecemeal jobs, but they were still respected for getting up each day looking for some kind of job" Nothing like the face of man returning home with a bunch of* **we ain't hiring now papers in his empty pockets"**. *Melvin Pitre*

*Old-timers would also tell stories of families hiding clothing and personal items to avoid being caught when the* **Housing Authority** *came knocking.*

**The Ward and June Cleaver Leave it to Beaver** *families* **were not part of our world**.

*"Our worlds weren't all black and white like our televisions, if your family had one" T Warren*

*"Man! Some of us had to go to someone' else's house just to watch TV, that's what made the neighborhood special, everyone was welcome in each others house" Glen GT Taylor*

*If the* **Cosby's** *were on television back then I'm not so sure for me the show would have been believable.*

**Good Times was more of what life for us was like.**

*"Everyday wasn't a walk in the park, we had our share of troubles, disputes and difficulties but there were many good times to remember" Annete Hughes*

*"I think there is a difference between living in poverty and being poor. To me being poor is a state of defeat" Glen GT Taylor*

*"Sunnydale by far was not a Fatherless community, there were men in the neighborhood we looked up to. They were not broken in spirit by the oppressive conditions stereotypes placed on then" Eric Peters*

**Ironically** *over time,* **the absence of the black men** *in the household along with the number of other infestations in the black communities would ultimately contribute greatly to Sunnydale's decline.*

*"Didn't make a whole lot of difference to us kids if your dad was missing in action, the fathers that were in Sunnydale did what they could to have a positive impact on most of us without one" T Warren*

*These uninvited changes ripped the heart, soul and spirit out of the people who once clinged to their unselfish pride, sense of community and respect for one another, and the next door neighbor.*

*'The neighborhood like most of our communities just wasn't ready to fight back. Sunnydale had the capacity for communityship but in reality lacked the understanding of what was really happening around us, and to us. We faced an enemy, not just the drugs and the*

dealers but the widespread greedy motives of those we had never seen or knew before" T Warren

"Drugs spread like wildfires through the neighborhood" it's not as if people gave up on living, we took to using drugs to escape many of the hardships of oppression and dimly lit futures. At the time it didn't seem all that bad being on cloud nine" Coyle Jefferson

There were so many of the intangibles that as a young boy I didn't understand.

"The shipments of drugs to our communities, whether Black, Brown, Yellow or White is by design, and taken its toll, the impact has been deadly and those cats on the upper echelon side of the game, responsible for transporting the stuff, they are the ones who have benefited the most and cared the least" Otis Bubba Hughes

"Drugs caused more than havoc in our community. It wasn't one family not infected by the impact of drugs in our community. But it could have been worse if not for our resilience, and love for one another. That's not to say tears were not shed and folks turned their backs on people addicted but anywhere else I'm sure it would have been worse. That's how Sunnydale back then got down" Levi Bryant

"It was sad seeing some of your childhood friends strung out on hop" Maxine Hughes

In developing **this composition** a realization came to me that back then everything and everyday was by far not all fun, games and playtime.

In other words, we never knew where the next meal was coming from, it didn't matter, nevertheless everyday **there was food on our tables and clean clothes on our backs.**

*"My mom could make 50 meals outta a pound of ground beef" A Burleson*

*"We faced our hardships, suffered through the pain and shared in the joy of living in Sunnydale. For me the good outweighed the bad. R Taylor*

*"Those who were without the basic necessities seldom went without because the families in the neighborhood shared what little they had' Melvin Pitre*

*Brookdale started at the corner of Santos Street and ran up the hill all the way to Geneva Avenue with private homes down the street across from* **Castle Bowling Lanes Alley** *a few yards from the* **Geneva Drive In.**

**Gone but not forgotten are the times we spent there and the Bowling Alley.**

*"We stayed at the Bowling Alley until the staff chased us away, and even that was fun running away being chased back to the projects" Glen GT Taylor*

*"We played from sun up to sun down, everyday all day" A Hughes*

*Blythedale Street ran from the corner of Hahn Street all the way up to the top of the hill connecting with Brookdale, there were parking lots and community playgrounds, outdoor basketball courts, washhouses throughout the neighborhood.*

*"For us all kids, growing up in Sunnydale, all we could think of was playing outside, we didn't care about anything else but going outside and having a good time. There was always something fun to do" Melvin Pitre*

*"The beautiful thing about the Sunnydale Housing Projects was*

*that we had freedom, to go to friends' houses, play board games, enlighten each other with dreams of being more than what we were. We were poor but didn't know we were poor as we always had food and had plenty to share with friends who came over for dinner."*
*Rafiki Webster*

**The Cow Palace** *hosted the* **Grand National Rodeo and the Ringling Barnum and Bailey Circus,** *crazy as it sounds, we used to sneak into the circus through the back gates where they kept the caged lions and tigers.*

*"We were part of the landscape, we knew every which way to sneak in the Cow Palace" B Freeman*

**Man! Sneaking into the circus! Was that krazy?** *If we had only known how dangerous it was, like they say "curiosity kills the cat" but I'm not so sure about that.*

*"Us sneaking into the Cow Palace where they cage the lions and tigers, now that was really stupid. Fun but stupid!*

*We were foolish but lucky because we were within arms distance of those big cats, sometimes even stopping to tease them before one of their handlers chased us away.* **Talk about Stuck on Stupid...**

**Playing cat and mouse with real tigers ain't something you should run home and tell ya' momma about. If'n ya' live to tell you about it.**

*"It wasn't one of those things sneaking into the circus at the Cow Palace through the back gates where they kept the big cats, we didn't run home and tell Moms about" Al Burleson*

*"We the families from Sunnydale have come a long way since the early days in the projects. In many ways we were like pioneers, we didn't discover Sunnydale but what the people in the community did discover was a devoted compassion to look out for one another and*

*care for the well being of our neighbors and our community" Melvin Pitre*

*"I think there are many communities throughout the various neighborhoods that are rich in history, community pride and involvement but the system is designed not only to keep these communities down but to keep them from sharing, knowing about our storied past among them. I would like to see a National documentary dedicated to the people who grew up in public housing communities like Sunnydale" Randy Roc Minix*

*"Underserved communities have the potential to rid themselves of negative influences, but it will take the entire community to fight for and implement those changes" Leon Booker*

*The structure and well being of our communities have been overwhelmed, flooded by the infiltration of drugs, of neglect, disparity, and isolation resulting in poor economic opportunities, lack of viable resources, poor education, understaffed schools, drug addiction, crime and poor outlooks on life.*

**Too many, they are convinced their condition is the way of Life and no more than a bad hand dealt in a game of chance.**

**Sunnydale of our past was no exception to these ghetto hardships but in many ways for us, ole Man Hardship, proved to be a worthwhile challenge, a comforting antidote, a rallying cry among our people who refused to succumb to a bad hand dealt.**

**Our community was led by community outreach leaders like the Broomstick Brigade, staff from the EOC, den mothers from the Rec Center and the people themselves who placed the well being, safety and welfare of the children ahead of anything else.**

*"I have no doubt that the communities today, facing these same enormous hardships and obstacles, are more than willing to address*

*these concerns, deal with adversity head on and become capable of employing a community involvement approach to overcome immeasurable odds. No doubt the people yearn for change, their survival depends on community engagement and more importantly I am convinced they are Up For The Challenge" Melvin Pitre*

# CHAPTER 5

# VISITACION VALLEY - AKA VIZ VALLEY

## One Block Away-So Close Yet Miles Apart

## A Whole Different World

*"We were one of the first families of color to move into the Eichler Townhouse Homes. I can remember as a young boy going to those townhouse meetings and listening to people in the Eichler community complain about the young Black kids from Sunnydale coming down to our community" Noel Smith*

*"We do have Blacks who live in gated communities but the gates are in the front of our houses" F Collier*

*The Eichler Homes*

*Visitacion Valley. aka Viz Valley and The Dale were/will always be connected, they are cut from the same cloth but strangely enough disconnected solely due to economic disparity.*

*"Visitacion Valley was not a gated community in the traditional sense, but the presence of racial equality was quite apparent" F Collier*

*"Oftentimes every day if we ventured out of the neighborhood one block away ugly stares of being unwanted and racism was there to greet us" A Burleson*

*"There was nothing on the other side of Hahn Street closed to us by a perimeter of walls and fences. The people living in homes on Hahn Street kept to themselves but many of them were cordial and would*

wave to the brothers standing on the corner and going about their business" C Jefferson

"We went down to the Valley, jumped over backyard fences, stole fruit then came home with pockets full of peaches, pears and apples we took to our Moms who made homemade pies and preserves. We would tell our mothers some man who felt sorry for us was giving away free fruit. Yeah right! We never figured out we was telling the same lie over and over everyday we came home with pockets full of free I mean stolen fruit" K Burleson

"Take one step on the other side of Hahn Street and walk a block to Sawyer Street and we were in Viz Valley, A Whole Different World" Glen GT Taylor

"Gated White communities are designed to deny entrance. In the Black community iron bars on doors and windows represent gated communities and the severity of hard and violent times" F Collier

There was huge division among the people who lived just a block away from The DALE.

"People living in residential plush communities throughout this country high atop the hillsides put their petal to the metal drive through communities like Sunnydale, ignoring the people like us down here on the ground" T Warren

How can Sunnydale be located in Visitacion Valley and not be a part of Viz Valley because the division was solely based on those living in **private homes** and those living in **public housing**, a true definition of **economic, racial disparity and separation**.

"All I know is for me both Sunnydale and Viz Valley felt like home to me but our family experienced more than our share of snooty you don't belong here looks and remarks" Noel Smith

*"Nobody felt the pain and disparity more than us kids from Sunnydale who attended Viz Valley Elementary School. Our parents instilled in us, to be smarter than our white classmates and study much harder. Our homework had to be immaculate, turned in on time and our behavior had to be respectful of all staff from the janitor to the lunchroom staff we kids from Sunnydale throughout the school year dealt with alot"* Lexie TC Caracter

*"Man! They can find a cure for so many things. It's just sad that Racism won't be one of them. If only someone, whoever could find a cure for racism the world would be much better off. Racism, it's a deadly disgraceful destructive disease"* K Burleson

*"We never knew about the kids, from Sunnydale our childhood friends who left everyday going to school in Viz Valley had to deal with all the racism going to and from school"* Randy Roc Minix

*"I don't know much about the smiles on Ronald, Steven and TC's faces when they left for school, to me they seemed excited, but I sure as hell know there was a difference about all of them when they got home from school, all of them with this aura of sadness. There were times when Steven, Lil Jeff, Ronald and TC didn't want to come outside and play right away. Never knew exactly why"* A Burleson

*"We thought our friends going down there to school were living large, involved in sports and playground activities, playing ball on a team with uniforms. To some of us, having a baseball uniform was the ultimate because our sports programs in Sunnydale couldn't afford them"* Glen Chop Porter

*"There were people in Viz Valley who showed their true colors and ill feeling about living just a few blocks away from Sunnydale"* B Freeman

*"Crossover that line on Hahn Street that separates Viz Valley from the Dale and either you was going to fight or run for your life"* Glen GT Taylor

*"We couldn't see that divided line in the middle of Hahn Street but we could feel the racial inequality"* Bubba Hughes

*"We were told to stay away from going down there, but the Valley to us had everything we saw on those TV shows. Little did we know about how some of the people felt about us"* E Peters

*The original Sunnydale and Hahn street businesses were meant to serve working class Irish and Italian immigrants who lived in Viz Valley working in nearby factories like Schlage Locks on Bayshore Boulevard and at the Southern Pacific Railroad.*

*There are no signs or border walls that separate the two because The Dale is in Viz Valley and therefore they are one in the same, a difference of private vs public residency.*

***"A You Ain't Wanted Here"*** *sign would have been more appropriate"* Glen Chop Porter

*However over the years the division grew and there are those who still argue that the communities are separate, although there are no San Francisco southeast sector county records to indicate this.*

*I know this to be true because after my first year attending John McLaren Elementary School {below notice the JM class diversity} at the top of the hill*

*My mom then made a decision to transfer my older brother **Victor** and me to Visitacion Valley Elementary School.*

## Busing Kids Without The School Bus

*This was at the time a different version of busing black kids down the block but without the yellow school bus so those of us who went, walked to school.*

*Needless to say there were a number of whites from Viz Valley highly opposed to our attending school there and the risk was far greater than many families imagined.*

*Some of the Viz Valley folks, I guess, felt they had their quotas of blacks going to school there already.*

*Those blacks who lived in Viz Valley homes in the neighborhood were quite sufficient I'm sure. Well at the time it seemed that way.*

*"The welcome mat wasn't always so welcoming" W Francis*

*"It does not matter how old you are ya' know when ya' not wanted"*
*TC Caracter*

*Quite frankly busing students is not solely based on the need to integrate the schools but economics play a significant role.*

*In other words, an empty school house with empty classrooms is least likely to receive funding for educational/training purposes.*

*But a school with a substantial student body, well...it's easier to bus the economically challenged students across town without much fanfare or resistance than to bus those from the suburbs across town to the ghetto.*

*What happened to the children in Sunnydale back in the day was the **school district's slick way** of using black children to increase their minority enrollment and capture a few bucks under...*

## Visitacion Valley School 8 or 9 blocks away

*There were black and hispanic kids at the school who lived in Visitacion Valley but few from Sunnydale*

## Mr Baines

**There was only one Black teacher, Mr Baines** *who was not my teacher but Ronald and Steven were enrolled in his class.*

*I remember my classmates snickering about him and at times there were white kids in the schoolyard who refused to obey his instructions during recess time,*

*Sadly through* **my own ignorance and disrespect** *I found myself doing the very same thing and not knowing why.*

*The Children from Sunnydale Were Introduced To Classrooms Like This At Visitacion Valley School*

*Mr Baines* *always conducted himself professionally and deserved much better treatment especially from me.*

*It was still very confusing to me that every day before school started the entire student body stood in the courtyard pledging allegiance to the flag.*

*Then shortly thereafter one of them same white kids with his or her hand over their heart would be calling you a...*

*If taking undercover abuse from some snotty nosed white kids was happening to **Mr Baines**. Well... it's easy to do the math. **Racism speaks for Itself.***

*Many families to my understanding were giving the opportunity to enroll their children in the school but for the most were resistant to change.*

*A few families in Sunnydale made the decision to enroll their children in the school but not many accepted the offer. {above} this still represents a subtle way of implementing busing.*

*Disparity has always existed between the Dale & Viz Valley which is a prime example of a system working hand in hand to alienate the privileged from the poor.*

*"I think deep down inside me those kids from Viz Valley really wanted to play with us it was their parents who forbid them to" Glen Chop Porter*

*There were those families from Viz Valley who embraced the people from Sunnydale, Ms Ellis, and her daughter Valerie, the Tolivers, the Joneses, George and Leo. the Camarino family.*

*Raul Rico, his older brother, his mother and father, the Smith family, Noel, Leon {Pumpy} and their two sisters who lived in the Eichler homes were real good friends in the neighborhood.*

*"We all thought Noel lived somewhere in Sunnydale, hell he was everywhere in the neighborhood, from top of the hill to down on the Front everyday" B Freeman*

*Raul, went on to international acclaim playing percussion for Carlos Santana, and his brother Jogre who formed the latin soul group Malo, dated one of the Camarino sisters. "Dude brought his congos to the corner everyday, played music and drank with us all day long" L Bryant*

*Raul, harnessed his percussion skills with the brothers on Sunnydale and Hahn, a Sunnydale tradition sipping white port and lemon juice at the bus stop.*

*New friends in a new neighborhood going to school in Viz Valley, for me, were hard to come by and old friends from Sunnydale became not so easy to get along with.*

*In the classroom both Victor and I excelled, mom was a stickler for reading and writing and all of us Theresa, Coyle, Victor and I found enjoyment in books and whatever literature we could get our hands on.*

*But in my classroom raising my hand to answer the teacher's question, I was seldom called on.*

## Friends For Life

*One day in school, Dennis B a white classmate in front of the entire class asked Ms Delalmo an Hispanic woman "why is it that you never call on Darro, he always raises his hands"*

*She turned beet red and Dennis and his twin sister Diane were reprimanded, and had to stay after school for detention.*

*I waited outside for them for 45 minutes after school and the three of us became close lifetime friends.*

*Their parents came to the school and met privately with the school principal and Ms Delalmo.*

*At the time I had no idea, years later, that upon entering Jr High School at the top of Sunnydale Avenue, I would be standing up for some of my white classmates who had to travel by city buses right through the heart of The Dale in route to Luther Burbank Jr High School.*

*The Sunnydale welcoming committee back then wasn't always so hospitable and a lot of those white kids took some severe ass kickings by a select few of our sick black brothers in the name of what...*

*These guys were simply bullies and bad news.*

*Their hatred of these innocent young white teenagers was no more than retaliation and ignorance...*

*Some of them even retaliated and threatened me for yelling at them to stop.*

*Of course I had little to fear. I was "Little Jeff" Coyle and Victor's lil' bro and that carried helluva' weight.*

*Sunnydale was a community that we could call any of the big brothers to take care of things and put punks and neighborhood bullies messing with you in their place.*

*Needless to say the following year when we exited Ms Delalmo's classroom the same thing happened again and again with yet another teacher.*

*In the meantime I was now being accepted by a few more classmates and their families after they had heard what had happened.*

*There were still many days when I felt all alone with no outlet or avenue to express my feelings.*

*I never was chosen to be a yard monitor, milk monitor, or toilet monitor, even though I raised my hand countless times.*

*Mr Baines on the other hand selected Steven C to represent his classroom, so at least Viz Valley had one black student milk monitor.*

*A small step in the right direction, even though Steven would heist the milk money, hoard the cookies, be short on his count and then on the way home after school buy thirty six chocolate malt balls from the Penny Store with the money he stole.*

*Viz Valley was rapidly changing and the families in The DALE were starting to become alienated victims of what was being said publicly about our community.*

*I could sense from my daily school travels and visiting the homes of my white classmates those in private homes were turning their backs on their fellow neighbors taking on their own separate identity,*

*The infiltration of guns, drugs and violence didn't help relationships between the folks from both communities, and the absence of strong black fathers was equally contributing greatly to the neighborhood's decline.*

*Sunnydale like many communities was being held hostage, accountable responsible for their own undoing.*

*Not a single brother imported a shipment of guns, traveled abroad, had major drug connections and flew back to the hood in a private plane full of drugs and of course having the money to finance major drug and weapons operations.*

## From Infestation to Incarceration

*But like in every community and on every street corner the people in the community suffered the most, victims of this vicious enterprise.*

## The Eichler/Geneva Towers

*This rapid change became evident, especially when in 1964 the Eichler/Geneva Towers two private story high rises were built on Sunnydale and Schwerin streets a few blocks from Bayshore Boulevard.*

*Two giant story apartment buildings two blocks fromThe DALE that could be seen for miles by anyone traveling on Highway 101.*

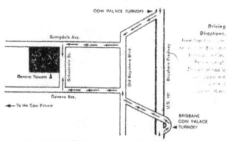

*"A lot of strange feelings started to unravel between us brothers and sisters when the lower Dale started attending school down in the Valley" Randy Roc Minix*

*There was no formal debriefing or training by the school district to prepare our parents for what we were about to encounter.*

*Sunnydale and **Victor's** friends meant the world to him.*

*He was a product of the community and the thought of him attending a lily white school in a lily white neighborhood wasn't his idea of a picnic in the park. My brother was **oh so right...***

*The three year difference between us and the other big brothers was significant then, so his having to separate from his partner was more difficult for him than me.*

*The thought of going to a new school was exciting for me, but little did I know this transition would introduce me to **a world of the haves and have nots.***

*The challenges for Sunnydale's older siblings were significant because many of them spent their early childhoods elsewhere before moving to Sunnydale or had grown up in the community and were ready to exit their preadolescence unlike me and my friends who thought life was one big candy store.*

*The school of life caught so many of the older brothers and sisters early due to hardship and family responsibility.*

*Their childhoods were forfeited and grew up much too soon and way before their time.*

*I know this because even one of my childhood friends, **Ivy,** who used to shine shoes as a kid became one the household breadwinners before the age of ten.*

*Ivy* was an honor roll student with enormous family obligations.

*The family's survival and his ability to put food on the table was mandatory.*

*He shined shoes well past his teen years to help put food on the table.*

**Racism immediately reared its ugly head in the classroom and on the playground it even pitted Sunnydale blacks kids against one another competing for approval, acceptance and friendship of our white classmates.**

*There were many days that* **Steven, Ronald, TC** *and me were chased home after school by white teenagers.*

*But as long as we made it to the corner of Sunnydale and Hahn the white boys would turn cowardly, turn back and run back home to the Valley.*

*Back then the site of The DALE never looked so good,*

*The brotherhood on the front didn't take too kindly to what had happened.*

*Our big brothers were our safety net but they always cautioned the four of us to be on the lookout for those white dudes down at Viz Valley Park, a very dangerous place to be without backup or a plan of escape.*

*What got most of the kids from Sunnydale in mischievous trouble was our deep inner desire to explore the unknown.*

**How could the community climate one block away be so different?**

*The unfortunate thing about the division left many children residing only a few blocks away in both communities with many permanent scars.*

*"Playgrounds were meant for children to play, no matter the color of their skin, denying our children the opportunity to engage in fundamental games of play should have nothing to do with economic or residential status, kids just wanna have fun" Randy Roc Minix*

*On the first day of school after summer break a group of us grade school kids from Sunnydale were excited about returning to school at Visitacion Valley.*

*I waited outside our house for my childhood friend Billy B. We were going to start the new school year as third graders.*

*Billy was one of the white kids who lived in the building in front of us.*

*Decked out in my brand new school clothes, to my mother's and my amazement Billy came out of the house ready for school dressed in the exact outfit I had on.*

*When the rest of the kids joined us we all headed down Visitation Avenue passing by white adults going to work waiting on the bus to downtown.*

*They stared at us kids, especially Billy and me, I'm sure wondering why Billy and I were dressed the same.*

*Without conversation our mothers had brought the identical outfits.*

*Upon our arrival at the schoolyard to my and Billy's amazement there were at least 9 other boys wearing the same clothing.*

*That day together on the playground JC Penny's brought together a schoolyard of black and white children sharing in the joy, laughter and excitement of returning to school without a care in the world.*

*To us youngsters that day wearing the same clothes enjoying the time of our young lives Racism didn't exist.*

*"Playtime is just that, playtime is fun and games color ain't gotta damn thing to do with it. Randy Roc Minix*

# CHAPTER 6

## THE MAN IN THE GREEN CADILLAC

*"This man was one insane brother, couldn't stand us kids from Sunnydale" Glen "Chop" Porter*

*Always waiting lurking on the lookout for us looking out his front window or upstairs balcony was* **THE MAN IN THE GREEN CADILLAC** *as we crossed Sawyer Street.*

*Every time he saw us or sensed that we were headed that way without warning he would run to his car* **THE GREEN CADILLAC parked in his carport and come full throttle with reckless abandonment headed in our direction, a Black mad man on wheels** *scaring the life out of us for no apparent reason.*

*"I never ran so fast in my life. Dude was out to get us for what we'll never know" A Burleson*

*The four of us never did anything to him but* **THE MAN IN THE GREEN CADILLAC** *had it in for us.*

*"That man was one sick son of a bitch" Randy "Roc" Minix*

*He would chase us towards The Towers or back home to The DALE, imagine* **a black man** *that did not want us in his neighborhood a block away from Sunnydale.*

*"He was the one at the community meetings always complaining about the people in Sunnydale" Noel Smith*

*Oftentimes he would come without notice up Sunnydale hooking a mad left on Hahn Street fishtailing terrorizing anyone in his path.*

*This black man was making a statement* **"I do not want the people from Sunnydale in my neighborhood".**

*There were times on foot when he flew out of his house and chased us.*

*"Why us* **Al, Roc, Chop** *and me always thought. We even thought about getting* **Mr Porter,** *who always carried his Silver bullets.*

*"We were afraid to tell Mr Porter. Chop's dad would have busted a cap in his ass" Randy "Roc" Minix*

**Chop's dad wasn't a joke.** *I remember a girl Chop had a crush on in the Towers, her father told* **Chop** *to stay away from his daughter because he wasn't "good enough for her"* **Mr Porter** *had just brought* **Chop** *a brand new wardrobe, and a badass mint green wrap around leather jacket so when* **Chop** *came home early unexpectedly.*

*"My father knew something was up with us when we came to the house all four us had the shakes and we didn't even drink" Glen "Chop" Porter*

*Well the man shouldn't have said that.* **Pop Porter** *went to his house to check his ass. End of story....*

*Not everyone including our crew were headed to The Towers but to Bayshore and Sunnydale or Leland Avenue for groceries and essentials.*

*There were countless reasons why people fromThe DALE traveled in that direction. It wasn't against the law...*

*For years and even to this day, no one knows for sure why this angry black man **IN THE GREEN CADILLAC** had it in for us.*

*Ironically comparing notes with others the same torment by this enraged individual was experienced by those walking across his path.*

*"You know what's funny there were a lot of brothers who went down to the Eichler Homes and the Geneva Towers and got chased by that Man In The Green Caddy, but he really had it in for Alvin, Randy, Glen and little Jeff" Levi Bryant*

*His actions, behaviors were a prime example of ignorance, **a black man's hatred against his own people who lived just a block away.***

*It was more about private home ownership vs poor folks living in the projects.*

*Just a question I leave with you the reader to ponder.*

***Why would a black man not want us in his neighborhood? a block away from Sunnydale!***

*Imagine the opposite if the people in Sunnydale had retaliated against those Viz Valley families black or white dependent on grocery shopping on Hahn Street at the Little Village Market.*

*I wonder where this irate brother shopped for his groceries since nearly everyone in walking distance shopped at the Little Village neighborhood market.*

*By 1970 the prima ballerina towers were converted into low income public housing apartments and was well on its way to becoming one of the city's most notorious places to live and one of the city's biggest housing disasters and ultimately was destroyed*

*Ironically, even some of the folks in The DALE started disassociating themselves from those living in the towers.*

*Another prime example of **separation and division**, no one was claiming communityship in Viz Valley, The DALE, the Eichler Homes and the Geneva Towers.*

*It seemed as if everyone was shame based, pointing fingers and separated by pure ignorance.*

*The Eichler Homes and the Geneva Towers were the first beneficiaries of neighborhood revitalization.*

*While Sunnydale remained a community in transition with promising economic potential but lacking social services and residential leadership.*

*Unfortunately The DALE will always be a neighborhood haunted*

*by its recent past and must rely on the commitments of dedicated investors if the community is to shed its black eye.*

*There are a number of dedicated individuals and organizations involved in the day-to-day operations of bringing revitalization to this marginalized community.*

*Their task is not an easy one. But this cannot be a valuable story of recovery and discovery without the old and the new.*

**Therefore the Sons of Sunnydale want this composition to serve as a blueprint for moving the process forward.**

*There is no doubt if communities like Sunnydale are to move forward, changes must include physical and psychological revitalization as well.*

*The DALE will experience a total transformation on all fronts with shared partnerships and dedicated commitments on all fronts if proposed projects are to succeed.*

**Changes that investors are hoping for must extend far beyond the intricate lives of those living in the community but expand its boundaries to individuals, communities and those stereotypes that exist far outside its domain.**

*The key will be helping residents develop a sense of community, provide them with necessary resources and leadership training skills to self govern themselves and take pride in their community outcomes, involvements and neighborhood affairs.*

*Transformation is often difficult especially when dealing with histories of false promise, self defeating mindsets, confrontational attitudes, poor core values and reluctant willingness to accept change.*

**But there are those investors such as Mercy Housing committed to change and revitalization.**

*The DALE like a number of low income communities have been cautiously hesitant to welcome in outsiders and have learned to self isolate, often accepting what life circumstances they feel has provided them, in other words the community cannot revitalize itself without shared partnerships and trust.*

*Construction of new and renovated housing will not lower crime, provide economic growth, develop healthy relationships, supplement depression or provide long term visions to overcome insurmountable obstacles.*

*Once again we cannot emphasize enough, the task is not an easy one.*

***Our communities must rid themselves of falling down and can't get up mentally and stop wagering the future of our children on a fast horse in a slow race.***

*It's like wearing new clothes, splashing yourself with dollar store cologne, not taking a bath, and expecting no one to detect the smell of funky armpits, or putting a bandaid on a bullet wound trying to conceal the internal and relying solely on the external.*

***Painted fences and cosmetic facelifts will not erase pain and suffering but for so many of us we will find solace in the Power of Prayer and validation in Community Involvement and Social Commitment...***

***Histories of being misled by development weighs heavy on the residents, many unwilling to trust those who propose change as well as those who even advocate for change.***

***The proof can't be more evident than when professional sports teams including the beloved San Francisco 49ers who tore down Candlestick Park moved the team to Santa Clara miles away taking with them many of our neighborhoods seasonal sources of income.***

***In return developers offer the replacement of those facilities with the proposed building of affordable housing, shopping malls and jobs, that residents will have first source opportunities to.***

***The promises have miserably failed to support the aforementioned developments from happening.***

*Our communities are left behind in the dark. Below is more than a sign of simple neglect, boarded up buildings and dying grass, these are only a few visual signs of neglect, because there are other significant contributing factors. Long Gone Are The Crayola Colored Green Manicure Lawns*

*"Papa Scales is turning in his grave if he saw front lawns like this"*

# CHAPTER 7

# 1523 SUNNYDALE AVENUE

## 1523 Sunnydale Avenue
## - The Jeffersons

*From our backyard window I had a birds eye view of life on* **"The Front"** *Man!* **Television didn't compare!**

*To this very day I can remember our home telephone number Juniper 587-5657.*

*In Sunnydale school children were Latch Key Kids way before the term became popular.*

*We were Latch Key Kids without the keys. Back then the doors in Sunnydale were always unlocked.*

*Momma used to tape money in the bottom of my shoes and give me bus fare to ride downtown to pay a bill with strict instructions not to stop and talk with anyone.*

*Our parents did not have the luxury of picking us up from school.*

**When we got out of school there was no one home to greet us.**

**We let ourselves in the house, fixed a peanut butter sandwich, did our homework, changed into our play clothes and watched television.**

*I used to listen to all of the gossip, hear the arguments, watch the fist fights and see things playing out right before my very innocent eyes.*

*Whoever would have thought that one day **fist fights**, **verbal arguments**, **misunderstandings would become extinct**.*

**They have been replaced by senseless violence, drive by's and turf wars...and Loss of Life...but that's not to say Sunnydale back then did not have its share of violent times.**

*I didn't need a zoom camera to see sharp looking dudes with mini skirts wearing women driving fancy cars.*

*Casinos didn't exist, but streetcorner craps did. I could hear the clatter of dice shaking every day.*

*The fun part was watching' impromptu streetcorner romance, and common folk having the time of their lives.*

*However what was far more revealing than my backyard vantage point was when **Al and I** started delivering the San Francisco Chronicle early morning newspapers at 5AM.*

*The two of us also delivered the afternoon papers.*

*One Day while out playing we forgot about delivering the newspapers and our mother's after working hard all day had to deliver the papers to some irate customers.*

*Neither one of us will ever forget the look on their faces when they finished doing our jobs. Sometimes the ghetto-ish fun was too hard to let go.*

*I blamed him. He blamed me, nevertheless we never heard the last of it, because **Momma and Mae** had to fend off **Kennedy and Nixon, two** aggressive notorious **Labrador** dogs that chased everyone from the top of the hill down to Hahn Street.*

*To date in talking with the brotha's about **Kennedy and Nixon** no one really knows who their rightful owners were.*

*Sunnydale had some dogs that were as popular as some of the dudes in the neighborhood.*

***Ms Agnew** and her son **Larry's dog JoJo**, a pure bred German Shepherd rescued a young white boy from falling down an unattended sewer.*

***JoJo** was awarded a **Service Dog Award** and was featured on the evening news.*

*__Ms Agnew a white woman and longtime resident, would__ walk to the **Little Village** in between the brotha's with **JoJo** holding her purse in his mouth. **What Not nobody messin' with Ms Agnew. Nobody!***

*What **Al and I** saw and heard behind closed doors, in the backseats of parked cars, in the bushes or behind the storefronts was live early morning triple XXX rated ghetto lust.*

*Doors were left open, curtains weren't drawn, windows were not fully shut and the sounds of **"give it to me daddy"**, love making bump and grind were a part of our daily routines.*

*The crazy thing about all of this was we saw a lot of creeps' and knew the participants.*

*Somebody's motha', somebody's fatha' somebody's sista and brotha' was gettn' their groove on.*

*A couple of times we got paid to keep what we saw and knew on the under...*

*I vividly remember some of those love making scenes and sounds that have lasted me a lifetime.*

*Delivering the newspaper early one morning to a young single woman, a friend of the family, I stumbled upon her and her boyfriend having sex like two feral cats going at it in the backyard under the moonlight.*

*From that day on, every morning the door to her house seemed to be left a little more open.*

*Then to my surprise, one day the boyfriend opened the door and made me come in and sit and watch them go at it.*

*Of course I was warned, told to keep my mouth shut...*

*Being forced to sit and watch two grown ass adults having sex has to be some **sick form of perverted sexual behavior** that I cannot describe and refuse to find the correct terminology for.*

*The experience would be a prelude to the **Dark Sexual Abuse and my Hidden Secrets**, I would be exposed to.*

*The only thing I knew about sex was peeking through the pages of nudie magazines at **Daniel's Drug Store**, but a young boy entering puberty seeing the real thing couldn't ask for more...*

*Al experienced some of the same...funny some of the looks we got... knowing more than what we were supposed to know...*

*When we weren't delivering newspapers we would take the extras and sell them to people going to work on Geneva Avenue.*

*But being outside in the early morning had many disadvantages as well, there were those shady characters who laid low in the cut, thick bushes and the buildings near the golf course.*

*Delivering the papers in the morning darkness was creepy, especially when one of our schoolmates in **1968** a young white teenager was raped and murdered inside an apartment next to the house where I delivered the newspaper.*

*The crime would go unsolved for **37 long year**s before **DNA** caught the sick perpetrator who killed our classmate*

# CHAPTER 8

# GOING BACK HOME
## With Skip Roberts

### *Son of Sunnydale*

*The Family*

*If there was ever a brother in the community born with an infectious smile, a contagious personality, was well liked and had more energy than a five hour energy drink he would be the son of Skip Roberts.*

*Roberts who now resides in Stockton, California shares his valuable time coaching youth track and field, fine tuning his golf game and has by far the perfect descriptive nickname. His grandfather gave him the name Skipper, the brothers in the neighborhood shortened it. Part of our culture.*

*Who would have thought a brother from Sunnydale would take an interest in downhill skiing and then become affiliated with the National Brotherhood of Skiers nbs.org, like Don King proudly states "Only in America " without a doubt Sunnydale first!*

*His natural boundless energy if manufactured, bottled and were placed on the shelves at **Walgreens** or **CVS** he would be a millionaire.*

*Skip's laughter, humor and spirited personality may have been his coping mechanism to deal with ghetto conditions surrounding him.*

*Nevertheless, because of his expressive humor he was able to turn away from many of the confronting pressures that so many others were unable to escape from, succumbing to negative influences that haunt our communities.*

*His outlook on life was looking through a lens of laughter that was the foundation for shaping him into the man he is today. No doubt he started each day with a **glass of "Personality Plus or a glass of that Act Right Juice".***

*Roberts never married but had five children, four daughters, 9 grandchildren and a deceased son; he spent 3 years in the US Navy and retired in 2003 having worked 32 years for the DOD.*

# Going Back Home

*With Skip Roberts*

*"We lived at one time in Hunters Point before our family moved to Sunnydale in 1965" first residing at **77 Blythedale Street** then moving to the top of hill where me and my siblings attended **John McLaren Elementary School.***

*"When we first arrived in Sunnydale I was introduced to a diverse group of new White, Mexican, Asian and African American friends.*

*Sunnydale growing up was a wonderful place, well kept and the people were friendly.*

*It was a Melting Pot for single moms. My mother raised 6 of us, Jackie, Deborah, Michael, Pedro, Punchy and me.*

*Growing up I wasn't worried about getting in trouble with the police, my mom saw to that.*

*As kids back then, the friends I played with knew that getting in trouble disobeying mom's law was much more trouble than anything we felt the police could do to us.*

*Sunnydale was a close knit community with an abundance of year round recreational and social activities to help us build our character.*

*We played basketball, baseball, football, tennis and learned to swim at John McLaren Swimming Pool.*

*In the summer the EOC and the Mayor's Summer Youth Employment Program provided us with summer jobs!*

*Young brothers got together to choose sides and played sports all day long.*

*That's what I remember the fun! The brotherhood! And Big Brothers are looking out for us.*

*Many who put our safety first, perhaps they saw something in us that we could not see for ourselves, keeping us on a straight arrow and making sure we didn't make the mistakes so many of our brothers from Sunnydale did growing up".*

## <u>Grateful Am I To Contribute To This Story</u>

*His mother, **Ms Hopkins**, worked alongside community activist **Geogre Davis, Ms Frierson and Tony Harrison at Sunnydale's EOC program.***

*While in Atlanta, GA at a conference on **Single Women Parenting and Working in Social Services** in the **early 90's**, there were several incredible workshops that I attended that dealt specifically on single mothers like Ms Hopkins working, providing services to others, and* *learning how to manage their time to have energy leftover at the end of the day to address the needs of their own family.*

**How Does the Caretaker Take Care of the Caretaker,** *was a fascinating eye opening session that focussed on parents, men and women working in the social services field from school programs, community advocacy, criminal justice and childcare, providing direct or indirect services to children, young adults, seniors and vast populations who rely on the program services, but more importantly rely on people, the staff who provide these services.*

**It's one hell of a balancing act that Ms Hopkins performed admirably.**

*No doubt **Ms Hopkins** fit this never ending criteria especially living and working in the same community.*

*If she walked home from work, I am sure she encountered people along the way in need.*

*The work of a provider living, working in the community is never ending.*

*For her there had to be little separation from getting off of work, heading home and having to raise six children on her own, only turning back the next day doing the same damn thing, countless times over and over again.*

***It's an enormous task** not excluding the many times there were frantic knocks on her front door after work from people needing her assistance.*

*Living, raising and family and working, helping the needs of others in the same environment presents unwritten challenging dynamics to social workers and community advocates.*

*I can testify to that because a former client of mine saw me out with my family one evening having dinner at a window table and invited himself into the restaurant to vent his frustrations about looking for a job and being unsuccessful.*

*It's part of the territory, not listed in the job description but a tough balancing act that comes without allotted, designated time to put the day at work behind and more importantly address the needs of our families.*

*A case can be made from this by the many police, fire and emergency personnel who serve and protect our communities but have great dysfunction in their homes and personal lives because they do not have the skills and understanding to take care of themselves, putting the stress of the day behind them.*

*Unfortunately sadly many of these dedicated individuals become dreadful servants and regretful victims devoured by their own good will.*

*People who perform these tasks are remarkably awesome individuals but they thread a thin line between burnout, addiction and resentment.*

# CHAPTER 9

# "THE FRONT"

*The Legendary Little Village Market At Sunnydale and Hahn*

*Sunnydale and Hahn, Back in the day **"The Front"** typified commerce and more importantly community.*

*"Got to wait your turn earn your stripes before you could hang out on the Front"* Coyle Jefferson

*"Send your black punk ass home in a minute if you wasn't ready to hang on the Front""* R Taylor

**Black's Liquor Store** *sold groceries, hot sandwiches and household essentials throughout the day and sometimes after hours on the under.*

*"I showed up on the Front everyday at lunchtime, the Front was the place to be"* Leon Booker

*Underage children could bring a note from home and purchase alcohol and cigarettes for older siblings from* **Black's or the Little Village Market.**

**Mr Manuel Big Black's assistant was always on full display. No doubt about it he had a small man's complex.**

*"I would go inside Black's Store without a penny to my name, tell Black I was hungry and come home with a bag of groceries. He knew all of us kids and our families"* Harold Williams

**He was always angry about something and would curse you out as soon as you walked through the door.**

*I do think it was a strange coincidence that* **Mr Willlie's Barber Shop**, *home of the red and white clad* **Sunnydale Jets** *baseball team and* **LC and Obie's Record Shop** *was between a Bible* **"Saving myself for the Lord" tambourine bang'n Choir Singing Church.**

**There was a preacher you could hear shouting and screaming the Word way up** *at the top of Brookdale.*

*They say **the Lord moves in mysterious ways** but there is something about having a place where **All Sinners gathered in between an All Saints Church.***

*"It might be wrong saying this but a lot of them church going folks seemed a bit tipsy to me, they wasn't going into Black's to buy bottled water believe me" G Chop Porter*

*"The early Sunday morning music and the preaching didn't set to well with the people who lived across the street from the church, especially those that had been up all night partying on Saturday night" Harold Williams*

***My God**, there had to be a better place than to have a barber shop with loud dominoes playing wine drinking sinners, a record store blasting loud secular music right next to **The House of The Lord.***

*What always puzzled me, to this day I am not sure what neighborhood the members of their congregation came from but a lot of them folks I know for sure didn't live in the DALE.*

*Mr Odom, on full tilt told them, if they didn't like going to church next to the Liquor Store or the Barber Shop they could attend services at Sunnydale's other church, but the churchgoing folks weren't gonna let some gin and juice steer them away from getting their praise on.*

***After services there was always a finger pointing holy water throw'n Bible toten' Brewsky drinkn' war going on between the Saints and Sinners.***

*"Papa Odom was at his high as kite best come Sunday morning" T Warren*

***The cursing language was so bad Jesus would have put his hands over his ears.***

81

*"There was a lot of that you're going to hell holier than thou finger pointing going on after Sunday Services" B Freeman*

*The concerns the people from the Church folks had with the fella's gathering in front of the Church was bigtime on Sunday after services when the **Sunnydale Jets** and their fan base gathered to leave for a game at Balboa Park.*

*"Back then on Sunday in Sunnydale the Lord was busy" L Bryant*

***The juice would be flowing, the music would be blaring and the language was curse word after curse word and the fellowship wasn't having any of it.***

*"Sunday on Hahn Street was better than going to the movies" Harold Williams*

*The **Jets** were Sunnydale's **Bingo Long All Stars and Traveling Motorcade** with **Mr Odom** on full tilt as their number one cheerleader.*

*The old' adage of mixing oil with water or **Sinners and Saints with Mr Odom leading the way led to some close but no cigar donnybrooks, and "ya' gonna rot in hell" confrontations.***

*"Pop Odom had no pain didn't feel no shame going up in a church, telling them church going folks what they didn't wanna hear" L Bryant*

*"Some of them church folks I'm sure when they got home had to take a little nip" Glen GT Taylor*

*"Not so sure Jesus and the Juice was meant to be together" K Burleson*

*Ironically with all this going on there was a row of private homes on Hahn Street across from the projects but the people who lived in those homes pretty much kept to themselves and few of us knew anything about them.*

*An ole' white man **Mr Peabody, Bless His Soul** loved his gardening and didn't bother anybody unfortunately he lived in the first house right next to the building on Hahn Street where everybody all of Sunnydale cut through the hood, coming and going, many running from the police.*

*People used to mess with that man for no reason at all. He just had a creepy way about himself.*

*Sometimes even today when reminiscing I can recall many of the households by going door-to-door down memory lane.*

*I remembered the family who once lived in Ms Henrietta's new Hahn Street ADA apartment, which was remodeled to help with her aging mobility issues.*

***Ms Horace's Bar b Que**, located in the middle of the block served some scream'n spaghetti in a cup. **The bag of grease was separate.***

*Most of the cats came in to flirt with her super fine thicker than a motha' f.... high yellow fine daughter **Patricia**.*

***I'm sure when Patricia was on duty sales were up - way up...her brotha's David and Willie were legendary, a little rough around the edges and not the sharpest knives in the Bar b Que Pit.***

*You could smell the aroma of **"the que" blocks away** and when some of those older cats saw that look of hunger in your eyes and felt sorry for us sometimes they'd break us off with some left over, once bitten chicken to split between us.*

*We thought that was really generous of them, but those older dudes knew we had no business at that time being down on Hahn Street.*

*In Sunnydale, youngsta's hanging on The **Front** was forbidden.*

*The EOC building where community matriarch/community advocate **Ms Frierson, worked relentlessly with Tony Harrison and George Davis** who would later earn his doctorate degree and become a renowned San Francisco senior service advocate in BayviewHunters Point.*

***Davis helped** brothers get jobs and families with whatever assistance they may have needed.*

*The office building was at the corner of Sunnydale & Hahn across from the original Little Village Market.*

*The community had a neighborhood watering hole, **Sammy's Bar, Sonny's Dry Cleaners, Daniel's Drug Store**, a laundromat shop, a thrift shop and shopkeepers who genuinely cared about the people.*

*We used to watch the soda truck for the drivers doing deliveries and we would get our choice of whatever soda we wanted.*

*All of us would choose **Nehi Grape**, personally I think before drugs came into our community entire families were hooked on **Nehi Grape Sodas**.*

*If only the people would have kept their lust for **Nehi Grape Sodas**, which were far less addicting than when **Tramadol and Red Devils** pills made their **euphoric narcotic** Sunnydale debut.*

***The Front** was where all the action was and where those who hadn't earned their stripes need not be.*

*I remember when **Siro stole the Gallo Truck**. All of Sunnydale got drunk for weeks.*

People who did not drink indulged, even **Rin Tin** Al and Kermit's german shepherd dog got loaded...

**The Front** was **New York City** alive and kicking 24/7.

By far the main attraction at the corner of Sunnydale and Hahn was **John's Ice Cream Parlor** that had a jukebox **Big Walter Harris**, a future **Golden Glove boxing champion, would drop coins in all day long.**

**Big Walt** must have spent a fortune in that jukebox playing **James Brown's Sex Machine** over and over again.

"Man at times it seemed like Sex Machine was the only record in that damn jukebox, but no one dared to challenge Big Walt" K Burleson

DARRO JEFFERSON

# Sunnydale's Tribute
# to Walter Harris

*Man it was a sad day in Sunnydale when he died in a plane crash aboard a plane headed for Poland with his USA teammates and coaches.*

*"Walter didn't smoke or drink but he was always out at night doing what I don't know but he was a brother everyone liked" Melvin Pitre*

*"At the recreation center there was a boxing ring that's where you find Walter working out with Wesley Simpson who went on to win the Golden Gloves" James Nelson*

*"Someday they oughta make a movie about the brother he came a long way from shadow boxing on the street" B Freeman*

***Big Walt*** *was always shadow boxing and harnessed his skills behind prison walls before his storied boxing career ended suddenly.*

*"Losing him is something I will never get over"* Harold Williams

*"That day the plane went down was one of the saddest days in my life"* Leon Booker

*"He was well on his way to bringing home the Gold Medal home to Sunnydale"* T Warren

*"Big Walt will forever be the Champ in our community"* B Hughes

*"All of Sunnydale's hearts went down with that plane"* Melvin Pitre

*"A true deserving member of Sunnydale's Hall of Fame"* A Burleson

*"He got the Gold Medal when the Lord called him home"* K Burleson

*"There weren't many brothers like him. I'm not talking about boxing but about the Man, he was cut from the same cloth but in a lot of ways, the way he carried himself made him different and special. His life took many a turn but who He was inside, a kind hearted Man who cared about His Family and His Community"* Randy "Roc" Minix

*"Rest in Paradise my brother you will always be remembered. Thanks for the memories"* C Jefferson

*Those of us who knew him, and the others who left us all too soon my brother Victor, Danny "Danko" Danny Ray, Sharon and Loretta, Norma N, Jesse R, Maryann, Debra O, Theresa J, Kent, Otis, Bucky, Sonny P, Simba, Burnis O, Big Butler, Bobby F, Kermit F, Steven, Leroy and Vernon C, Stephen, Stevie G, Roy Nelson, Leo Toastie Nelson, Andre B, Dexter G, Ted {aka} Knukky, Sam P, Blain P, Big Black and of course John Jr, aka Daddy O, and Uncle Ike.*

*"Everyone of these brothers and sisters left their signatures all over our community"* Glen "GT" Taylor

*"Sunnydale laid to rest some wonderful sisters and brothers and their lives need to be remembered somehow someway" Harold Williams*

*Unfortunately some of the above losses were attributed to some of the same individuals listed above.*

*"No community is immune to the hazards and challenges the cards in life deals us" Kermit Burleson*

*So many others of **OUR** neighborhood's sons and daughters **will be forever remembered.***

***A Song for Ms Henrietta** pays homage to them and continues to mourn their passing.*

## The School Of Life

*Was unforgiving, from young high school couples facing the harsh reality of unexpected pregnancies to our young brothers and sisters succumbing to drugs, the fast street life, gangs and violence, the SOL and the streets of our inner cities are without "A" doubt unforgiving.*

## Dark Days

*As so many of the contributors have shared, The Dale was a safe place for young children to play.*

*Perhaps because of our youth, innocence, and ignorance, we the children of Sunnydale had no idea that dark days and dark things surrounded us.*

*It was as if Drugs and Violence creeped over the hill, and people started dying around us*

*Sunnydale back in the day was no exception to the rule and had more than its share of senseless violence that ended in the loss of precious lives.*

*Drugs and the streetlife contributed greatly to the death of many of our brothers and sisters.*

*While the community mourned, the funeral business was booming big time.*

*The cemeteries are full of our brothers and sisters who succumbed to street violence and drug addiction.*

*There was one funeral business that paid us kids to go door-to-door passing out and posting low cost burial leaflets and business cards.*

*The competition among funeral parlors was intense, they even used catchy phrases to get people to sign up for their services. Imagine receiving a leaflet in your mailbox "You Carry We Bury"*

*I have no doubt that Ms Henrietta was there to comfort all of our families during times of hurt sorrow and loss.*

*You could have called her cough drop because she was Sunnydale's soothing medication.*

*I can remember one Sunday afternoon we were sitting down to supper after my mom had come from the Kingdom Hall.*

*Danny Ray, running from the police, without knocking entered our back door and begged my mother to hide him from the cops'*

## *Car 54 Where Are You*

*Car 54 was a popular television police comedy program. On top of the squad car were the numbers 054 quite a coincidence, since that was the number on the squad car that patrolled Sunnydale.*

*Moms agreed to help Danny Ray but made him wash his hands and sit down at the table just as the police came knocking at our door, "excuse me ma'am", the officer said but "we're looking for a young man we thought may have lived here"*

*Moms calmly told the officers "we're about to sit down and eat Sunday supper. "I'd be obliged if you let me feed my family".*

*They went away, but for his reward. Momma made Danny Ray and Coyle, Danny Ray's partna' wash the dishes and stay for Bible Study.*

# CHAPTER 10

# DANNY RAY HARRIS

## Brotha Brotha Brotha

*"Yeah, Danny Ray and I had many Heart to Heart conversations outside the game.*

*He was a victim of the Street Life, a product of the grip of the neighborhood where drugs and the absence of role models were few and not always present.*

*My brotha' was awesome, a great athlete and forever a Son of Sunnydale". Coyle Jefferson*

*"He could out run and out jump anybody in the neighborhood"*
*Melvin Pitre*

*"It's sad to think what became of Danny Ray and the others heroin*
*had no pity on its prisoners" Dennis Pettway*

*"Danny Ray could have gone pro but them damn drugs sucked the*
*life right out of him" Leon Booker*

*"When we were young boys a day never went by without us seeing*
*Danny Ray playing with a football, baseball or doing something*
*sports related" K Burleson*

One day at Hertz Playground behind the backstop some of us watched
Danny Ray shooting up some dope then started playing in a pickup
football game, he was unstoppable but started to nod as the game
wore on.

*"Dude was a natural born athlete chiseled from head to toe" D Martinez*

*"Drugs in Sunnydale were devastating, cruel and had no mercy on*
*those who got hooked. Brothers nodding on street corners, women*
*selling their bodies was not a pretty sight. All of them were family*
*and friends in the neighborhood" Dwayne Robbins*

*"He had his faults, his demons but for the most part he had your*
*back. The brother had a damn good heart" R Taylor*

*"I think with all his natural abilities and being well liked there was a*
*sensitive nature about him that he kept to himself. My brother Kerm*
*and I spent a lot of time with him, we only lived a few doors away*
*from the Harris family. I think it was hard being him, there was a time*
*when Danny Ray could do no wrong, outside of silly ghetto games*
*that all us participated in. No doubt about his gifted athleticism but*
*deep down inside there had to be some kind pain and uncertainty*
*he sheltered about just being himself and to me I am convinced he*
*protected that inner Danny Ray" A Burleson*

# CHAPTER 11

# THE KING'S ARRIVAL

*"Junk Man Standing On The Corner, Selln'*
*Death No Conscious Has He"*
*The Temptations Take A Look Around 1972*

*Not even the compassion of **Ms Henrietta**, nor the courageous community activist efforts of **Geogre Davis** or the countless pleas of Sunnydale mothers aboard the **Teardrop Express** could save Sunnydale from the arrival of the **King-King Heroin**.*

*"Junkie walking through the twilight" Lyrics from Gil Scott Heron's Home Is Where the Hatred Is" 1971*

*"Every family in Sunnydale one way or another was victimized by the King". T Warren*

*"There is not one inner city community that can be held responsible for bringing drugs into their neighborhoods. Our inner city people are victims of criminal, social and well devised plans to keep us down. But within our communities we do have the abilities to be resistant through street advocacy and awareness. People in the community can hold themselves accountable for not taking action to help assure the safety and well being of their communities" Coyle Jefferson*

*The King hit Sunnydale hard, delivering **Tyson-like knockout blows** throughout the neighborhood. Addict after addict got on board the King's drug train.*

*"When the King came to Sunnydale a lot of junkies, white boys from Viz Valley showed up in the neighborhood" D Hughes*

*Undoubtedly many contributing factors can be attributed to the devastation and demise of those who boarded the **King's Train**, but the absence and presence of strong black role models was not the sole culprit for the King did not discriminate nor have mercy on his prisoners he captured.*

*"All of a sudden there was a whole different breed of new faces hanging out in the neighborhood" W Francis*

***The King** was a killing machine, a volatile vulture at the top of the food chain-preying, hovering and capturing anyone who crossed his destructive path.*

*"I've Been Through The Desert On A Horse With No Name" song by folk rock band America 1971.*

*Heroin was also called horse among many other dope cultured names.*

*"Much of the crimes, break ins and burglaries in Viz Valley were blamed on the brothers in the Dale but a lot of that stuff was committed by junkies who came to the neighborhood to cop their dope" T Ferguson*

*"Most people think drugs in the Black community is common thing a way of life, but when drugs spread to the suburbs people became alarmed and started saying oh my God this can't be happening in our community became their cry for freedom" K Burleson*

*Crazy as it may seem, Al, Roc, Chop and I made a game outta watching the brothers nod on the bus stop at Sunnydale and Hahn.*

*We would bet between us which of them would nod, then suddenly snap out of their dope syncopated performance before falling face first on the hard concrete.*

*"These were our brothers and sisters hooked on heroin nodding out in front of everybody right there on the corner" G Chop Porter*

*What we thought was an impromptu ghetto ish game was a serious life threatening powerful disease that was ripping the heart and soul out of our community.*

*"The King hit Sunnydale hard, worse than a sledgehammer upside the head" B Grant*

**The King** *did not waver on his seek and destroy mission-not stopping entering households without an invitation from an unwelcome guest, refusing to leave.*

**The King** *left his epidemic trademark signature like a dog pissn' on a streetcorner fire hydrant and consumed all willing to take a whiff* of his awful smelling addictive aroma, stripping the life right out of our brothers and sisters and anyone else who became a victim of his irresistible joy and false elation.

**The King** knows to rid him of his devastating and destructive ways there is no magic wand, but countless people have found the strength and courage to reclaim their lives.

"The King wasn't nothing nice he destroyed a lot of good people and a lot of good families" K Burleson

People have the capacity to take back their communities, address risk factors that can contribute to the well being of their families and communities through education and prevention.

**Communities and People Can Change when they Make Demands for Change in their Lives.**

There are few who once boarded the train and lived to survive are shouting with glee **Long Live The King**

# CHAPTER 12

# HAROLD WILLIAMS

## Sunnydale's Native Son

*"The changes going on in Sunnydale I totally support. For me it was a proud moment driving through the community seeing all the construction, buildings going up, people in the community working in hard hats but the changes have been much too long coming. the people there deserve much more than what they have experienced over the years. My only hope is that the people there like when grew up take pride in their community like we did back in the day" Harold Williams*

**Anthony, Harold Lonnie Williams**
*Sunnydale's Native Sons*

*Of* all the contributors to our story Harold Williams is the true Native Son of Sunnydale having been born there in 1959 to Ms Vivian Williams a single mother who also raised two other sons.

**Williams** now resides in Sacramento California helping to raise four grandchildren while being active in youth sports programs, a passion he developed in Sunnydale playing in SF REC AND PARK, Police Athletic League Pop Warner sports programs.

*"When I heard what was going on in Sunnydale, I drove from my house in Sacramento with the quickness back to the neighborhood. When I got there I was shocked but proud. I even went and knocked on the door where we use to live and introduced myself to the people living in our old house on Blythedale" it brought back memories, I mean we didn't have much at all, some of us only had a few pennies to live on, but back then a penny could buy you plenty".*

*"I always had an interest in the wellbeing of my community. Through sports I learned teamship, camaraderie and leadership, these are qualities that my brothers and I learned growing up with in Sunnydale. Sports can be a blueprint for getting families and communities involved in their community. Playing in organized sports programs we were taught the values of having your teammates back on and off the field. I am a product of that kind of uplifting participation".*

*"I remember Ms Henrietta was always spreading joy, giving hope and understanding to the people who lived nearby us. She wasn't one of those I told ya' so folks, always pointing the finger, all up in your business kind of people. She was just a downhome kind hearted women who was downright concerned about the people in Sunnydale"*

*Back in the day **he was** known for his sprinting abilities and will argue, brag and boast, to this very day, even bet you a few twos and few dollars that he can still outrun some of his youth team members* *in the 100 yard dash, all the while sitting down in his favorite recliner chair laughing, eating donuts before dozing off taking in an afternoon senior citizen nap.*

*"The kids who I coach remind me so much of us youngsters back in the day playing pick up games, balling all day at the schoolyard, in between the buildings, out on the streets dodging between passing cars.*

*Man! Sunnydale was always popping' Some things, most necessary like constructive activities our youth today need to be exposed to. It's sad because some of the games our children our youth play end in serious arguments. They get into petty things over nothing that have significant consequences and it should not be that way"*

*Growing up in Sunnydale from our backyard window we could look out and see the brothers who didn't play sports getting into all kinds of trouble"*

*His laughable signature smile and Colgate Toothpaste grin are the things that made **Williams Sunnydale Special**.*

*Harold never let us forget he was born and raised in Sunnydale. He constantly reminded everybody that he was a Native Son. If back then he had the money I wouldn't doubt for a minute the brother would have hundreds Tee Shirts with pictures of his brothers and him printed up to remind everyone in Sunnydale they was born and raised in Sunnydale" Glen GT Taylor*

*"There was structure in the community when I was growing up I had mentors who were big brothers and a system of support for me" Harold Williams*

*"We would actually hide from Harold, he was younger than us by a few years but he was one of them dudes, Man! We couldn't get rid*

of him. Believe me we tried to ditch him. Sometimes he was at our hideout places before we got there" Randy Roc Minix

"A damn straight up pest was he, but in a good kind of way. Always on the prowl to hang with the brothers. But Harold wasn't no dummy, he knew who to hang out with and who to stay the hell away from." Thomas Warren

"Dude was at our house everyday. My brother and sister thought Harold was either a little brother Mom's never told us about or he was part of the furniture" Kermit Burleson

"Young Harold had a thing for throwing rocks. Walk around with a pocket full of rocks. One day, he threw a rock at Lil' Jeff, damn near busted his head open then took running, laughing like it was the thing to do" Glen Chop Porter

"He would follow us around all day long until all we could do was accept him into our click, give him his membership card and hope the hell he doesn't have one of his crazy rock throwing fantasies" Al Burleson

"When I heard he went out to Sunnydale to check out what was going on with the development. It came as no surprise. I thought no doubt he was back in Sunnydale pestering the hell outta' the people especially those people living in his old house" Thomas Warren

# CHAPTER 13

## SUNNYDALE'S BLACK PEARLS

### With

## Lexie TC Caracter and Eddrena Peters

Mrs Caracter, TC & Phyliss Henderson

*I*n 1969 during some difficult times in this country. R&B artist Sonny Charles and the Checkmates released a powerful thought provoking song *"Black Pearl Precious Little Girl"*

The song was a romantic song about a Black Man serenading his girlfriend, giving her validation and courage to realize her Beauty and Blackness.

**Charles** sings about Black Women being **"in the background much too long"** the lyrics are inspirational, a plea for social equality and social consciousness and address the second class systematic portrayal that not all Black Women are domestic workers, housekeepers, maids only capable of only working menial jobs and those that do have nothing to be ashamed of and can take pride in themselves.

*."Black Pearl Precious Little Girl" is a love ballad of revolutionary consciousness. Telling All Black Women ``you've been in the background much too long"*

Black Women throughout our communities are frequent riders of the **Teardrop Express** buses leaving the inner cities headed downtown or to the rich white folks homes in the suburbs at the wee wee hours of the morning on their way to work oftentimes leaving their children sleeping in bed, all the time Praying that upon their return home from work they will not be greeted with troubling news about their children having been left behind to fend for themselves.

*"The Teardrop Express travels down Weeping Widow Single Motha' Avenue, turns right onto the Empathy Expressway, exits on Kleenex Boulevard before' stopping on "HELP ME LORD DRIVE"*

*Noone but a Black Woman forced to leave her children behind while working menial jobs knows what this pain feels like...*

*"I had more family responsibilities than my peers looking after my younger brothers and sister because both of my parents were involved in the community". Eddrena Peters*

*I remember seeing women going to work everyday then coming home from work. They all seemed to be on the same schedule. I was proud of them because they did what they had to do to put food on the table" TC Caracter*

Eddrena and TC are two Sista's of Sunnydale who grew up in families with five children. Both of these remarkable Black Women held unique positions in the family structure.

Both women have positive outlooks on life and offer strong encouragement to young Black girls growing up in our inner cities.

Eddrena was the oldest of five children and TC the youngest of five and the only female in her family.

They are separated by several years in age and therefore their roles, and upbringings in the family household took on different challenges and responsibilities.

*"Sometimes being the oldest I felt all alone, I didn't have time for all the fun and games other young girls were having but that didn't bother me because what I did for my family was rewarding and helped me mature into a grown woman" Eddrena Peters*

One was the protector, the other the protected. TC lived within walking distance of the Front at 1547 Sunnydale while Eddrenna resided at the top of the hill at 1864 Sunnydale Avenue.

*"I was grown up before I was grown. Looking out for my brothers and sister was a full time job" Eddrena Peters*

*"I was sheltered and protected by my older brothers, there was little I could do without my family's permission. A lot of the kids in Sunnydale didn't have this kind of support" TC Caracter*

*"When I got time to myself I would walk from my house by myself over the hill through Crocker Amazon Park all the way to Geneva*

*and Mission and back that's what I did with my free time" Eddrena Peters*

TC attended Visitacion Valley Elementary School having to walk eight or nine blocks through the unwelcoming Viz Valley community while Edrenna could open her back door and damn near be inside her classroom at John McLaren School.

Born in San Francisco in 1956 TC graduated from Abraham Lincoln High School before obtaining her Associate Arts Degree at SF City College.

Initially she wanted to follow in my mom's nursing career footsteps.

*"Black girls must be exposed to positive role models and those sisters who've made out of the ghetto must give back to their communities, not just financially but through that straight up in your face, tell it like it is, honest to God check yourself before you wreck yourself reality", TC Caracter*

*"Our young sisters don't need to hear about successful sisters they need to meet with them face to face, get to know these women, then they will begin to feel and believe in themselves" Eddrena Peters*

Mrs Caracter was a registered nurse but TC had second thoughts when her research revealed *"The unbelievable stress, people bleeding, spitting puking on you. Nah I had second thoughts but respected my mom and Ms Johnson for doing what they did". TC Caracter*

Both women have accomplished careers, TC, a long distinguished career with the Department of Motor Vehicles. Eddrena worked as a County Health Worker, she is retired and maintains a close relationship with her brother Eric.

TC lives in Sacramento California. Spending her time reading and conversing with a few close friends.

Inside the family house at 1547 Sunnydale Avenue, she recalls growing up watching cartoons. Her favorite show was Top Cat, a fitting coincidence to her legendary initials.

Eddrena was a fan favorite of the Ed Sullivan Show. *"When that show came on TV Sunday Night, I would watch it get ready for bed and get up the next day doing the same thing I did yesterday and the day before"* *Edrenna Peters*

The Caracter family were Seventh Day Adventist and were not allowed to watch television programs like the Three Stooges or allowed to partake in Saturday afternoon activities because the SDA held services on Saturday.

*"There was nothing wrong with studying the word. Some of readings and bible studies I enjoyed and were very inspirational"* *TC Caracter*

She talked about growing up with four older brothers being sheltered and protected, sometimes flirting with the temptation of going outside when she was told to remain in the house.

*"I would look out the window and see young girls playing outside, it looked like they were having fun, but inside the house I was content entertaining myself with the things my parents provided"* *TC Caracter*

*"When I was young growing up I stayed away from those street sisters who showed me exactly what not to do. They were into some things I didn't care to get involved in"* *Eddrena Peters*

Most significant in their lives and upbringing were their mothers who were both active in the community.

Mrs Peters was a community activist and Mrs Caracter worked as a healthcare professional. In fact Mrs Caracter was a highly educated Black woman who attended a pretious Black southern university in Florida.

*"My parents left me in charge of the house. When they left in the morning to the time they came home at night, I did everything clean, cook help with homework everything" Eddrena Peters*

*"My mom was my role model, but there were many women in the community I looked up to. Our young sisters should have more exposure to these hard working dedicated Black Women" TC Caracter*

The two excelled in the classroom and presented little opposition to the rules of the family.

*"Not only did I have to take care of my siblings but after school in High School to help out I got a babysitting job, I was always taking care of somebody's children" Eddrena Peters*

Both came from homes with a father figure in their lives. Mr Peters was a stabilizing influence in the family home and the community while TC's father was a frequent visitor to the family while living in an apartment in the Fillmore District.

*"My dad was a fun loving high energy man with interest in a lot of creative things and maybe a few other unsavory things" TC Caracter*

*"Our father was there but because he was involved in so many community activities sometimes when he was home, he wasn't really there. It's sort of hard to explain" Eddrena Peters*

Young men with a healthy back and willing to work could find work, day to day labor jobs with Mr Caracter painting or doing odd jobs at some of the apartment buildings Mr Caracter helped maintain.

Even with sound minds, a somewhat protective shield around them and future aspirations the two young women were not immune to the neighborhood's dark sides of temptation, exposures to ghetto life, and the inner city hazards that lurk and prey on our young Black sisters.

*"Things may look exciting out there on the streets, but our young sisters need to know there's nothing on the streets but trouble. We heard that alot" TC Caracter*

*"Some of those sisters just threw their lives away chasing after some no good wanna b ain't gonna amount to nothing brother. It's sad. Really sad." Eddrena Peters*

The two Sista's of Sunnydale offer their unique experiences, perspectives about young Black girls growing up in inner city communities and more importantly provide insightful commentary and opinions of the challenges young inner city sisters must overcome on their roads to adulthood.

*"You know nowadays they have girl gangs, thugettes, hochie' mommas and all that kind of crazy stuff going on. It's in all our communities". TC Caracter*

*"Some of our young sisters got some mouths on them. Make you wanna close your ears, ashamed hearing the things they say to one another" Eddrena Peters*

*Sunnydale has a chance to address these quality of life situations and put in place some positive programs of reinforcement for Women of Color" TC Caracter*

*"So many of our sisters try to play the tough girl role but deep down inside they ain't really that tough. It goes the same for some of our hard headed brothers" Eddrena Peters*

*"One time Ms Henrietta's daughter Sharon and I got into it, for what to this day I will never know, something silly like one of us didn't like what the other one was wearing but our argument was over before it started. Can't say that about these young people today, our kids are killing each other over nothing and that's a damn shame" TC Caracter*

*"In Sunnydale the transition from the old to the new doesn't come without challenges because people cannot just be told to have a sense of pride; they must see others in the community going out of their way to keep it clean and safe. Being nice to your neighbor watering the lawn picking up trash those simple things that show people you care about your neighborhood": Eddrena Peters*

*"There needs to be more mentorship programs and development activities that empower our young Black girls. I am not talking about forcing them into programs, forcing education and awareness down their throats but providing them with a start to finish blueprint. A life map that helps them make healthy realistic life choices" TC Caracter*

*"Young girls growing up having babies need to learn parenting skills, some don't even know how to budget, make out a shopping list but they sure as hell know how to get pregnant. You can't tell me these young women don't need something, programs and constructive activities to enhance their self esteem are needed" Eddrena Peters*

### *Sunnydale's Black Pearls*
### *NO LONGER IN THE BACKGROUND*

Kathy Stewart Kathy Frierson, Phyliss Henderson, Ann Pitre, Valerie Burleson, Donna Bibbs. Marva Thomas

Sunnydale's Annual Memorial in Stockton, CA To Honor Jackie Roberts

# CHAPTER 14

# GROWING UP IN SUNNYDALE

*Kathy Stewart*

Growing up in Sunnydale as a young girl was fun. My family came to Sunnydale in 1963. Kids were Kids.

We made tree houses, pitched tents in the front yard and slept outside overnight.

Sleeping outside in the projects today with all the drive by shootings and sick perverted souls out there I couldn't imagine.

Times are much different than when we grew up.

Young children nowadays aren't afforded the safety and luxury we had growing up. It's bad out there and so many of our children are at risk and living in harm's way.

Sunnydale was for me a place where everyone got along, neighbors looked out for each other and the children.

I spent many a day climbing on the Bear in the front of the Recreation Center. In fact I can't imagine any kid growing up in Sunnydale that didn't take his or her turn sitting on top of that Bear

I do remember Ms. Willliams and Family at the top of the hill sold those delicious Candy Apples.

Sunnydale as a whole was good growing up. The brothers and even a few of the sisters would play bongos on the brick bench on Santos.

Sure we had some tough times, our parents struggled to put food on the table and clothes on our backs.

We were poor temporarily but we weren't spiritually bankrupt.

The people in the community saw to that. Sharing what little we had and making the best out of bad situations when we were without.

I don't remember really ever going hungry and maybe I didn't get everything I wanted, especially things I saw on television that's just the way it was but from not having the things I dreamed of made my brothers and me more appreciative of the things we had.

Sunnydale provided me with the foundation, the upbringing to value what we had, what we ate and the clothes I wore.

I raised my own children with these very same values I learned growing up in Sunnydale.

Loretta Harris was my age and a good friend. They lived down on Blythedale and we lived up on Blythedale, but I knew the entire Harris Family.

It feels good to know Ms Henrietta and so many women in our community touched so many souls. May they Rest in Peace.

To be apart of this wonderful story not only brings back precious memories and a sense of pride but wonderful thoughts and visions of how all of our communities can be like

When we grew up there was a Bar B Que Place, a Grocery and Drug Store so many things sadly that don't exist in our neighborhood anymore.

It would be super nice if the changes in Sunnydale could have these things and our communities and children were not exposed to guns and violence.

The Sunnydale where I grew up was a place where everyone got along and neighbors looked out for each other and the children.

Kathy Stewart Kathy Frierson

# SISTA'S OF SUNNYDALE

Sista Debra "The Odoms" Sista Judy

Maxine Hughes Jimmy Nelson, Kathy Stewart and Patricia Horace Willis

TC Caracter, Debra LaBlanc, Lisa Burleson, Donna Doyle
Sandra Frierson, Phyliss Henderson, Maryann
Granderson and Reggie Price

*NO LONGER IN THE BACKGROUND*

# CHAPTER 15

# PRICELESS REFLECTIONS

## With

## Thomas Warren

*Thomas Warren, is a very unassuming well mannered, highly articulate brother, who was always a pleasure to be around, an amazing compassionate trustworthy thoughtful man who has shared*

*his own life experiences to help others lead productive independent substance free lives.*

*His journey back to Sunnydale and his memories are Priceless Reflections of days gone by.*

*He has a resounding laugh, is full of vigor and enjoys his days being with his grandchildren enjoying his golden years.*

*Talking with him you can feel the wisdom, compassion, excitement and see lightbulbs of concentration, thoughtfulness and exploration beam across his forehead.*

*When he reached out to share his priceless reflections about what growing up in Sunnydale he simply stated without reservation "I am delighted to be apart of this extraordinary creation"*

*TW, represents the challenges, personal discovery, the struggle for change and empowerment and his life growing up in the community and no doubt his experiences are woven into the fabric of who he is as a Man and who we were as a community.*

**"I came to Sunnydale in 1958, I was about 4 years old and we lived three, maybe four doors down from the Harris family. I remember Danny Ray from those days always being outside playing football and other sports outside in front of our house".**

*The Warren household was always a warm friendly place where Albert, Jackie, Pamela and Thomas resided under the watchful eyes of Momma Warren who was one the Sunnydale's go to Moms.*

**"Our dad was around but not all of the time. We was like most families in the Dale, raised by a strong Black woman, but unlike so many other families at least we knew who our father was"**

*Thomas still frequents the old neighborhood visiting his sister Pamela who still resides in the neighborhood so he has witnessed Sunnydale's transformation and the revitalization efforts waged by the Mayor's Office and other developers..*

**"Man it's good to see the changes but a lot of the mental stuff remains the same, and that bothers me. Families have moved out and been given new apartments, housing opportunities but there are still people there with the same street behaviors and attitudes of the past. Some are afraid of change, others simply do not know how".**

*Warren becomes further animated, almost agitated when comparing the old Sunnydale with the new.*

**"I hope the changes are not a sophisticated modern day way of warehousing our people.**

**Sunnydale, don't get me wrong, it looks hella nice on the outside but my concerns are what kind of programs are going to be put in place to help teach people to empower themselves.**

**There are a lot of nice looking ghettos with people who have ghetto mentalities, especially when many of the people there are from generations of the past, they survive and live solely by what they have been taught or experienced.**

**It ain't always easy, the revitalization of Sunnydale is more than building a kids backyard tree house".**

*His points are well taken and merit careful thought because there is no change without struggle.*

*Within the community there is enormous potential but Sunnydale's revitalization must not be an experimentation of massive exploration.*

*"Bruh people gotta want to change. When I was out there running the streets using drugs causing grief and havoc it got to the point that I was sick and tired of being sick and tired. I had to do something if I was gonna live my brother"*

*He proudly states that in 1989 a using buddy dropped him off at a Recovery Meeting and he has been clean and sober since that day.*

*"I got clean in Sunnydale",* he proudly states. *"I would pass by the same cats I shot dope with on my way to and from a meeting"*

*His contribution is greatly appreciated and the brother, Son of Sunnydale is a prime example that within all of us there are God Given qualities to walk away from despair while pushing on moving ahead in the right positive direction to productive meaningful ways of living.*

*"Growing up in Sunnydale I will never forget. I only hope that my contribution can be a source of inspiration to others. Thank You for letting me share my story, for me looking back is a Priceless Reflection"*

# CHAPTER 16

## TRUE SISTA'S OF SUNNYDALE
### Annette and Maxine Hughes

*"When Everyone Knew Everybody When Everybody Cared for Everyone"* Annette and Maxine Hughes

***Maxine Hughes***

*Annette has a contagious smile, an impenetrable personality, a Sunnydale Joy, a beautiful woman blessed with a beautiful voice and spirit.*

*Maxine is a kind hearted soul, expressive yet soft spoken, able to convey powerful thoughts with deep conviction.*

*The two sisters are products of Sunnydale with a bright outlook on life that was not darkened by the shaded obstacles many young Black girls often grow up with in our low income challenged communities.*

*The School of Life kept its ugly hands away from their childhood, but both were aware of its presence and steered clear of the streetlife.*

*Their roles in the family structure, being a positive influence on their siblings was not always easy, especially trying to keep pace with some very inquisitive brothers.*

*"I had a wonderful childhood, a caring family and friends that played together from the early morning until it was time to go home" A Hughes.*

*"We lived right across the street from the Rec Center. They had a lot of games and activities for us kids so it was easy to have fun and friends" M Hughes*

*"I used to ride down the hill on coasters just like the boys" she said with her voice starting to get excited about the "good ole days" as she called them. A Hughes*

*"We played outside until it was time to come inside. The boys in the neighborhood were silly just like the girls, but it all meant for a good time. Playing is what we did. It seemed like Everyone knew Everybody" M Hughes*

*Annette is the oldest of six children and embraced her role within the family to look out for her siblings.*

*Her revelation is a miracle when so many older children in our inner city communities are forced into adulthood before their time, forfeiting their youth because of circumstance and family obligations.*

*"I was fortunate to have a caring mother, who had a huge influence on me and a big sister to look after us. It's kinda sad that there were some families that didn't have that kind of big brother big sister, look out for one another thing and there's a lot of reasons why some kids got into trouble, but the people in the community were there for each other, they just couldn't be there all of the time, and that's the sad thing" M Hughes*

*Throughout our communities far too many of our children have had to endure these responsibilities and are simply kids raising kids.*

*"I have no regrets or bad feelings telling people where I grew up. Sunnydale was a good place to grow up. We could go outside and play and didn't have to worry about anything bad happening to us" A Hughes*

*The family moved to Sunnydale in 1955, with their parents and was one of the rare families in the Dale with Father and homemaker Mother.*

*They came from good stock and her sunny disposition is quite apparent when reflecting on her fond Sunnydale memories.*

*"I washed dishes, babysat and did chores around the house everyday now that I look back on those days. But it's what I was taught to do. To tell you the truth, it's what I loved to do" A Hughes*

*Both were good students at John McLaren Elementary School. Luther Burbank Jr High School.*

*Going to the Rec Center across the street from their house, playing with friends and going on field trips were some of the things they enjoyed most.*

*"I remembered the brothers on the corner or at the bus stop drinking their wine and playing the congos and the men in the community hanging out on the corner down on The Front playing loud music, gambling and playing dominoes". A Hughes*

*Annette worked downtown as a complulator at the Emporium as well as working for Levi Strauss and the Telephone Company.*

*Hard work was in her DNA, "I looked forward to going to work like when I was a kid looking forward to playing outside" A Hughes*

*"We lived by the bus stop and we saw the women in Sunnydale going to and from work everyday. It had a positive impact on me growing up because these were hard working responsible women who got up early everyday riding the bus downtown or where ever to and from work" M Hughes*

*Annette became a single mother and shared her empathy for those women, when she simply said "believe me raising kids on your own, ain't easy but you have to do what you have to do"*

*They both shared their thoughts on Sunnydale's hardships of not being above lives being lost to foolishness, drugs and neighborhood pressures.*

*"Since everyone knew each other it was easy to see and know who was doing what, getting sidetracked and being on the wrong page" M Hughes*

*"The sad thing about the people in Sunnydale who began to fall prey to wicked temptations was they all were just like family and we all shared their pains and suffering" A Hughes*

*The writers of this composition are pleased to include our Sista's Annette and Maxine Hughes sharing with us their story and more importantly allowing us to travel back with them in time to their early childhood days in Sunnydale*

## A Sista's Plea

**"We Need To Save Sunnydale's Children Because They Are The Ones Who Are Going To Carry The Torch For Generations To Come Every Child Deserves a Childhood There's No Shortcuts when it comes to the wellbeing of our children" Annette Hughes**

## Maxine's Words

**"I am so glad to be able to contribute to Henrietta' Story. I saw her many times out there in the neighborhood trying to bring goodwill to others. She, like my mom and so many other women in Sunnydale helped raise us kids, and taught us young girls how to carry ourselves and care for our neighbors. Sunnydale was our life, the community is all some people out there had. When there was trouble in the home, there was trouble in the community. Everyone pitched in to help that's what I remember most about growing up in Sunnydale"**

**"We could go outside and play and didn't have to worry about anything bad happening to us" A Hughes**

*"When Everyone Knew Everybody When Everybody Cared for Everyone" Annette and Maxine Hughes*

# Our Place On The Planet

*Gloria Ann Pitre*

*When I look back there are many things that enhanced our survival. Most impressive were love and music.*

*Mothers and Fathers who had left southern bigotry knew love was their super power.*

*They knew embracing every human being they laid eyes on was our healing balm.*

*Each household in Sunnydale was masterfully woven into other households.*

*Each household knew instinctively all the needs of each household would be met.*

*Some families struggled to stay in a position to share food, clothes, money or love when needed. Because no one knew when they might be called on for anything the goal was to always have an abundance of at least one.*

*Also vital to our survival was our music. Bobby Blue Bland and BB King playing in every living room in Sunnydale laid the musical foundation for congas and drums on the corner of Sunnydale and Hahn.*

*No one I think had formal music training. No one I am more than sure could write a note on a music sheet.*

*But the beats and the rhythms captivated all ears on Sunnydale, Brookdale, Blythdale, Santos and Hahn.*

*Moreover, the rhythm and blues hiding out in Sunnydale would be heard on albums by Santana all over the world.*

*Raul Rekow, Santana's percussionist lived in the Eicler homes and harnessed some of his skills in Sunnydale jammin' drink'n with the brothers playing congas in Sunnydale*

*Music brought us together on the corner of Sunnydale and Hahn.*

*Most importantly, music eased our soul when the worst of our secrets were being kept.*

*Peace and Harmony*
*Gloria Ann Pitre*

## Memories

*Back in the Dayz'*
*We Waz Tighter*
*Than 10 Toes in a*
*Sock*

*Siro stole the Gallo*
*Wine Truck All of*
*Sunnydale Got*
*Drunk even Rin Tin*
*the Dog*

**OUR PLACE ON THE PLANET**

# CHAPTER 17

## OUR COMMUNITIES HAVE SEEN MORE THAN ITS SHARE OF REVITALIZATION AND GENTRIFICATION

*Photo SF Heritage*

*"Man I couldn't believe the Sunnydale back in the day photos. They really did have white picket fences before we moved there? I can only hope when the Revitalization is complete the new development will be a prideful community like where we grew up. Who knows maybe even with white pickets fences like they have in the avenues" Thomas Warren*

*Warren's heartfelt compassion about Sunnydale's Revitalization is exemplified and shared with many others in inner city communities who would like to see residents become shareholders who collectively decide what they value in their community.*

*"Man if San Francisco, the people in the neighborhoods ain't seen enough. I know it's a good thing but we gotta remember this ain't our first rodeo" Thomas Warren*

*With his temperature rising and deep patterns of contemplative thought unable to lay dormant, appear across his forehead his concerns about Sunnydale's Revitalization are constantly at the forefront of deep rooted apprehension. Especially his concern for the well being of Pamela, his younger sister residing in the community today.*

*Pamela among others still in Sunnydale, are a part of the early years, weathered through the Swamp and have had birds eye views from their backyard windows, when the mesh fences went up, the groundbreaking ceremonies took place and the bulldozers arrived in the community.*

*Sunnydale has suffered over the decades from neglect, crumbling infrastructure, vandalism, crime, and violence. Source The Internet*

*"I am not interested much in the dismantling, the replacement of old buildings, the reconstruction or anything cosmetic in Sunnydale. As a longtime former resident with family ties still in Sunnydale*

*to this day, my concerns are solely that the project and community advocates provide the residents with after-school tutoring, job placement, addiction treatment, health care, personal growth and self development training programs to help shed themselves of being less than mentalities and street behaviors that have far too long plagued our community" Thomas Warren*

*Eradicating "ghetto mentalities' '' 'can be very difficult for some, especially if they are often wrapped up and consumed by defeating thoughts, overwhelmed by negativity.*

*Many in our communities have strong feelings about redevelopment and the warehousing of people.*

*This country has an ugly history of shifting people from neighborhood to neighborhood from ghetto to ghetto forfeiting on promises then expecting people in our communities to be excited about new developments.*

*There are people in our city who have been moved or relocated to every housing project in the city*

*I am not so sure that the failures of development are no more, not much different than that of one of our sisters going to the hair stylist, leaving the salon highly upset and unsatisfied with her new weave and hairdresser.*

*The difference is her stylist wants to do nothing more than to fix things, and do whatever she can to make things right. But when development fails there is little they will do to make things right*

*Community Development projects should be designed to help people change their lives not to enhance the community's appearance.*

*"There are those stereotypes placed on our communities from outsiders.*

*Many who are afraid to venture into our neighborhoods but come election time or the promises of potential development, I always found it ironic that those same outsiders ain't afraid to come into our communities any more.*

*The bottom line. development and votes fill pockets of greed"*
*Thomas Warren*

*Public housing across the nation began to deteriorate in the 1960s, a process that accelerated and, with rare exceptions, has continued to the present day. Source The Internet*

*Gentrification has long been the leading contributor of displacement and mistrust, having displaced countless communities of color and restricted their access to important opportunities and resources.*

*"Don't get me wrong, I do feel good about what's happening in Sunnydale now, I have to, my sister lives there.*

*If any community deserves a new opportunity in San Francisco, Sunnydale should have been at the top of the list years ago" Thomas Warren.*

*People of color have every reason in the world to not trust developers. They don't always have our best interest in mind.*

*There was a time there were Black Communities and Black Townships all across this country, destroyed by economic greed and racial hatred all in the name of Gentrification and Revitalization*

*There are many today, ancestors of brutality from the horrors haunted by the memories of attacks by armed mobs in the Tulsa Race Massacre in a neighborhood called Greenwood, which included a thriving business district sometimes referred to as the Black Wall Street.*

*The violence began on May 31, 1921 and left hundreds of black residents dead and more than 1,000 houses and businesses destroyed. Source The Internet*

*Sadly today only thirteen Black Townships remain: Bolley, Brookvillie, Clearview, Grayson, Langston, Luma, Redbird, Rentievillie, Summit, Taft, Tatum, Taitullahasse and Vernon.*

*The demise of our Black Townships and the Gentrification in our communities have forced residents to seek refuge in ravaged communities much worse than the ones they resided in.*

*One of most conceiving examples of displacement of people of color was The Dawes Act (sometimes called the Dawes Severalty Act or General Allotment Act), passed in 1887 under President Grover Cleveland, it allowed the federal government to break up tribal lands.*

*If they accepted the allotment divisions, the Dawes Act designated 160 acres of farmland or 320 acres of grazing land to the head of each Native American family. These acreages were comparable to those promised by the Homestead Act, but there were important differences between the two acts*

*The Homestead Acts encouraged Westward expansion. The more people homesteading in the Midwest, the greater pressure for Native Americans to assimilate.*

*What is assimilation?*

*Assimilation is the process of taking individuals or social groups and absorbing them into mainstream culture.*

*More than catchy phases regardless of what they are called displacement is one in the same.*

*If there is a fine line between Revitalization and Gentrification, it's important that the people in the community know the names come in many forms and different titles but can result in significant consequences if the people in the community are unaware of their meaning.*

*It's not ironic that both Gentrification and Revitalization have coexisted in areas close in proximity but the people in nearby communities have been equally alarmed when the bulldozing crews appear.*

*There are significant and vast reasons why both Revitalization and Gentrification projects have fallen well short of providing job opportunities through First Source Hiring.*

*First Source Hiring. The promise and potential of employment opportunities can be misleading.*

*The first thing developers tell us is that their projects will provide jobs, construction work and 50% of our people will be guaranteed employment.*

*But what they don't tell our people is that they are primarily proposing general labor job opportunities that are not longterm and the skilled labor jobs many of our people are not qualified for.*

*Undoubtedly before construction begins there must be neighborhood needs and community value assessments, education and informational training self awareness sessions facilitated by Community Development Staff to orientate and familiarize the people in the community of the projects in greater detail and understanding.*

*The community should be able provide a roster of those seeking employment and the skill sets of potential job candidates to contractors*

*First Source Hiring opportunities are one of the most misunderstood components of both development projects because residents are not informed that the job opportunities are not guaranteed when skilled positions are required.*

*If in the community there are no skilled electricians, plummers, heavy equipment operators, residing in the community contractors are afforded the opportunity to look elsewhere to fill those skilled positions.*

*Contractors simply contest these arguments by saying there are no skilled workers in the community available, many of the jobs are union jobs and require up to date payment of union dues.*

*Over the years, there have been numerous protests from community members who argue contractors are in non compliance, even shutting down work projects.*

*Falling short of hiring compliances, upset with work stoppage in some instances some contractors have been willing to settle their compliance obligations in a court of law.*

*If qualified skilled union affiliated community workers, individuals who have lapsed in paying their union dues are not current, funds and resources for them should be set aside and made available to them.*

*These are key elements the people in the community need to be made aware of.*

*General labor jobs are temporary and not needed when the projects require skilled labor.*

*Undoubtedly people in our inner city communities need to be made aware of these First Source contractual components.*

*Residents need to be informed, exposed to job training programs to pursue skilled job opportunities, and provided financial resources to purchase work boots and tools.*

*Contractors should be brought in to provide basic labor orientations so that residents can pursue long term career paths.*

*Quite apparent when the work shortage bogs down or is shut down by protest ill feelings of mistrust and betrayal surface over and over again.*

*Our communities have long experienced more than our share of Revitalization and Gentrification, let down, disappointment, heartache, and our communities left in the dark. Call it what you want. I think of Excitement and Apprehension when it comes to development go hand in hand.*

*Changing the neighborhood fabric in our communities won't be easy but we can Pray and Share in the Vision of those who have taken on the task.*

# Sunnydale Hope SF

## Revitalization in Sunnydale Is Coming

CHANGING THE NEIGHBORHOOD FABRIC IN SAN
FRANCISCO'S SUNNYDALE HOUSING PROJECTS

*" I support all the things their doing in Sunnydale. that's where
I was born" Harold Williams*

# CHAPTER 18

## COMMUNITY IDENTIFICATION & RESISTANCE

### What's in a Name

*"The Swamp or Swampe' D"*

**"Shedding the neighborhoods negative identification is a job in itself" Melvin Pitre**

*By many accounts because of the violence and other illicit activities in Sunnydale, The Swamp or Swampe' D became synonymous with people outside of the community.*

*Noone knows or can rightfully claim ownership to the originality of the name, and by all accounts it doesn't really matter.*

**"We were outside playing the congas. *The almighty hawk, the wind was blowing hard, the wind was swirling around through Sunnydale and one of the brothers said the wind is blowing through Sunnydale like a desert Swamp. That's how the Sunnydale SwampeD got its name" Dennis Pettway***

*I am convinced the name is not registered in the recorder's office at City Hall, in the Yellow Pages or with the USPS.*

*But nicknames in Black Culture have always been a part of some form of Identification.*

*Nicknames such as The Swamp or Swampe' D have not always by any means had an positive uplifting impact on, or in our communities. But that does not mean that the name has to be associated with negativity.*

*People take pride in living in Pacific Heights, and other upscale communities, however does that not mean there is not some kind of dysfunctionality, crime or 911 calls of criminal behavior in those communities.*

*In fact by many accounts there is an unwritten law that sweeps unlawfulness, domestic violence and white collar crimes under the table in those upscale residential communities.*

*When crime does happen in residential communities. People there are quick to respond **"it doesn't happen in our neighborhood"** as if crime doesn't exist and is limited only to communities of color.*

*Why can't Sunnydale be referred to as a Residential Community?*

*People in Pacific Heights, and those in Sunnydale have the same opportunity if nothing else to take Pride in the name and community where they live.*

*Granted The Swamp or Swamp' D is not the most attractive of names but neither are **Whitesville, Coontown, Colorlordsville, or Spanish Harlem.***

*For the most part when inner city communities high five, chest bump and identify themselves with various nicknames it is a symbol of Identification and Resistance.*

*Pride in its most minute form is often the only cherished thing communities can cling to.*

*Often it's the only thing the people and their communities can to grab ahold of because social, economic inequalities have stripped them of everything else, therefore community names do not always represent negativity and at times are the only no more than a source of inspiration.*

*The name of our communities have little to do with the well being of the people who live there.*

*Swamp can easily mean that the people of Sunnydale confronted with enormous social and economic challenges found a source of salvation, a strange form of identification in a name that does not represent challenges as hostility but simply a way of life and need to endure oppressive times.*

*The name of the community belongs to its residents.*

*If the Swamp was given its name by media outlets or even those from outside the community it only represents stereotypic identification and systematic racism, that points its ugly fingers towards inner city communities to convince people they deserve nothing better.*

*It is therefore necessary that people understand that some of the nicknames in our culture are significant forms, means of identity, resistance and at times endorsements of acceptance.*

*Sports teams are a prime example of this and people have denounced their nicknames and team mascots, including the Blackhawks, Redskins, The Redmen, Indians and their mascot Chief Wahoo, The*

Braves and their mascot sitting in a teepee Chief Noc-A-Homa, The Bullets, The Tribe, and in London, a city in Ontario, Canada a professional baseball team was once named The Rippers, paying homage to the serial killer known as Jack the Ripper.

Quite obviously these names are derogatory and falsely represent the meaning behind them.

Many have prospered from the sales of nicknames and mascots.

The name "The Swamp or Swamp' D' therefore does not have to represent something bad.

Yet for years developers, real estate investors have set their sites on primetime properties in inner city communities regardless of the names of the communities.

Their eyes as big as silver dollars are focussed on a name change to attract potential profits.

In San Francisco this is no more illustrated than what happened and is happening in the Fillmore, picturistic Potrero Hill and the Bayview Hunters Point districts.

To attract business and home buyers developers add catchy acronyms, phrases such as **Heights, Villas, View, and Park**, aimed at bringing in new families while displacing residents and countless families.

No doubt this gentrification increases property value and forces people out of their neighborhoods, by using catchy terminology, cultural reversal nicknames that attract commerce.

History of these ambitious name changes have been met with opposition and resistance.

*It is the residents and the community regardless of name that must accept the identity and identify themselves with it.*

*Not all nicknames, ghetto sign signatures, graffiti represent bad things*

*"The Swamp or Swampe' D' can represent a symbol of ethnic and community pride.*

### *Sunnydale on the Decline*

Chronicle / Lacy Atkins

**"How can they expect us to take pride in our community when we are afraid and in fear, ashamed of the conditions where we live" Dennis Pettway**

*"I thought they were going to build new apartments to get people involved in the community but it's going to take more than that to bring back that sense of pride we had when we grew up in Sunnydale. We had a lot less but we wasn't short on community pride and looking out for our neighbors" Randy Roc Minix*

*"Many of us had moved on before things started to get out of control, and the neighborhood started going downhill, but we never forgot where we came from" Eric Peters*

*"We had some family visiting from out of town. They wanted to see the neighborhood they knew we had grown up in. Driving through the neighborhood was a culture shock to all of us. Decline was everywhere. Nothing like when our folks visited us years ago" Coyle Jefferson*

*"I was out there still connected to the old neighborhood. People and families still there but it didn't make me feel good that they were calling Sunnydale the Swampe D" Butchie Freeman*

*"It wasn't our Sunnydale anymore. Hard Times, drugs, street violence took over but there were people I knew from back in the day still living there. The blood in their veins ran deep with Sunnydale of the past. The name of the Swamp meant nothing to them. They were all Sunnydale true and true" Glen Chop Porter*

*"Sunnydale the Swamp was always in the news. The media made it like the people were living in a war zone" Glen GT Taylor*

### Sunnydale on the Rebound

*"The revitalization of Sunnydale is more than building a kids backyard tree house".* Thomas Warren

*"From what I've read, Mercy Housing has proven they are an organization concerned about the community as a whole. They're just not taking down the old, building the new without talking with the people. It seems the input of the people there is valued"* Skip Roberts

*"Nothing wrong with change as long as the people in the community have something to say about it"* Al Burleson

# CHAPTER 19

# IT'S NOT ABOUT THE STRUGGLE

## Rafiki Webster

## It's About Perseverance and Joy

I lived in Sunnydale from 1964 until 1975. Driving through Sunnydale seeing the new changes and developments, remembering The People - The Projects My Soul Felt Refreshed.

Being back in the neighborhood, took my breath away. Fond memories forged friendships, pick up football, baseball and basketball games. I thought how every kid in communities like ours deserves just a chance, a safe opportunity to go to the playground and play without care for hours and hours.

Far too many of our young children are not afforded this simplistic opportunity and it's not based on the people and conditions in our communities as much as it is the systematic conditions placed upon us

Our parents, working mothers were involved in our lives. My father did not live with us but every week I could expect him to visit with me, it was a proud moment, there were friends that gravitated towards me because of my father and that really became a constant theme between the Father's in Sunnydale, few in between yes, but sometimes just a minute with them made a positive impact on those without a Father.

Mr Peters who started the Sunnydale Boys Scout Troop was living proof of how much a positive role model could help influence a young child.

In my life experiences I have come to the realization that people don't need to feel trapped by economic and social conditions.

The solutions rest within the people in our communities. These conditions will cease when the people realize they are the most valued and powerful sources to eradicate their own hopelessness and despair.

There is no better remedy to uplift our communities than the "each one teach one"

"It's About Perseverance and Joy. It's Not About The Struggle

Within our communities those who contribute mostly to the decline, despair and fear given the encouragement and training can become the most productive members of our communities once they realize and understand their life experiences can become the blueprint for changing lives.

Drug dealers, gang members, street thugs, have their own loved ones and families to look after.

It's a matter of convincing them they can become contributing factors to the wellbeing of their communities, turning their negative behaviors, life experiences, failures inside out and becoming productive role models in the community.

I feel the Black Panther Party was a strong proponent of understanding the rich values of community outreach and community involvement. There are countless street soldiers among us willing, ready and capable of delivering the messages of hope and resistance.

To do this in Sunnydale, organizers of the development must provide key essentials including jobs, paid job training and mentorship programs to inspire people to value themselves and the community.

Growing up in Sunnydale negative influences were everywhere but there were countless programs, dedicated individuals and mentors who valued their work and the people they served.

Throughout our inner city communities we have countless examples of young men and women who have turned their lives completely around and are making positive impacts in the community.

Theirs are the voices that need to be heard.

It is with my deepest hope our journey through time will enlighten you and give struggling communities the fortitude to move forward.

"It's About Perseverance and Joy. It's Not About The Struggle

There is no better remedy to uplift our communities than the "each one teach one"

# Sunnydale Lives Newspaper
## The Revitalization of Sunnydale is More Than

### "Building a Kids Backyard Tree House".
### T Warren

**Things Are Changing In The Swampe'D Melvin Pitre**

**Sunnydale on the Rebound**

*"Where we grew up every parent is your parent and they could beat your behind, no doubt for sure you are growing up in a community that cares" R Taylor*

# CHAPTER 20

# GEORGE DAVIS

Sunnydale's Anchor
*Caring For The Greater Good Of His Community*

The George Davis Senior Housing Community Facility in Bayview
**May He Rest in Peace**

***George Davis*** was Sunnydale's anchor, devoted to the community leading the way forging the path to neighborhood success, empowerment and stability.

*'He was the mastermind with a vision of all good things to come to Sunnydale. The first thing he tried to do was reach out to the young men in the community standing on street corners, playing the congas or drinking liquor in front of Black's Store. They didn't give Mr Davis the time of day but he never gave up, so he started visiting our homes talking with the mothers in the community and going to the Housing Authority which was so screwed up they were out there taking pictures of the young men and turning the pictures over to the police. His plan was to start a Women's Group which most of us single women joined. Some of us had more than our share of hard head boys and young men. Eventually his efforts would pay off and he reached out to some men who were very interested in what Mr Davis was proposing. The talk of jobs, and job training programs, grants for attending school, starting an organization in the Community, The Sons Of Sunnydale had them knuckle heads listening"* Donna Billups

*"George Davis wasn't like that Underdog cartoon character on television "coming to save the day" he was a real live Black Man, a brother truly committed to helping his community"* Coyle Jefferson

*"My mother would come from work at the EOC on Hahn Street and talk to us about how committed the staff at the EOC was about helping the people in the neighborhood"* Skip Roberts

George Davis was a Man among Men, who went about his business without any fanfare, just a desire to provide practical solutions to benefit people and bring them together.

*"He didn't wear any fancy suits to work. If the brothers were hanging out on the corner you can bet George would be right there too. He was as much a part of the neighborhood as those of us who lived there"* Kermit Burleson

Davis himself was no stranger to the inner city community, he grew up in Oakland and Richmond's public housing projects learning the values of community and dedicated his life to helping others.

He worked in community development for more than 30+years and had a storied career.

*"Brothers like George are not rare I think there is a Geogre Davis in all of us"* Randy Roc Minix

Davis put all of Sunnydale on his back, climbed the mighty hills of despair with richness and cared for the community not only on his back, but closely in his heart.

His influence made an impact on education, and the quality of life in Sunnydale. A man who left his mark on the brotherhood and sisterhood of the community.

He inspired people to lift others up. His powerful voice, commitment to serve made him an advocate for change.

*"He could talk with the best of them. He was street when he needed to be and the sharpest talking tool in the tool shed when he wanted to be" Levi Bryant*

Davis was on a mission to make Sunnydale a better place to live.

*"The brother was committed to helping people anyway he saw fit. He was one of the guys most of the time but not all the time, I mean George would respect you and support you but in return he wanted his respect to" Butchie Freeman*

His street advocacy changed faces in the neighborhood, gave us hope to reach new heights, pursue obtainable goals and helped make Sunnydale a safer place to live.

*"Don't let it be basketball season. If George wasn't in his office he was hooping it up at Hertz Park" Levi Bryant*

*"The only time I really saw him come out of character, not himself, was on the basketball court, he wanted to win just like everyone else. George wasn't going for any of them rinky dink bogus calls. He could flat out ball" Al Burleson*

Tall, strikingly handsome, scholarly looking, quiet with a resonating baritone voice and wide eyed grin to make people happy, Davis was known throughout the community.

He was more active than verbal. He loved the people in Sunnydale and would have walked a country mile, jumping through a blazing fire to help them change their lives.

The people loved him and respected him, gave him his props and stood by him. Davis was a transformation seeker. A visionary not a dreamer.

Davis brought the brothers together and helped them start the Sons of Sunnydale long before they became the SOS.. He knew the benefits of Community organizing and provided the blueprint for the birth of the organization.

He had an understanding of people and was sensitive to their needs, he knew when to reach out and he knew when to step back and let people make their own decisions. He wasn't an I told you so kind of person.

As an organizer Davis developed outdoor sporting activities and social events that brought the community together. He would make time for families in crisis and visit brothers in jail.

In an effort to share his vision Davis teamed up with Tony Harrison, Ms Frierson, Ms Hopkins and many other community activists, while working for the EOC, the Economic Opportunity Council on Sunnydale and Hahn Streets, an organization dedicated to help empower struggling communities.

Davis work continued when he earned his PHD and left the community to become Executive Director at the Bayview Hunters Point Senior Center where a 121 one and two room is named in his Honor

# CHAPTER 21

## REMEMBERING THE PEOPLE
## IN THE PROJECTS

*The Outrageous Steven Caracter*
*Rest in Peace*

# For No Reason At All

*Few words can rightfully describe the Outrageous Steven Caracter, but if there were a MOC Most Outrageous Character award given out Steven Caracter my childhood buddy would have won the award hands down.*

*There are those people who wake up every morning needing their morning coffee, morning Words of Inspiration, a dose of Act Right or Personality Plus but Steven began his days with his own remedy, a tall tall glass of FNRAA For No Reason At All Juice to stimulate his brain. For No Reason At All for him worked to perfection.*

*Before he even went outside the house he had ole' man trouble looking for a place to hide and begging for Mercy.*

*He had people in the neighborhood scratching their heads until their hair fell out. Their pondering faces of disbelief were mesmerized in sheer amazement from the things he would do.*

*Clinically there is probably no professional diagnosis for what was ticking inside his head.*

*"Steven wasn't a bad dude by any means. Take your eyes off of him for a minute and he would do something no one could imagine. He just did some crazy ass things that were uncalled for". Randy Roc Minix*

*One day Mrs Caracter had me go to the therapist with him.*

*Steven went to the little boys room before seeing his shrink, a man came down the hallway screaming the toilets were stopped up and the water in the sinks were flooding the bathroom.*

*By the time the session was over the poor psych doctor ended up on the couch, dropping tranquilisers like skittles candy.*

*On the bus he would purposely sit next to an elderly person and catch imaginary insects then put them in his shirt pocket patting them while talking to the insects as if they were his pets, scaring the living hell out of the unsuspecting elderly person.*

*Sunnydale's maintenance worker Mr Bruce had just cleaned up the play area of broken glass behind the Caracter's house and took a smoke break.*

*Steven found some Coca Cola bottles and threw them right where Mr Bruce had swept up. For what? No Reason At All.*

*He was outright funny, charming and outrageously unpredictable and the Black version of Televisions Eddie Haskel on Leave It To Beaver. He was Sunnydale's very own Dennis the Menace. "PEST" should have been his first name.*

*"I thought Steven was going to make it big in show business. He was entertaining and funny. He could make everybody laugh at the same time. I heard he wanted to be the next Bill Cosby, Steven was just that funny" Val Burleson*

*He studied music, played the trumpet, took foreign language classes and was raised a Seventh Day Adventist.*

*Most of his corruptive behavior took place every day but Saturday because on Saturday the family attended Bible Study.*

*His fatha' LT,* didn't live with the family.

*He was a handyman who came across town every now and then, got toasted and cooked a huge pot of red beans that lasted the family more than a month.*

*The family developed a huge dislike for red beans and rice. Mr C was a penny pincher, he used to mark the pots and pans with a screwdriver. Always screaming to his kids "somebody ate over the line"*

*One day Steven threw a bucket of sand on a freshly painted house in Viz Valley right in front of the man who stopped to admire his work.*

*Another time he broke out all the windows in John McLaren Swimming Pool just for the hell of it. For No Reason At All*

*That day most of the kids were at Hertz Park and later several of the youngsters were taken to Juvenile Hall who had nothing to do with it while Steven went on his merry way.*

*"Man dude took a water hose and put it through Ricky's mailbox flooding the entire house" Al Burleson*

*"We were at Hertz Park for baseball practice. Steven played back catcher and was talking shit to little Jeff who had enough of his teasing so Jeff turned to Steven warning him to stop his teasing then out of the clear blue sky, hit Steven over the head., Bam! Smack right over the head with a baseball bat. Finally Jeff, his lower Sunnydale partna' I guess had enough of Steven's bullshit. We laughed for days" Glen Chop Porter*

*"He was a good kid but did some things nobody else would do like going down to the Eichler Homes Swimming Pool and throwing some motor oil in the water. That's part of the reason they didn't want Sunnydale down there" Randy Roc Minix*

*Cars coming down Woodrow Wilson Hill were unsuspectedly greeted by large tree branches or rocks Steven would drop down on the hoods of the cars from high atop one of the pine trees.*

*"I remember that one time he hit the wrong brother's car. Dude crept up on Steven out of nowhere, took him home to Mrs Caracter. Thank*

*God that brother didn't hurt him, beat his ass but he was mad as hell. The next day Steven was back at it again" Al Burleson*

*At school during lunchtime he would go around the school yard walk over to some of the white girls licking an orange juice bar take his hand rub his crotch then take his finger run it up and down the girls juice bar who didn't want it anymore then give it to him and he would kiss away the germs up to God.*

*He was the gram cracker monitor who would bite off the crackers, drink some of the milk while the students were outside at recess.*

*One Day a teacher brought fried chicken for her lunch that he bit off then swore before God he didn't have anything to do with all the while with fried chicken and breadcrumbs dripping from his mouth.*

*Mr Polier, my six grade teacher, was missing thirty six dollars from his wallet and on the way home from school Steven brought thirty six dollars worth of chocolate malt balls from the Penny Store that he hid under his mattress. Mrs Caracter found them cleaning up his room.*

*Man this dude lived in the next building from me and I got many an ass whuppin' for hangn' out with him.*

*Steven found an old box of bullets and stole a book of kitchen matches from his house, went outside and on the side of the building started a fire, threw the bullets into the fire and bam! The bullets went off everywhere and damn near killed several boys shooting one of the boys in the leg stupid enough to stand around watching the fireworks.*

*Once the three of us Andre D, Steven and I were over at an apartment building his dad was working on in the Fillmore District.*

*Mr Caracter, left specific instructions for us not to mess with the paint cans stored in the basement of the building where he was working.*

*The first thing my crazy ass buddy did when we went downstairs was open up several cans of paint and start a paint throwing party.*

*When LT came back later and found paint everywhere I will never forget what he said to Steven.* ***"Didn't I tell you not to mess with that paint"***

*Steven's reply* ***"I didn't! The paint jumped on me"****...For No Reason At All. It was an ass whuppin' I will never forget.*

*Ironically this trumpet playing community clown, my partna' was a straight A student at Viz Valley Elementary when he wasn't stealing fried chicken out of the teachers lounge. For No Reason At All!*

# CHAPTER 22

# THE MAGIC THAT MADE SUNNYDALE OUR PLACE ON THE PLANET

## With Gloria Ann Pitre

*BA Political Science and Black Studies*
*Masters in Social Work 1996*

*Street Soldier Organizer Sista of Sunnydale*

### She Wore Her Sunnydale Badge of Honor with Unconditional Love And Faith As Those Women of Our Communities Have Worn The Badge of Honor Before Her

The Magical Community is a term used to refer to a community of good magical beings living in the world. These beings are known to regularly interact with each other and come together in times of need.

**"One day while working at San Francisco General Hospital seeing all these brothers and sisters from Sunnydale coming to the clinics and different departments for various services, it donned on me there was a need to reach out to them, keep our neighborhood connected and provide a platform for all of us to stay in contact with one another. It was easy, the Sunnydale Reunion was what was needed. The birth of the Sunnydale Reunion seemed almost magical" Gloria Ann Pitre**

"I can see why she chose the words magic in our story. Sunnydale was our Playland at the beach except we didn't have any ferris wheels and clowns running around the neighborhood. There was a certain magic in the air, back then green grass was everywhere. Playing outside us kids made our own magic" Al Burleson

"To me Sunnydale was just that A Magical Place. Today when I think back about those times growing up there, in spite of the economic, social and racial challenges we faced, people being there for people made our community extraordinary. That's the Magic I am speaking about" Gloria Ann Pitre

"We went outside and played without a care in the world. I guess growing up in the inner city today with all the violence and things happening to our children, if they could go outside and play like we did, I guess that would be magical" Annette Hughes

*Ann Pitre was not a magician nor a miracle worker, simply a beautiful Black Woman, a product of the community with God Given qualities to put her family and community first.*

*She was a gifted treasure, the neighborhood's very own Sista of Reconciliation Recovery and Remarkable Commitment to her Community.*

*"There were so many down to earth Women, Sista's of Sunnydale like Ann Pitre who made a positive impact on our community that deserve recognition, believe me they had to deal with a lot of stuff growing up in the projects" Coyle Jefferson*

*"Sunnydale had a boat load of beautiful Black Women and young sisters like Ann Pitre. I know because I tried to hit on all of them" Levi Bryant*

*"She was much more my brother than a pretty face" Randy Roc Minix*

*"Pretty Polite and Positive was she" Glen GT Taylor*

*"Good thing for Momma and Pops Pitre they didn't have cell phones back in those days the phone would have been ringing off the hook" Levi Bryant*

*"A breath of fresh air in times of despair" Thomas Warren*

*But the respect of the people in our marginalized communities, trust they bestow upon someone is not to be taken lightly.*

*From her community involvement, Ann Pitre would be the first to tell you this. "Community Organizing is a tough job your heart has to be in the right place" Gloria Ann Pitre*

*Perhaps there were many who thought she may have possessed magical talents, a magical smile, anything to help make things better.*

*"Everyday the sun didn't come out in Sunnydale but she hung in there going toe to toe with hardship and peer pressures knocking at her front door" Kermit Burleson*

*Her upbringing, in a two parent home, concern for her neighbors contributed greatly to her cordial qualities and desire to take in part community organizing events and activities,*

*If she was a drug she would have been a soothing medication however she would be the first to tell you there was nothing magical about her at all.*

*"I came from deep southern roots, down south where the livelihood of the community depends on one another looking out for one another" Gloria Ann Pitre*

*She was not a bowl of Lucky Charms Breakfast Cereal and the people of Sunnydale were not the seven dwarfs and there were no Cinderella's or Tinkerbelles residing in the community.*

*"Magically delicious was Ms Henrietta, Sunnydale's real Lucky Charm" Glen Chop Porter*

*"Like that song by New Birth, she was a Wildflower growing up in Sunnydale no doubt she faced her share of the hardest things you could imagine" Eric Peters*

*"A beautiful sista' with a beautiful Heart. A wonderful Woman with a wonderful Spirit" Thomas Warren*

*"In our ghettos there are no magic wands or David Copperfield pulling rabbits out of hats tricks that can address the issues of poverty". Kerm Burleson*

*"Ain't no rubbing two sticks together going to impact the lives of poor people" Levi Bryant*

*"People in our inner city communities without the basic necessities, like food on the table cannot make people believe they are not hungry, stomachs of young children growling is an awful sound more than enough of harsh hungry realities to ignore" Gloria Ann Pitre*

*Throughout her social advocacy career, Ann hasn't attempted to sugarcoat her advocacy. How could she? She knew from her own experience she was not exempt from the harshness that comes with living in a challenged community.*

*She was among many of the young women in our communities to follow in the footsteps of Courageous Women Street Soldiers, Members of Broomstick Brigades who were not called to duty but stepped forward on their own accepting the challenges.*

*"Being involved in the community does not come without challenge and criticism. Community involvement requires extraordinary patience often taking a backseat to one's Compassion yet should never over ride one's Spirit" Gloria Ann Pitre*

*To her it was better being a part of the team than being the shot caller, the conductor, captain of the ship.*

*Those special God Given Qualities enhanced her commitment to serve others, and be of service in her community*

### TV Show Host Truth Today BETV Berkeley California

### Activist Dick Gegory, Professors David Covin and Robert Smith

*Her keen ability to listen to the concerns of the people in her community helped to bring out the Spirit in Sunnydale working with others to bring together past residents and lending a helpful hand to organize several of Sunnydale's Reunions.*

*Call it Magic if you'd like. Ann Pitre brought her very own sense of* **Magic That Made Sunnydale Our Place On The Planet**

*"The inner city challenges that exist in our communities today are no different than those of yesterday. Sunnydale back then had a sense of kinship and was led by some strong role models Women and Men, trailblazers, dedicated to the cause like our Sister Ann Pitre. Young brothers and sisters growing up today can learn from this kind of community advocacy and need to be ready when the torch is passed on to them. That's what Ms Henrietta wanted more than anything"* *Thomas Warren*

# CHAPTER 23

## AL'S DREAM COMES TRUE

*Al* was the event planner with his "let's go for it" brainstorming, and always the chief, our *HNIC* while ``Chop and I were the Tonto's…

*One day Mister Know It All* was by himself cruising on his bike down to Viz Valley park, by himself after some other dudes from the DALE left him.

Some white boys spotted him and the *"get that nigga" chase was on.*

*Many a time our curiosity took us down on Bayshore Boulevard, we hung out in front of a biker club checking out the motorcycles and when those punk white boys from Viz Valley Park came chasing us, members of the motorcycle club would check them then put us on the back of their bikes and escort us back to Sunnydale.*

*The brothers on the corner and the bikers had their brief stare down moments then checked our crazy asses for going down on Bayshore Boulevard.*

*Blazing foot speed was Al's forte, his God given solution to escaping most of the situations we got into.*

*There's no doubt he harnessed his running, jumping and athletic abilities on the schoolyard, backyards and playgrounds of The DALE.*

*That's why Al turned those skills into a pro football career, and was originally drafted by the Los Angeles Rams, played in the USFL then became an All Pro Defensive Back with the Calgary Stampeders in the Canadian Football League which was his dream come true.*

*These were the lucky numbers 18, 86, 40, 27 Al wore on the back of his jerseys should you decide to play the lottery. They worked for him.*

AL BURLESON

Calgary Stampeders

Endorsed by the
CFL PLAYERS
ASSOCIATION

*"I wanted like most Black athletes to buy my mom a house. I think I thought of that everytime I put on my uniform"* Al Burleson

*He and Valerie* are the proud parents of *four wonderful sons Al Jr, Lyndale,* and future *NFL Hall of Famer and CBS Television's Nate Burleson and NBA Rockets G League Head Coach Kevin Burleson.*

*Everything we did was based on running, jumping and athletic abilities, but being chased by some drunk white dudes jumping a fence near the S&W factory to get away ain't what I think Al had in mind.*

*"If there was one brother who lived and breathed sports it was Alvin. He had a flair for the dramatic, truly a gifted athlete"* Willie Francis

*"I don't even think Alvin knew how good he was but he was. Never bragged about his abilities but had every right to"* Skip Roberts

*"His middle name shoulda' been Track and Field"* Glen GT Taylor

*Bike exploring through Viz Valley riding outside our boundaries and community comfort zone was a recipe for a potential ass kicking. Alvin almost learned this the hard way. But it was his athletic quest to explore the sports activities outside the neighborhood that helped him perfect his skills.*

*"On the track or on the football field dude was tough as nails but if you really knew him. Alvin was as sensitive as a baby taking a bath in Mister Magic Baby Bubble Bathing Water. I mean dude would do something great like return a punt 90 yards for a touchdown then damn near cry about it almost feeling sorry for the other team. But that was AB.* Glen Chop Porter

*"By far he wasn't the fastest, he just refused to finish in second place"* Willie Francis

*"Alvin wasn't cut out for street life. I can't really remember him getting into any real trouble but all of us kids in Sunnydale have a story to tell about coming close to getting into trouble" Robert Butchie Freeman*

*"I will say this about Alvin because my mother and Mae Burleson were close. Not sure what butt whupping he got or how many, but one of them you better mind extension cord butt whupping from Ms Mae kept him outta trouble for a lifetime. Now his brother Kermit that's a different story. Funny of the two Kermit may have been the better athlete" Thomas Warren*

*"I think my little brother loved his sports so much I wouldn't be surprised if he slept in his uniform" Kermit Burleson*

*"At the time back in High School I think my future husband loved his damn sports so much he didn't even think about taking me to our Junior Prom instead Alvin went to the Fresno Relays. That's how much he payed attention to me back in High School" Valerie Burleson*

*Before High School Al played Pop Warner football with Roc, Chop and me on the Gladiators and Steelers teams at Crocker Amazon Park over the hill from Sunnydale.*

*I started playing several years before the three of them joined our team.*

*Playing Pee Wee football was no different experience from what today's modern day star athletes encounter, it's the same house nigga field nigga, light skin dark skin mentality Malcolm spoke about.*

*"It was in so many ways, playing sports being involved in constructive activities was a way for us to deal with the oppressive times the ghetto and street life that swallowed up so many of our inner city youth*

*many who never got the chance or gave themselves the opportunity to showcase their potential and talents" Randy Roc Minix*

*Not all the time did talent prevail, a number of times teammates got to play in games because they had parental participation driving players to the games providing financial support, some coming from two parent homes outside the area.*

*Warren Wilson was the brother from the neighborhood who the PAL coaches selected to recruit Black youngsters from Sunnydale.*

*Our team would travel outside of the city.*

*All of our teammates white or black stayed with the host team's families when the games were out of town.*

*We traveled by bus to cities like Fresno, Redding, and others that were far enough away for us.*

*Man this one family I stayed with had a swimming pool and beyond the pool ran the Sacramento River.*

*We caught fresh fish right from their backyard and upon arriving home, I found myself asking my mother "Why can't we live in a nice house"*

*Little did I know Momma was putting aside every hard earned penny to make HER dreams come true.*

*This time momma put it to me plainly and for the first time in my young life I knew that living in Sunnydale growing up with friends and family was more precious than gold and a number of things were beginning to make sense.*

*Especially my understanding of the "world of the haves and have nots".*

*Momma and Mae Burleson used to volunteer washing our white team uniforms with Snowy Bleach and hanging them outside on clothes lines to dry.*

*My mother would make homemade milkshakes for the coaches and team, jump on a bus and bring them to where we practiced after a hard day's work cleaning houses across town for Doctor Halde in Buena Vista Park and Doctor Sheeler in Lake Merced, a helluva commute on public transportation.*

*Oftentimes her employers would give momma a ride home and even stop at the grocery stores to let her shop for groceries before bringing her home.*

*Not once did any of those white coaches offer either Momma or Mae a ride home from the practice field, after washing, cleaning, folding our uniforms and catching a bus to drop them off.*

*I could tell this bothered Al some but not as much as me.*

*It really hurt and rubbed dirt in our faces.*

*At the end of the season there was always an awards banquet and Mae and Momma never received a simple acknowledgement while the white mothers always got all the glory.*

*Not one "wham bam thank you Maam compliment"*

*"We may have been too young to understand all of it but Jeff had more experience dealing with it having been on the team growing up and going to school in Viz Valley" Al Burleson*

*I started to withdraw, finding solace and escapism in reading and writing.*

*There was no avenue for me at that time to express my anger, a deep inner hurt that lay dormant because there was no one, and no place to vent my frustration.*

*It was the first time I started to disengage from sports.*

*Al and I were cut from the same cloth, but our experiences growing up in so many ways were miles apart.*

*Al persevered maybe because his childhood experiences were different from mine even though we came from the same neighborhood but attended different elementary schools, but nothing was going to stop him from playing pro ball.*

*Without a doubt playing pro ball was Al's Dream Comes True*

*"Through sports I have been awarded a wonderful life, a loving wife and family. One promise I made good on to both my Mother and my Wife was to get my college degree and I did with the support of my family and supportive friends" Al Burleson*

# CHAPTER 24

# THE AMAZING GLEN GT TAYLOR

## The Man Who Loved To Laugh

*E*veryday hanging out with GT, there were never ever two days the same.

The things us childhood friends shared with him, from entertaining ourselves everyday with goofy unannounced make up a game on the spot ghetto games to running down the hills and fairways of the McLaren Golf Course, playing dodgeball, or shooting hoops at Hertz Playground.

He and I entertained ourselves with toy army men or digging for make believe lost treasures or whatever our imaginations could create.

Being with Glen the things we kids did together with him was more than a fulfillment of memories that will last all of us a lifetime.

Those who chose not to hang out with him will never know what they missed.

Hanging with GT was a belly full of laughs and more than likely his laughter I'm sure substituted for many of the hardships and complex issues that young children growing up in our inner city communities are confronted with.

His friendship and laughter sometimes made it easy to forget our stomachs at times were empty but being outside with him playing in between the buildings, the schoolyards, taking wooden popsicle sticks and watching them glide down a running street stream of water or laying down outside on the concrete looking up in the blue sun shiny skies letting our imaginations run wild, being with him was always fun and enjoyable.

He was known throughout Sunnydale for running the second leg of our Park n Rec winning 440 relay team at Kezar Stadium in his legendary full length green trench coat running with an infectious smile laughing and grinning until he handed off the baton.

That green trench coat went with him wherever he went. But there was one eventful occurrence that I will never forget that took place with GT during lunchtime at Balboa High School.

I am sure his better half Mrs Taylor has never heard this crazy story before.

The outrageous unpredictable Steven C and another brother, sensitive ass Lloyd C were playing the dozens in front of a group of students, with Steven getting the best of Lloyd.

Steven talked about Lloyd's momma so bad everyone was either laughing or crying.

LC was one of those brothers who could dish it out but couldn't take it, dude was so sensitive some of us thought he had sugar in his tank.

Nevertheless if anything we all felt he had to be first cousin with Crybaby Ronald Johnson.... .a box of kleenex between the two didn't stand a chance.

Steven got on his knees and pretended to see a clan of pincher bugs crawling down the street.

He began talking to the pincher bugs capping on Lloyd's mother. *"Ms C Lloyd's gonna be late coming home from school"*

Everybody was on the ground laughing when Lloyd started to cry *"don't talk about my momma like that"* he pleaded but Steven's antics got worse.

Everyone was laughing at the brother but nothing like GT', he was doubled over unable to contain himself.

Lloyd, embarrassed, couldn't take GT's laughing anymore and turned his anger and frustration on him.

Out of nowhere Lloyd pulled out a spatula and a butter knife! Of course Steven took advantage of this and started saying *"Mrs C ya better come quick Lloyd done took your favorite spatula and butter knife to school"*

When GT saw the knife he calmly said *"you're gonna stab me with that knife"*

All of sudden without notice from inside his trench coat GT produced a large afro steel cake cutter comb and Lloyd's demeanor suddenly changed.

As this harmless merry go round of ghetto calamity continued between them, everyone still laughing, Steven C, continued his brutal pincher bug attack saying *"Mrs C ya better come quick GT getting ready to cut your son"*

One can only imagine the hilariousness of what a butter knife kitchen spatula and an afro cake cutter comb can do to bring out some insane ghetto non stop laughter.

GT was taller than many of the kids and a whole lot taller than some of the older cats in the Dale, but that made him even more special because his height gave our hanging out crew yet another dynamic that I am sure made passer bys on the busses going through the Dale or folks driving through the neighborhood take a second glance at our crew I can imagine those people pondering to themselves *"damn that's a weird looking group of kids".*

There was nothing weird about us. We were just poor kids with holes in our hand-me-down clothes, patches on our shirts and jeans to hide the wear and tear, shoes with no soles and pockets full of poverty and not a care in the world.

GT had an infectious personality that ran in their family. I wonder if Momma Taylor made her children drink a glass of Personality Plus every morning before they went outside or to school. Dude's smile was as bright and wide as his height.

That's not to say that the brother like a lot of us kids growing up in Sunnydale didn't make few left turns into one way traffic in his young life but none of were immune to temptation peer pressures or the insatiable need to show off fit in prove ourselves to who and for what, a lot of that bullshit comes with growing up in the hood.

But there was nothing complex about our brother at all.

GT was an important part of our childhood, a missing link that prevented many of us youngsters from being caught up stumbling over blocks and short changing ourselves from reaching potential productive opportunities in our lives.

## MY STORY

*Glen GT Taylor*

*I*n 1975 over 1000 miles away from Sunnydale projects, at a parry in Seattle Washington, Two young men shouted out the name, Sunnydale! Sunnydale in the house!

Back in the day, sometimes we would hear that coming from a group of men who grew up in Sunnydale Projects.

*It was one of our "Ya better recognize"* signature identifications. An expression of pride of where we were from.

This kind of ghetto recognition is common in the inner city communities.

*"Once when I was attending Magic Johnson's party on a rooftop at the Super Bowl in San Diego in 2003 and I couldn't believe I was shouting out Sunnydale in the house"*

Sedalia Taylor, moved GT and his two older sisters Sharon and Joyce to Sunnydale from the Fillmore District at the age of 7 in 1962.

Before settling in the Dale, *"I think we lived in every public housing project in San Francisco, a lot of times staying with relatives for awhile".*

The family transition did not come without a rude awakening to the neighborhood.

*"We were welcomed to the Dale by someone who broke into our house after a week being there".*

At John McLaren Elementary School in the second grade the heavy harassment continued. *"It was all in fun unless the jokes are on you"*

His classmates decided to make a circle around him, the new kid on the block teasing the brother because GT had holes in his shoes, pants and big ears.

His elementary school indoctrination was a prelude to his ghetto acceptance. *"I started to cry, fought back pushing and the next thing I knew, my black ass was looking up from the ground"*

This kind of childish rough housing in our communities is damn near extinct. School yard disagreements today end in violent actions often ending in senseless loss of young lives.

In the old days playground fights were settled with fist, not with a barrage of bullets. Back in the day the beefs were over forgotten about and young kids would become friends for life.

*"One of the kids who punched me, knocked me down, stood over me with a mouth of missing teeth, helped me up and introduced himself as Glen "Chop" Porter, who met me after school and we walked home together".*

Later that day GT received his unofficial Sunnydale Badge of Acceptance and Chop introduced him, Alvin Burleson. *"I think the brothers accepted me because after they jumped on me even though I got my ass kicked I cried but even laughed a little"*

His laughter contagious smile and upbeat personality became his signature calling card throughout all of Sunnydale.

*"That day my life in the neighborhood began my journey living in Sunnydale and something I will never forget. I also realized that in order to survive I was going to have to stand up for mine"*

## Welcome to the Neighborhood

*"My first assignment with my new found friends a week or so after meeting Al, we went down to Visitacion Valley Elementary after school with his older brother Kermit and other older kids to pick on the kids down there".*

This behavior occurred often Black kids from Sunnydale coming down to Visitacion Valley trying to enforce their will on White kids and even threatening Black students who lived in Sunnydale attended Viz Valley Elementary or Blacks children who lived outside of Sunnydale.

*"Looking back to earn my stripes this kind of foolishness didn't make any sense. I would stand sometimes in amazement because of some of the Black kids I recognized from the neighborhood. I was glad when my partners found something else more worthwhile to do. Not always positive, but I just went with the flow.*

*I quickly learned my pass outside the house depended on me telling my mom I was going to Mae's the Burleson house. My mom knew I was going to be ok. She knew Mae was a strong black woman".*

GT's development to who the Man he is today did not come without Sunnydale stumbling blocks, speed bumps and hazards in the road.

*"Getting into trouble, peer pressure was a strange badge of ghetto honor"*

## His Testimony His Transformation

*"Between the ages the 12 to 16 I stayed in some type of trouble, mostly fighting or cursing someone out.*

*My mom cussed a lot and that is where I got it but also when I look back on things, I had a lot of anger in me.*

*She tried to get me into the Big Brother program but it was a long process and I never got in.*

*I got paddle so many times in elementary school and junior high school and even my first year of high school that it didn't even phase me.*

*I got kicked out of Luther Burbank and Denman Junior High School. On June Friday the 13th 1969,*

*I was fourteen, Man! I have to go to court for truancy, skipping school, assault and battery, fighting and burglary. We broke into the park thinking that the lady working left money in a file cabinet. I saw her put it in there, but came to find out she set us up.*

*So on that Friday the 13th, I was sent to a boys school,*

*Hidden Valley Ranch until I got out, February Friday 13th 1970.*

*Bruh, it took a long time before I went outside for many years on Friday the 13th. It was one of the best things that ever happened to me going to Hidden Valley because I had to go to school six days a week so when I got out, I was so caught up on my school work that I was in high school.*

*I do remember the first week at Balboa High, I got into a fight and the principal pulled my record and found out I just got out of the boys school and I made the statement that I wish I was there and he told my mom that. I know that must have hurt her because of all the things I had to go through while I was there and not having a car, trying to find ways to visit me.*

*Once I got into sports at Balboa things changed for me, plus my oldest sister Sharon told me that she would give me anything I wanted until I turned 18, if I would get good grades and stay out of trouble".*

## From Sunnydale to Seattle

*"After living in Seattle for over forty years, I graduated from University of Washington and raised a family: my two daughters and son and my grandkids.*

*My wife (who I meet through Al sister Lisa while she was going to San Jose State, I am now retired and living in Arizona. House on a lake and pool. Yes, that kid from Sunnydale.*

*I thank God, my mom who never gave up on me and my cousin Al and his girlfriend Val and my right arm of support, my better than better half, my loving Wife, for letting me follow them to Seattle to get out of the projects.*

*At one time my dream was getting a job for $10 an hour, getting a car and living in Sunnydale all my life where I felt so loved and safe not believing there was anything better. Life is good now.*

*Respectfully Glenn GT Taylor*

*An Amazing Friend Who Loved To Laugh*

# CHAPTER 25

## SOME UNFORGETTABLE MOMENTS WITH SOME UNBELIEVABLE CHARACTERS
### Their Claim to Ghetto Fame

*Steven C,* lived up to his last name Caracter, getting in trouble was his game. *For no reason* he broke out the windows in John McLaren Swimming Pool Luckily the pool was closed.

*Patsy,* how could a girl so fine beat the *living hell outta me* in front of everyone in the hood? The good thing is I still got the *you know what* in the bushes. An ass whuppin' worth taking'

*The ToeTickler,* no one really *knew who he was,* maybe a few, but this dude tormented the community by climbing through bedroom windows and tickling women's feet. Rumors have it, it could have been_____?

*Siro,* on roller skates, in broad daylight, jumped in the front seat of the *Gallo Wine truck,* drove the truck to Hertz Playground getting everybody in the Dale wasted on Gallo wine. For days the Gallo Company never even came and got the damn truck

*Judy O,* girlfriend was tough as nails, whatn' no joke, one fine *PYT'* rub her the wrong way and pay the price

*George L, "Lyons"* what an appropriate last name for a *fabricating,* put too much on it don't believe a word he says storytelling' brotha

*Willie B,* faked like he attended State College walkn' around campus with an *encyclopedia*, and could barely *read and write* wearn' eyeglasses with no lenses looking like the scholarly type.

*Will M,* big time Will one of the first brotha's to date outside his race, got chased home many a time for chasing' the wrong skirts

*C Dunston,* by far the strongest brother in the Dale, dude could damn near lift a motor out of a car by his damn self

*Rin Tin, JoJo, Kennedy and Nixon*, damn ghetto dogs make the list

*David S "Simba"* fastest man to ever lace up a pair of track cleats, ran the 100 yard dash at All City *barefoot and won*

*Bernis O and Thomas W,* Sunnydale's version of Ralph and Norton of the Honeymooners Jackie Gleason Show

*Black Harold,* laugh in ya' face, give ya' a high five, then throw a rock upside ya' head and take off runn'

*Reggie,* this sister had a face, to go with an afro the Jackson Five could have put on the front and back of their album cover

*Sherman P,* coolest cat in the neighborhood, with a rap all his own a legend in his own mind

***Roy B***, dude was outhere. He had his car with no tires sitting on milk crates asking people for a jump

***M Fleming***, no one knew where this brother was getting those leather coats from but he sure as hell didn't pay for them

***B Barringer,*** fool ran away from home with a forged note from his mother, just in case he got lost

***M White,*** in front of everyone at Kezar Stadium he won the 880 in record breaking time but was disqualified because his little pecker came out during the race

***Berle G,*** mista' sweet tooth, must have had some stock in the sugar cookies and candy he brought at the Penny Store or at John McLaren School, how could a brotha with flat feet run so fast, jump so high? Had to be the suga'

***Willie and Don N,*** Mr Willie' the barber's sons, his heart and soul, rock steady all of the time young brotha's

***Willie F,*** start off in dead last, when his head went back this 440 yard running brother crossed the finish line first

***Pete and Melvin P,*** Sunnydale do it all soul brothers, primetime dudes give you the shirt off their backs but not one of their baseball gloves

***Booker,*** SF's Cable Car Conductor, a sho nuff Sunnydale' loyal 49er faithful took brotha's to Candlestick in his RV just to have a damn good time

***Baby Ray,*** coulda' shoulda' made it to the big leagues could play some shortstop, worshiped the game of baseball

*John Jr. "Daddy O" taught* us youngsta's a thing or two about' drinkn' downhome in the bottle moonshine

*Maryann G,* we called her *Two Lips* always had some coins to contribute on the drink, unfortunately once you passed her the bottle you could forget about getting another sip

*Danny B*, he may have been blind but his handicap never stopped him from hangn with' the fellas running the streets and causn' havoc

*Darrell C*, would make Perry Mason proud, never lost a ghetto argument

*Lawrence C,* brotha was allergic to the barber shop, *his natural had a natural his afro had an afro...*

*Vernon C,* we never knew the boy had that much *suga'* n his tank

*Ronnie C,* teenage pimp brought a lime green convertible Coupe Deville without a driver's license with cash money stashed in a brown paper Safeway shopping bag

*Randy C,* Sunnydale's leading man, the epitome of a ladies man this dude had more' women than fingers

*D Martinez* aka *"Danny Boy"* this *left handed legend of the game'* could dribble hit the jumper way before they had a three point shot and played hoop til' the sun went down

*Glen Q,* pound per pound may have been one of the Dale's greatest athletes, sold five dolla' weed match boxes on the side

*James "Bug" N,* Sunnydale's *Satchel Paige* starting pitcher for the Sunnydale Jets Baseball team

*"Buchie"* placed in the backseat of a squad car *suspected of* tryn' to have sex with a sheep at the Grand National Rodeo denys it to this day the part about the sheep

*James R,* celebrated his birthday hustling drinks for three months, kept on saying "it's my birthday" "it's my birthday" for three months"

*Jesse R,* never buy a television or anything else from this cat

*Levi B,* knew mo' bout Cowboy flicks than John Wayne, dreamed of being the next Fetus on Gunsmoke, he was the Rifleman without the rifle

*Robert T,* good banana pudding making mother f....charge ya' for it to

*Danny "Danko" D,* couldn't go wrong hangn' wit' him he always had ya' back, he will be missed by his faithful pit bull Capone

*Sam and Earl P,* Sam would show' you love by punchn' the hell out of you. Earl was at least two french fries short of a Happy Meal

*Steve and Emory F,* Emory fell in love with a girl from Lakeview. Steve fell in love with watching Herman the Monster, looked just like him

*Leotis "Toastie"* talked mo' shit than anybody

*Steve "Skip" R,* had more' energy than a *Five Hour Energy Drink*

*"Chop"* the King of the *Dozens* game talk so bad about ya' momma you wouldn't wanna go home and *iftn'* you was dumb enough for a nickel you paid him to watch color TV on a black and white TV set with one of those fake color TV screens

**Sonny P,** a downtown plaid shirt, shoe shining' loudmouth no sense making talkn' straight to the bone goofball, a ghetto clown without the circus

**Kermit B,** even at a very young age trouble ran away from this dude, one day for no reason at all from his bathroom window for fun he shot pellets at unsuspecting people with his BB gun, dude had an insatiable desire for being in the right place at the wrong time

**Lisa B,** *sista'* missed her true calling' woulda' been an ideal FBI candidate, telephone, telegraph and tell it all Lisa B

**Uncle Ike,** Sunnydale's *favorite uncle*, his smile was contagious, country strong

**Al B,** the original jump off a two story building for the hell of it, Sunnydale's Evil Knevil' jump off the roof' daredevil, bet him he couldn't do it and...yo' money was as good as gone...

**Paul J,** Sunnydale's adopted Lakeview son crazier than a road lizard

**Michael and Woodrow T,** one day these crazy fun loving cousins showed up in the Dale and we couldn't get rid of them. Rumors have it that Woodrow wore a dead man's shoes to the dead man's funeral

**Cindy and Jimmy N,** top of the hill finest how could **TWO** sista's be so fine? **RIP Brother' Roy**

**Ronald B,** the **neighborhood bully**, all the hoods have one and this cat was no exception, nice guy probably when he was sleep, in elementary school the brother looked like he was in High School

**Zelda W,** her beauty was skin deep, one fine drink of water

**Sherri D,** was every inch of 6' 9''feet tall, fine from head to toe

*Zeke B,* one of the *oldest looking teenagers* you ever laid eyes on. Dude had to show his school ID just to get into school. His sister' was drop dead gorgeous

*Michael Kathy and Billy S,* the entire family was good look'n. Today *Michael* is a criminal justice system advocate

*Robbie B,* this cat seemed to get off start'n s…..t This cat was straight out always f….k in' with somebody always *starting something for noth'n*

*Ronnie M, "McKnight '' the heart of a lion, the soul of a lamb,* the mystery man, you never knew what he was up to but believe me the brotha' was up to something. Believe me…up to something

*Glen T,* ran on Sunnydale's 440 winning relay team in a full length double breasted lime green trench coat that he never took off. I think he may still have that trench coat

*Jimmy and Dwight H,* don't know where these brotha's bought their flashy clothes probably Howard's on Market Street but they was always sharp

*Ted "Nukky"* always good for a nip, kept his bottle in his back pocket, inside coat pocket, his socks always good for a nip

*Pam S,* Harold's sista' too fine for her own good

*Harold S,* Pam's *off the hook brotha'* the elevator didn't always go to the top, in fact a lot of times his elevator was out of service

*Darnell H,* had the coolest' walk in the neighborhood when he wasn't *runnin' from the po' po's*

*Peanuts,* instigator extraordinaire good brother, weird dude

***Noel S,*** dude lived in the Eichler Homes next door to the ***Crazy Man in the Green Cadillac,*** going to his house was a no no…so he came to Sunnydale so much we all thought he lived in the projects

***Eric P,*** dude looked so young and handsome, the brother is going to have hell proving he's old enough for SSI

***Blain P,*** must of learned a lot being around Mom and Pops maybe that's why he opened up his own bakery on Geneva Avenue

***Hayakafa,*** how could a 14 year old brotha', drink a half gallon of Carlo Rossie, Gallo, Annie Green Springs, or Rot Gut by his damn self

***Douglas L,*** book smart, white sock wearn' never bet on this brotha in a race, the slowest brotha' to ever try out for the track team, smarter than a schoolbook slower than a snail

***Big Gary S,*** good two for one sandwich eating brother, put the fat Man on the map

***Jesse R,*** worked for the city in the daytime, was a second story crook after dark

***Nuell N,*** pimping was his game, straight up player, the stuff people write about

***Joe Pete,*** a sho nuff certified playa' might not have invented the game but certainly lived the life, he was true to the game

***Mac Duff, TB,*** had the stuff legends were made out of or so he thought

***Crybaby Ronald J,*** has a mugshot with tears in his eyes, cry for' nothn'

**'Roc** '' *my partna' but I could never figure out why he was always at my house eating sandwiches.* "*Yo' mom bruh makes the best sandwiches I ever tasted*" *knocked* R Moody from Fillmore out cold in the third floor bathroom at Balboa High School for talking' shit about Sunnydale with one punch, he hit em' so hard the boy went through the bathroom stall doors and landed upright sitting on the toilet seat.

DARRO JEFFERSON

# BROTHERS OF THE ORIGINAL DALE

## Kent Lloyd & Royce Lloyd

**Not The Swampe' D**
**Jessie Ruiz Kerm Burleson Preston Baker**

**Roc, Walter Harris, Chop, Royce**

**Al Burleson and Randy Roc Minix**

**Eric Peters, Steven Caracter & Douglas Latham**

**Sunnydale's Very Own Smokey Robinson**

**Vernon Deverney**

**Darnell & Anthony Hughes, Gregory Griffin, Legrand Varner, Pete Pitre**

**The Unforgettable**
**Bobby Ferguson, Victor Collins James "Bug" Nelson**
**Joseph "Baby Ray" Pitre**

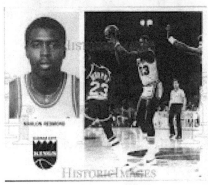

**High School Legend, USF Dons and NBA Star**
**Marlon Redmond**

**Ronald Butler, Blaine Peters, Clifford "Meat" Murray & Dvaughn Frierson**

**Berle Grant**  **Sunnydale's Leading Man Randy Cambell**  **Roy Batte**  **Zeke Brown**

**Robert "Butchie Freeman**  **Andre Bell**  **Ricky Graham**  **Sunnydale's Uncle Ike**

**The Legacy of David "Simba" Sterling Lives On**
**David Sterling III and Proud Grandmother Patricia Willis**

# CHAPTER 26

# LOOKING BACK WHEN WE WAS LITTLE NAPPY HEADED BOYS

## With

## Leon Booker and Melvin Pitre

Sunnydale's Real OG'S

Melvin Pitre and Leon Booker are true products of the Sunnydale community.

They are two silver headed hair great grandfathers with wrinkles of wisdom etched across their foreheads and proud contributors of A Song for Ms Henrietta

Their reflections provide a unique perspective of wisdom and insightfulness.

*"Silver hair is a crown of splendor and glory, gray hairs of experience" PROVERBS 20:29*

*"Growing in up in Sunnydale we were so young we didn't know no better than just to go outside and play, just some little nappy headed boys who knew how to play' that's what we did day and night until we had to go inside" Melvin Pitre*

*"Like that old saying, we didn't know shit from shinola but what we did know was how to go outside and have fun" Leon Booker*

*"All we had to do before going outside to play was do our chores and make sure we washed our face and hands" Melvin Pitre*

The brotherhood between Leon Booker and Melvin Pitre started in their early childhood and teenage years in Sunnydale and continues to this day.

The two and Melvin's other brothers Pete and John everyday were in and out of the Pitre household at the parking lot on the 1500 hundred block of Sunnydale Avenue.

*"I always thought why did I have to comb my hair, wash my face and do all those things, to get ready to go outside and play, because when I came home from playing I was so dirty my parents wouldn't let me in the house" Melvin Pitre*

The two men were well respected in the neighborhood and their contributions to this composition has significant meaning and further describes their living and upbringings in the early days of Sunnydale.

*"Our basic motivation was to play and play hard we was having so much fun we wasn't interested in or had time for getting into trouble" Leon Booker*

They were part of a generation of older brothers who withstood many of the challenges and temptations that many of their peers fell victim to.

In Sunnydale their youthful transitions to adulthood did not come without sacrifices to overcome predatory influences that rocked the neighborhood.

It's important that we acknowledge these two men because they paved the way for those brothers who followed in their footsteps and not those behind them who chose to walk in the shoes down unforgiving paths of individuals in Sunnydale who got caught up in the madness or opted for the calling of the wild streetlife.

With great pride the writers and contributors of our story are proud to journey back through time when these two iconic brothers Leon and Melvin who recall the days gone by in their precious community.

*"I remember the Harris family when they lived on Sunnydale Avenue, before they moved to Blythedale Street. Napoleon and I were real good friends growing up and I remember their father, Ms Henrietta's husband. The Harris family were a two parented family, something a lot of people didn't know that's how far back my days growing up in Sunnydale go" Melvin Pitre*

*"Recently I had been thinking about Sunnydale. Man when I drove through there a few weeks ago it was a different place from when we grew up there, I wondered if anybody from back in the day still lived there" Leon Booker*

*"All we have is the memories now. I like the changes, new buildings going up but I am concerned if the people there now will embrace the neighborhood and care about each other like we did when we grew up in Sunnydale" Melvin Pitre*

Melvin and Leon are well into their 70's and have remained lifelong friends.

Each of them have a unique story of growing up in the neighborhood.

Melvin came to Sunnydale at three years of age while Leon lived with his family in a home on Esquina Drive near the Geneva Drive In but was a regular fixture in the community.

Both were from two parent homes and beneficiaries of strong family structure upbringings.

They are proud to share their experiences of what Sunnydale was for them *"When They Were Little Nappy Headed Boys"*

*"I use to jump the fence on Velasco Street to hang out with the brothers from Sunnydale" Leon Booker*

*"When we moved to Sunnydale there weren't many Black families there but that didn't make any difference to any of us kids Black, White Hispanic it didn't make a damn bit of difference" Melvin Pitre*

In Sunnydale these youthful experiences were building blocks for lifetime friendships that endure them through the good and bad times and served as a kinship for their development into adulthood.

The relationship between Leon and Melvin was etched in the neighborhood landscape, they both went on to storied distinguished careers with the City and County of San Francisco.

Melvin retired after 28 years with the SFFD and Leon was a part of the city's historical Cable Cars crew working as a Conductor before his retirement.

*"People need to understand that Sunnydale for most of San Francisco was a place on the outskirts of town. To them we were outcast and the negative things they heard about our community they felt was suppose to happen and when and if it did for the most part few outside our neighborhood could care less or give a damn" Leon Booker*

*"There was a lot of pride in the people from Sunnydale. Our pride love, respect and care for one another kept us together as a community"* Melvin Pitre

*"We were the underdogs but as kids we were having so much fun nothing else really mattered"* Leon Booker

*"Our playmates no matter what color were from families and parents just like ours who faced the day to day challenges of putting food on the table clothes on our backs, there wasn't any time for the community back then to be worried about what your next door neighbor looked like"* Melvin Booker

Outside influences in our inner city communities are always lurking. Studies have indicated that without strong parental guidance, community leadership and economic opportunities, the likelihood of community togetherness and survival are nil.

Both Melvin and Leon experienced first hand how the aforementioned challenges can have a devastating impact on the community.

*"Of course there were families without a father in the household and a number of my friends had to fend for themselves. Brothers because of circumstance, no fault of their own, were growing up much too fast. The Black men in Sunnydale who tried to pitch in couldn't be everywhere at the same time and a lot of older sibling were not ready, or equipped to step up to the plate, so sadly a lot of my friends turned their attention to the streets"* Melvin Pitre

*"Melvin and I were the lucky ones we had structure in our homes and when we strayed a little bit south, today I am sure we both have the extension cord butt whupping scars to remind us of those days when a hard head made a soft ass"* Leon Booker

Those comments offer significant credence when our conversations steered towards the role of the Black Father and Black Men in our communities.

*"Of course times are different now. Back in the day I couldn't imagine a Black Man walking around with his pants sagging and his butt showing. What kind of fatherly example is that? Melvin Pitre*

*"Black Men in Sunnydale walked the walk and talked the talk. When they went out of the house they were well dressed even if they was just going to the Little Village Market" Leon Booker*

*"Man Mr Porter was always clean, crispy clean white shirts, pressed slacks and those shiny Stacy Adams shoes" Melvin Pitre*

*"My dad taught us how to play baseball, work on cars and kept a watchful eye out on the fellas that were on the verge of getting into trouble. He really cared deeply about the brothers in our community while raising his own family. Believe me, raising my brothers and me was a full time job. Sometimes my brothers and me wondered where he got the extra energy to lend a helping hand" Melvin Pitre*

As mentioned, the responsibility, task and challenges of a Black Man raising his own family while being committed to fostering other families is an enormous undertaking and along the way there were many disappointments these Black Men had to endure while keeping a positive outlook on life.

*"The sad thing is that there weren't enough Black Men in Sunnydale to be there for all of the young brothers. A lot of our brothers needed round the clock support, there just wasn't enough, just wasn't enough" Leon Booker*

*"The way the men when we grew up carried themselves, head up high, walking with pride and dignity we looked up to them. How come*

*and why should our young brothers today look up to a brother with his butt showing his pants sagging" Melvin Pitre*

*"I was Student Body President at Luther Burbank, had the grades to go to Lowell High School. I know for a fact that the influence Black Men had on me growing up gave me the courage to give back to the brothers in the community" Leon Booker*

*"For me helping others seemed like the right and only thing to do. That's how my brothers and I came up. That's what my mother preached and what my father did in the community helping others learn to help themselves" Melvin Pitre*

*"In the 60's Huey Newton came to Sunnydale trying to get brothers to join the Black Panther Party then the brothers from the Nation of Islam started coming to the Dale these were powerful prideful Black Men" Leon Booker*

*"George Davis was an unsung hero in the community without him we would have lost a lot of brothers to drugs and the streetlife" Melvin Pitre*

*"With great pleasure am I to share some of my feelings about growing up in Sunnydale. This is a proud moment for me. Leon Booker*

*"Our story may not mean much to others but if only they knew what is was like growing up in a neighborhood like ours, a neighborhood full of people who cared about one another" Melvin Pitre*

# CHAPTER 27

## A SIT DOWN CONVERSATION WITH

### LaFrance Graves

### Son of Sunnydale

*LaFrance Graves, was born in San Francisco and moved to The Dale in the early 50's.*

*He served as a community events consultant for the **Sons of Sunnydale and contributed greatly to the success and mission of the Sons of Sunnydale organization.***

*He was unsung among his peers.*

*When he talks it's sometimes hard to follow one of his stories from the other but he does make a point about growing up in Sunnydale he learned quickly to separate **"benefit from bullshit".***

*I caught up with him at his glorious two-level multi bedroom home a stone's throw away from picturistic Pacifica CA on a dreary November day in 2021.*

*He proudly reminded me this was not his first house, in fact he boldly emphasizes how he purchased his first house at **"twenty two".***

***"I got out of Sunnydale and bought my first house when I was twenty two" ain't been back since'***

*More than 20 years have passed since he has been to the ole' neighborhood.*

***"Ain't forgot where I came from but most of the cats I grew up with' well let's just say a lot of them ain't here anymore"***

*It was here at this part of our journey conversation about back in the day, I could sense and share in his pain, **"the trip down memory lane ain't always worth the journey"** he started sitting back in his lounge chair trying to conceal emotions that I was unearthing.*

*I had known him from my early childhood and his friendship with my older brother Coyle and Theresa my sister...Lafrance's jaw, I was told was introduced to a barrage of Coyle's right jabs that set the tone for their life long friendship,*

*At ten Coyle and LaFrance bumped heads in the John McLaren schoolyard and have remained friends every since their duke out*

*Graves was a frequent visitor to our house and often had to withstand the glaring **"grit her teeth stare down"** of my mother because of his association with Coyle, his partna' who made a few wrong turns, crossing against the red light in his younger days.*

*Another of Graves' childhood buddies was **Robert Taylor, the two have been knowing one another since kindergarten. The other, Levi Bryant, would arrive in Sunnydale from Kansas City in the Mid 60's.***

***We mention** this because Robert, Levi and Coyle formed a close knit association with Graves that produced contrasting outcomes... however in adulthood the three have achieved personal success and joyful friendships.*

*What makes a story of boys fighting so amazing is that **boyhood fights back in the day were thrown in the Sea Of Forgetfulness before the end of the day.***

***Now the vicious and violent choices young men today choose to settle their disagreements, with drive-by shootings, gang violence, stabbing's, ultimately ending with Life Without The Possibility of Parole, Family Devastation, long-term incarceration.***

***All a most significant waste of human life and for what? Over Noth'n!***

*My mom thought LaFrance was a drug dealer because of his cordial mannerisms and Coyle's prophecy for running with the wrong crowd and constantly getting into trouble but she, like so many other parents, found his politeness and respect to be part of his character. Lucky for him Mom was known for speaking her mind.*

**Growing up in Sunnydale** *represented few opportunities good or bad with the latter holding **Sunnydale's Trump Card.***

*Sitting down with him it was important to switch gears, become an explorer and delve into his character, familyship and his fortitude to courageously overcome insurmountable odds.*

*Graves and his brothers were raised by Ms Bertha, a single black woman.*

*Early on because of family responsibilities his quest to overcome the pitfalls of Sunnydale's harsh ghetto life was quite apparent if not a miracle in itself.*

*He and so many other brotha's and sista's in low income inner city communities across this country have truly been the exceptions to the rule.*

*However for every success there are those unfortunates who paid the price with their lives making his story serve as inspiration and worth sharing.*

*We idolize the star athletes but for everyone who has made it out of our inner city ghettos there are dozens who have been left behind.*

*Imagine the G.O.A.T. Michael Jordan not being good enough to make his highschool team. Star players themselves will regretfully tell stories of neighborhood buddies that were three times hands down better than them.*

*His contribution to **A Song for Ms Henrietta is most necessary and significant.***

*Graves, grew up in the time when so many of the brotha's his age took a wrong turn in their lives, succumbing to the fastlife, chasing falsehoods and farfetched dreams or destroying their lives using drugs and committing heinous crimes that landed them in and out of the criminal justice system.*

*He witnessed early in his young life what the devastation of drugs and violence was doing to his community.*

*At a very young age he made a solemn vow that he would not be one of its victims, a difficult challenge with adversity and despair staring him right in the face and the absence of a strong male father figure, and three younger brothers depending on his leadership made the odds of his day-to-day survival even more challenging.*

*Knowing this I cut right to the chase and asked him why and what made him travel down the road of righteousness avoiding the paths of self inflicted destruction.*

**"Man I got in trouble one time, went to juvy' and that was it. I think I was twelve, thirteen doesn't matter, once was enough. I knew life on the streets wasn't for me so I spent my time running track, playing sports, getting into things that would keep me outta' trouble".**

**"Guys around me were getting into trouble doing things that didn't appeal to me including your brotha' and most of my friends. I could see that kind of lifestyle wasn't for me".**

*Everyday 24/7 temptation and peer pressure sat outside his front door near the top of Sunnydale Avenue presenting unreputable opportunities, with baggage of no value and non-refundable/return policies on his life.*

**"Man I got out before I had time to get in"**

*At 73,* **"Graves' 'as** *my brother calls him, reminds me of Wylie E. Coyote cartoon character's cunning, hungry* **and unsatisfying need to be the center of attention.**

*He is outspoken, cantankerous, confrontational, highly opinionated, the* **Life of his very own Party.** *Loving every minute of engaging folks in discussions of political, social, economic and racial issues.*

**"If ya' wanna hear about the Red "n" Blue States" let yo' ears beware...**

*It's funny how he playfully ignites conversations when the topic is ten thousands miles from what is being talked about.*

*A master of deception* **"changing the pace"** *as he always says, Quite the cartoonish character he is in his own right...a legend in his own mind.* **"The Bomb"** *he calls himself.*

*After graduating from Balboa High School he served in the Navy was stationed in the Philippines and* **today is married to a wonderful Filipino woman,** *spending his time conversation, kicking back sipping on his favorite* **Cabernet Sauvignon, glued to Court TV, forever listn' to one of those 1 800 music programs while always opening his home hosting impromptu gathering with brotha's from the Dale who drop by unannounced.**

*He proudly reminds me that he was a successful business entrepreneur, owning a Limousine service that catered to the upscale Pacific Heights community and those affluent white folks...*

**"I hired brotha's from the Dale but some of them couldn't handle the responsibility or intermingle with our clientele, they were outta' their Sunnydale comfort zone".**

**You can take a brotha outta of the Dale but you can't take"** *end of story...*

*When I steered our conversation to **A Song for Ms Henrietta** I was shocked to learn that his opinion of **Ms Henrietta** and the **Harris Household**, was far different than I could have ever imagined and significantly different than others who will share their recollections and accounts of her in **A Song for Ms Henrietta** but everyone is entitled to their opinions and their contributions are respected.*

**Graves** *recalled* **Ms Henrietta being** *strict, always hollering at* **Danny Ray** *that's not uncommon among single* **Black Women Households** *responsible for the wellbeing of raising a family in a* **Fatherless home.**

*What's always talked about are the dynamics of **Single Parented Homes, young folks growing up too fast,** but what is never shared are the intricate behind closed doors feelings these **Black Women** in **Fatherless homes masked on a daily basis.***

*A number of Sunnydale's working mothers rode the 15 Kearney or 30 Freeway Express busses **together** sometimes 7 days a week, leaving children to fend for themselves, and look out for one another and ...**this responsibility was put in the hands of the oldest sibling,,,many who were not much older than the others...***

*Our house was no different. That responsibility fell on my sister Theresa's shoulders...**Coyle** was a handful...and **Danny Ray** even more so...*

***If Ms Henrietta was strict, hard on her boys, there is no doubt in my mind she had to be, doing what needed to be done to keep her hardheads in line...***

*I would watch Momma put extra handkerchiefs in her tote bag, having no idea she would be handing them out to a busload full of sobbing Sunnydale mothers.*

*These women all experienced the same hardships and day-to-day struggles of trying to raise a family, make ends meet and carry themselves with pride and dignity.*

**Graves' assessment** *is probably true but only another woman can experience the pains and frustration of raising children alone.*

**Ms Henrietta and Sunnydale Mothers,** *looked out for younger women but the majority of them every morning faced with the responsibility to put food on the table boarded the Teardrop Express.*

*Continuing the conversation with* **Graves**, *I realized that he did have a positive impact on a number of the brotha's...good for him, he convinced* **Taylor** *to join the military or succumb to a ghetto-ish lifestyle of criminal intent. His recollection is more than likely a stretch of his imagination.*

**RT opted out big time, went on to travel the world as a Merchant Seamen** *and we cannot give* **Graves total** *credit for* **Taylor's** *transformation.* **RT** *found something deep within himself, courage to change his life.*

## COYLE'S TAKE ON LAFRANCE

*Coyle and Lafrance with the **Posner Hair Straighter***

*I got a chance to read the Graves story….Man Graves left out all the juicy details and some of the funniest ones…I will have to pull your coat one day…lil' brother, just for starters ask LG about the time he and I and Danny Ray were at 1523 and we were trying to conk our hair (Posner Hair Straighter) Yep, you guessed it we wanted that Mighty Temptation's look.*

*That was when the Daniel's Drug Store was open…Man where it usually took the average Brotha about a half a jar or maybe three-quarters we had to piece our change together and buy three jars for LG, his hair was bad, bad, call it mailman hair cause every strand had its on route.*

*Well this Posners is really a jar of lye and the whole objective is to leave it in as long as you can stand it cause the shit burned but if you didn't leave it in long enough it would not take…well, LG kept saying take it out take it out of course me and Danka Ray was crackin' up…so I knew that momma would be coming home soon and this was not a sight she would want to walk into especially after a long day on her feet...bottom line I had to get Graves outta the crib fast and in a hurry.*

*We washed the goop out of LG's head and gave him a head rag and told him we would try it another time.*

*The lye from the straighteners will leave big sores on your scalp and they get crusty...you can't hide them bro they have to go away on their on...LG went home and his Momma Bertha look at his head and thought her son had been ran over down on Hahn Street she asked him what happened and of course LG spilled the beans and momma ask me what happened and of course I pleaded the 5th and shaded it over to Danny Ray....Yeah! BTW...LG had to wear a stocking cap to school for about two weeks,,,still makes me smile when I think about that shit...Lol, Lol Coyle Jefferson*

# CHAPTER 28

# TWO OF A KIND

## Levi and LaFrance

## The Dale's Very Own Fred and Grady

*A Sho' Nuff' Real 211 Gravity Beer Drink' Cabernet Sauvignon Wine sippn' no holds barred conversation about' absolutely nothing'.*

*As LaFrance and I were about to conclude our conversation coming down the quiet neighborhood street unannounced but making his baritone voice heard from down the block was no other than **Levi B,** Lord have Mercy on my ears and tape recorder it was going to get loud up-n-here.*

*The Battle of the Mouth's was about to take place. **A sho' nuff' real 211 Gravity Beer Drink' Cabernet Sauvignon Wine sippn'** philosophical opinionated, no holds barred conversation based on absolutely nothing'.*

***Levi** landed in San Francisco's Fillmore District in 1966 attending Poly High School, majoring in s...t talkn' 101, he moved to Sunnydale in 1967 after moving to the city from Kansas City to stay with his mother in the Fillmore district.*

***LB**, told me in order to get across town from Sunnydale to Poly High School everyday he stole a car to get to school.*

*This immediately solidified his acceptance in the community and obviously there was plenty of street in him before he got to San Francisco.*

*He lived near the Sunnydale Rec Center and immediately became one of the neighborhood's legendary figures.*

***Levi, I remembered** babysitting me. In fact it was **Bryant** who introduced all of Sunnydale to watch' westerns' on TV every Saturday morning.*

*Never couldn't figure out why he always came knocking at the back door.*

*I think it was a better place for stashing his short necks, half pints behind the garbage can, so momma wouldn't know he was drinking but he and Victor were tight...*

*He loved music, sang a mean second tenor and some baritone and even had his own band the Rivieras.*

*For years he was coaxed into volunteering during the holidays as Santa Claus in spite of weighing less than **200 pounds soaking wet**.*

*Man! Those kids must have wished Santa had some breath mints cause my brotha' was lit' up like a light.*

*Nevertheless the kids in the neighborhood got to see Santa. A lil' tipsy, feeln' no pain but to them he was still Santa.*

*Listening to **Bryant and Graves' pure** nonsense was more entertaining than watching **Fred and Grady on Sanford and Son.***

*They engaged in conversation without merit but loved going at each other.*

*Their long time friendship and brotherhood was quite apparent. The more oil the more lively and outrageous the conversation.*

*In their presence with the alcohol flowing non stop Sunnydale was alive and kicking.*

*It became time for me just to turn off my device, kick back and enjoy another one of my favorite episodes of **Levi and LaFrance** trying my best to conceal my laughter and careful not to critically examine their state of mind and hilariousness.*

*A Battle Royal of complete genuine B.....S! Between the **"211 King and the Sauvignon Kid".***

*They were like two big ass kids sharing an all day tootsie roll pop only to argue who was going to get the last lick.*

*Levi* is a remarkable individual and his contributions to the brotherhood and the neighborhood are well respected.

Inside each of us there are **God Given Qualities and the Desire For a Betta' Life...**

*Graves and Bryant* are the lucky ones but I find each of them today **not so self righteous and prideful** to have **forgotten the days gone by**....

*Today they are unlike so many other brotha's and sista's throughout our communities, some so **ashamed to look back at their past, with their snobby noses pressed to the sky looking down on our brotha's and sista's struggling to get out...***

*"We are all at times looked upon the same, therefore we Blacks must realize we're all cut from the same cloth...there are have nots and unfortunates in all of our families...But we cannot CHANGE OUR' STYLE NOW THAT WE'VE REACHED DA' TOP...*

# CHAPTER 29

# 1864 SUNNYDALE AVENUE

## The Peters Family

## With Eric Peters

**The Ever Present Eric Peters**

*"Three of my younger brothers and sister were born and raised in Sunnydale" Eric Peters*

1864 Sunnydale Avenue is located at the top of Sunnydale Avenue, in the parking lot two buildings down from John McLaren Elementary School near the entrance of the McLaren Golf Course.

Today the parking lot has little resemblance to the lot that Mr Peters and Mr Bruce, the community's custodian swept daily and kept clean of trash and papers that blew down the hill from the school

Residents living there now in either of the two parking lots on both sides of the street in the 1800 block double park their cars on the sidewalks without fear of their vehicles being ticketed or towed away.

*"Back in the day people didn't have to lock their doors and when kids played outside at night parents came outside to keep and eye on them" E Peters*

The area is a deteriorating scene of neglect. The parking lots resemble a pick your part auto junk yard, with abandoned cars and vehicles sitting on milk crates, a far cry from what people and golfers saw driving up and down scenic Sunnydale Avenue.

*"I remember when the city had those blue and white Scenic Drive signs posted on both sides of the street. People would actually drive up and down the block get out of their cars and take pictures" Eric Peters*

Eric's recollection is so true because with the John McLaren Park hillside, its lush forest green hills, pine trees in the backdrop is today one of the most beautiful sights in San Francisco.

*"John McLaren Park, Crocker Amazon, the golf course were a part of our daily ventures. We built tree forts, played hide and seek and played on the hill everyday". E Peters*

Proud are we to introduce The Peters Family from 1854 Sunnydale Avenue with Eric Peters inside the **Peters Family** household and of some of the **People in the Projects.**

Mr Peters was a veteran of the Korean War when the family moved to Sunnydale in 1953. Eric came to Sunnydale in September of 1954, his older sister Eddrena was about 2 or 3 years old at the time the family settled down in the neighborhood.

Younger brother Blaine was born in 1956, followed by sister Balita in 1960 and the youngest member of the family Zonel in 1964 all three siblings were born in Sunnydale.

Today he is married and lives in Novato California and has 28 years of sobriety.

*"Growing up the families in Sunnydale were more than neighbors we were more like family, it was the Sunnydale way"* E Peters

Unlike the veterans of recent years, Korean War veterans and those soldiers who fought in previous wars, soldiers returned home from the wars, when little was known about PTSD many suffered from their services to our country.

Their diseases lay dormant, few had avenues of support, resources and arenas to express themselves. Mr Peters found solace in helping others.

*"I think my father got involved in the community helping organize community activities like taking kids on fishing and camping trips was in a way his own way of putting the war behind him"* E Peters

*"My dad was a veteran of the Korean War. Sometimes I would see my father just staring in the distance, he was there but he wasn't there staring into the distance"* Glen Chop Porter

*"If you needed help Mr Peters was a man we could count on. He sacrificed a lot for the brothers in the community. He was always there for us"* Leon Booker

The impact Mr and Mrs Peters had on the lives of the people in Sunnydale was far more than heroic, they went above and beyond the call of duty to help others in the neighborhood. Their involvement had a tremendous impact in the community.

For years the Peters parents both undertook organizing community events, programs and projects to help the community.

*"I remember Mr Peters taking us brothers on camping, fishing and all kinds of outdoor activities outside our community. Not only did he help me get my first job but he helped a lot of cats find employment, even taking some brothers down to the DMV to get their driver's license.* Leon Booker

Mrs Peters spent time as a school crossing guard, a school yard monitor, a member of the PTA, volunteered at the food pantry, community board member and even a community fundraiser baking cookies and creating arts and crafts that were sold at the recreation center.

*"Sunnydale had its own Boy Scout troop, Mr Peters organized. We were a part of the Scout A Rama Boys Scout convention at the Cow Palace. I don't remember our troop number, that doesn't really matter, what matters is that we did have a Boys Scout troop and that's all that matters"* A Burleson

*"I don't know where my parents got that extra boost of energy, but helping others was always part of the conversation at the dinner table"* E Peters

Oftentimes parental and community commitment to others has a trying effect on those willing to lend a helping hand and their immediate families.

The demands of community involvement sometimes leave the children of these street community ambassadors with feelings of abandonment.

*"Seeing my parents out there in the community involved in all these activities was a proud moment for my brothers and sisters. Besides, my brothers and sisters received more than our share of support from people in the neighborhood. We had no resentments at all and my parents' community involvement helped us develop new friendships. I had all kinds of friends Black, White Hispanic and Indian friends"* E Peters

Recalling his youthful days in the neighborhood Eric talked about some memorable times.

*"What comes to mind is the brothers down on Front at the bus stop playing the congos. We could hear them playing at the top of the hill where we lived, so the kids up where we lived would jump on our bikes and ride down to the Front and hang out all day. That's where we met new friends, friends for a lifetime"* E Peters

Eric expressed deep feeling about the changes new developments going on in the community

*"My main concerns are the well being of the people in the community. I would hope that the residents there will not only take advantage of all the new things but among themselves become supportive of one another being there for their neighbors and participating in community activities rallying around each other"* E Peters

# CHAPTER 30

# DARK SECRETS

## All Of Us In Some Way Are
## Haunted By The Past

*There exist many forms of social racial and economical abuse that have left more than its share of permanent scars throughout World on People of Color*

*Not all abuse can be attributed to physical domination or exploitation.*

*Our children who are denied access to their rich ancestry*

*in our schools are stripped of their culture, made to feel less than and are the victims of an abusive system that has destroyed them emotionally and academically.*

*A known clinical fact is that those who have experienced any form of abuse, sexually, emotionally, socially and racially face enormous self esteem challenges, social attitudes, and stereotypes about themselves.*

*For young children it's a heavy burden to carry and often lays dormant well into adulthood. But adults, men and women are not immune to the same isolative masking internal pain abuse produces.*

*There are all types of rape and sexual abuse and can be defined in many different ways but one thing remains the same, it's never the victem's fault.*

*Perpetrators are often people closely associated with their victims and my assailants were friends of the family.*

*For so long for me there were those **Dark Days of Sexual Abuse and Deep Hidden Secrets.** I carried within me for years telling no one of what I had experienced.*

*It wasn't that I was afraid to tell on my perpetrators but I was more concerned about the reaction and retaliation on those if I had told.*

*My family would have not taken this lightly that I know, the circumstances were too close to home and the perpetrators were trusted friends of the family.*

*Even though for me there was this sense of community loyalty I knew exposing these sick freaks was the thing to do, but at the time I just couldn't I didn't want to bring this drama down on our family it was the worst decision of my life and only hope that those who suffer these experiences take the necessary steps forward to expose their perpetrators, confront the pain or sadly accept that if they don't address these deep issues their lives will be filled with days of unhappiness.*

*At the time when this happened to me. I had a deep hatred of these individuals who had wronged me, so over time I withdrew, found shelter within myself, finding solace becoming an expert on escapism in writing and eventually using drugs and alcohol.*

*Being forced to sit and watch two grown ass adults having sex was my indoctrination into my being abused.*

*Undoubtedly it was indeed some **sick form of perverted adult sexual behavior I was exposed to.***

*The woman would always find excuses for me to come over to her house such as going to the grocery store, washing dishes, mopping the floor, that sort of thing not to draw attention to her undercover motivation to have me come over.*

*She would be dressed in see through nightgowns, walk around semi naked, dance in front me, play with her breast, fondle me then masturbate in front of me.*

*When her boyfriend was there the two engaged in sexual acts and laughed at me.*

*This went on for a long time and continued with her when she and the boyfriend parted ways.*

*I never knew his name but knew where he parked his car and wanted badly to break out his windows.*

*To coax me over the woman started paying me money to sit and watch her perform these sick strip club X rated obscene performances.*

*I never said a single word, returning home with a few dimes and nickels that I bitterly tossed underneath my bed.*

*I had no idea the **worst was yet to happen** when two older brothers of my childhood friends engaged in physical sex in front of me which led to one of them raping me, one rainy night in the bedroom of my friend when I was forced to spend the night.*

*Between the two of these well known brotha's I was repeatedly fondled and raped.*

*For years I held onto these **Hidden Dark Secrets** but was strangely relieved in my adulthood when one of my real close lifelong friends while talking about the old days in Sunnydale angrily blurted out he had experienced the **same thing by the same perpetrators.***

*This impromptu revelation between us came without notice nearly **30 years later!***

***30 years later.!** All these years. We both had lived with these **Hidden Dark Secrets** telling noone and keeping these **Hidden Dark Secrets** under an emotional lock and key buried deep within us.*

*Today I am proud that these **Hidden Dark Secrets** demons of the past have been laid to rest.*

*I share this openly, forgive those and throw the experience in the **Sea of Forgetfulness. Amen***

# CHAPTER 31

## A SAD DAY IN SUNNYDALE
### January 25th 1973

*Victor Doran Jefferson*
*"Mac Jeff"*
*October 26, 1951 - January 25, 1973*

**On January 25th 1973** *on the "Front", Victor was killed by a bullet that we were told was not meant for him.*

*"Brother Victor was well liked he had a rare quality about himself"*
*K Burleson*

*"That day was hard on me. Victor's death. My girlfriend and I had given him a ride home to Bayview where the family had moved it hadn't been a week or two but in that short time both Debra and Victor were both gone because of some stupid shit"* *Dwayne Robins*

*"I spent many a day at Mrs Jefferson's kitchen table. My grandmother and her were close friends in the Truth. He was like a big brother to me. It was a sad day that day in Sunnydale"* *Randy Roc Minix*

*"That day I will never forget. Victor and I were tight. Some of us especially me never got over what happened"* *Levi Bryant*

*Sunnydale was in his blood and the neighborhood he could not leave behind. Ultimately that **Unconditional Love** for the neighborhood sadly cost **Him His Precious Life.***

*"You know sometimes when I look at Darro all I can see in him is his brother. His leaving us so early so young had to be tough on the family but it was tough on Sunnydale to"* *Al Burleson*

*To date we are not sure what really happened but a childhood friend of mine was convicted of killing my brother.*

*The loss of his young life was devastating to our family as is the loss of all lives that are taken without cause from unnecessary elements that plague our communities.*

*"Another brother was taken from us much too early."* *T Warren*

*"Victor was the **heart and soul** of Sunnydale and his death hit Sunnydale hard".* *Al Burleson*

*A tragic loss something and someone I will never forget"* *W Francis*

*"The brother was going to State College worked at Hertz Park was being mentored by Geogre Davis and there's no telling where in his life he was headed" Glen Chop Porter*

*The mourners at Bryant Mortuary wept with deep regret and hostile thoughts of revenge.*

*The day he was shot was on the birthday of my good friend and Victor's drinking buddy* **Douglas L, was equally devastating.**

**To compound matters, January 25th brought even more grief to our family because Chop Willie B, and I were in jail at 850 Bryant Street for running through a North Beach underground parking lot allegedly trying to break into cars.**

**It didn't help that the three of us were drunk under the influence and had no business being in North Beach.**

**When the police handcuffed us, they put us in the paddywagon with some street hookers and Chop and Willie tried to hit on them. Is that crazy or what?**

**Momma now had to deal with one dead son and two sons Coyle and incarcerated.**

**Me for the first time in my life and Coyle serving time somewhere at some detention facility.**

**The car burglary charges against the three of us were reduced to mischief behavior.**

*I found out about his death in jail.* **Willie H, told me** *and said don't worry* **"we gonna get that motha'.......**

**Victor and I** *were three years apart really close as were my sister and brother. It took a long time to put his passing behind me.*

*In March of the same year, my sister gave birth to a wonderful baby girl Erica Victoria that helped us through our loss.*

*I thought I had come to grips with his death. **I never did nor did many of his close friends in Sunnydale.***

*But then one day while working as an Employment Administrator for the renowned **Northern California Service League**, an organization that worked with ex-offenders.*

*While facilitating an orientation for recently released parolees, and going through the new case files of those parolees in attendance at the orientation, in front of me seated was the **young man convicted of killing my brother.***

*Our **eyes locked in on one another**. I excused myself, unable to facilitate the orientation. His eyes were **shame based,** with an **aura of sadness.***

*I shared this with **Shirley Melnicoe, Executive Director, who** encouraged me to call my mother at home, which I did.*

*My mother told me **"there is nothing son you can do to bring your brother back", she said "you are married now with a wife and young family of your own". "Put in all in God's Hands***

*Not only did the call home helped me but in that same orientation was a parolee who told his story of being incarcerated in prison and when a deputy opened his cell he was introduced to his new cellmate.*

*The new cellmate was the son he left behind who grew up fatherless and followed in his footsteps right to his cell in State Prison.*

*His story brought the entire group to tears, and for me a strange consolation of the heartfelt intricate pains we all feel no matter the circumstance.*

*To date both father and son have made successful transitions from incarceration to productive citizenship.*

*That day with my brother's killer in the orientation I delivered one of my most powerful heartfelt motivational presentations in my twenty three year association with **NCSL**.*

***Momma was so right "Put It All In God's Hands and He Will Do What's Best For You"***

*Years later I would learn that the **young man was killed allegedly by one of the brother's from Sunnydale.***

*I sure as hell hope not, for **retaliation and senselessness** have far too long destroyed the fabric of our communities, contributing nothing but additional **pain and suffering.***

***Every year on October 26 on his birthday and the anniversary of his death Coyle sends flowers to his gravesite and I go out to sit with him and Momma reflecting on the good times we shared.***

*MISSING YOU BROTHER VICTOR*

# CHAPTER 32

## PO' KID'S PARADISE

*Kenji Shibuya vs Bearcat Wright*
*Big Time Wrestling at the Cow Palace*

*We snuck into the legendary Cow Palace on Geneva Avenue and got to see big time musical acts from the Beatles, to the Jackson Five, Roller Derby and of course Big Time Wrestling.*

Estelle Chop's mom was a big time front roll seat go by her damn self die hard wrestling fan.

'Bruh at times I think my mom had a crush on Bobo Brazil or an addiction to wrestling" Glen Chop Porter

"People in the neighborhood, especially us kids, thought wrestling was real. In fact you couldn't tell us that it wasn't" A Burleson

"People went to wrestling before they went to church" R Taylor

Every Friday night Mrs Porter dressed up in a rainbow sherbet Baskin Robbins 51 flavored dress, drenched herself with Jean Natae' French smelling' perfume donned a multi colored flowered straw bonnet brought alone her shortnecks of choice and headed to her favorite ringside seat to religiously watch Big Time Wrestling at the Cow Palace.

Willie B was an excitable dude. So excitable and high strung that one night at Big Time wrestling at the Cow Palace he ran down to ringside and punched Kenji Shibuya right in the face then took off running.

*Shibuya had just beaten Willie's hero black wrestler Bearcat Wright.*

*Wrestling was as fake as Willie's gold watch but you couldn't tell him that.*

*The Japanese wrestler took off after Willie, followed closely by Cow Palace security and all of Sunnydale laughing our natural behinds off.*

*Man! It looked so crazy to the fans, many thought Willie was part of the act.*

*Mrs Porter would have loved to have known a good friend of the Sons who frequents LaFrance's crib in Daly City.*

*Brian T, is a younger first Samoan brotha with strong community ties and happens to be cousins with wrestling greats The Samoans and former champion Peter Mavia.*

*"Kids from the neighborhood would pay me for their autographs" B Thompson*

*One of his other cousins is NFL QB Jack Thompson.*

*BT proudly talks about how many of the legendary Cow Palace wrestlers hangn' out at the Lakeview family house on Caine Street.*

*"I can't believe you guys never paid to get into the Cow Palace" B Thompson*

*Man I'm thinking' had Estelle known Brian, she would have been to his house after wrestling every Friday night with her bonnet and all...*

*I can see them now BT and Mrs Porter looking through his priceless collection of vintage wrestling programs and magazines.*

*In 1964 the Cow Palace hosted the Republican National Convention where Sunnydale's own shoeshine boy Ivy F shined the shoes of Senator Kennath Keating live on national television.*

*"Dude never missed a day shining shoes but he did what he had to do to help put food on the table. For that alone you have to respect the brother" Glen Chop Porter*

*Not once can I remember any one of the brothers from Sunnydale ever paying to get into an event at the Cow Palace.*

*The venue provided hustling opportunities like buying booze for some underage white boys, watching the cars of people on the street, too cheap to pay for parking in the lot, then charging them for directions or places to eat in the city.*

*Everybody had a hustle. Some of the cats parking cars had fake ticket stubs flashlights and wore white parking attendant coveralls.*

*"Where the quick money was we found a way to make a few bucks" L Graves*

*"We had every uniform for every event, always looking the part. The Cow Palace should of hired us because some of us did more than the people they paid to work there" R Taylor*

*We knew every side door entrance, every nook and cranny and even climbed up on the roof and dropped down inside the arena during performances unnoticed.*

*"Sneaking in the Cow Palace was easier than sneaking in our houses after dark" B Freeman*

*The same thing went for the Geneva Drive-In as well, we saw every flick that came out, right there in our neighborhood backyard for free.*

*Raiding the snack bar for bags of our favorite zoo zoos and nothing but sugar coated wham whams, then sitting undisturbed in the bleachers, watching young white couples get their freak on while watching movie after movie we thought was living ghetto fabulous.*

*"Some of them white folks would feel sorry for us and buy us a bag of chips, sodas and a hotdog" Glen Chop Porter*

*"At the drive in, inside the back seat of those cars sometimes we saw more than just a movie" Al Burleson*

*Geneva Avenue was a poor kids paradise for fun and excitement*

*A few blocks down the block there was the pool hall that made some of the original Po' Boy sandwiches, but the pinball machines were by far the main attraction.*

*At Mayfair Market, we would enter and exit undetected through the electronic slide doors all day long stealing Italian salami, cheese and crackers, white powdered donuts and Nehi grape sodas.*

*We weren't hungry, or yearning to get into trouble but kids who grow up in the inner city with limited organizational recreational activities have to improvise.*

*The kids in the suburbs not only came from two parent homes but are afforded the opportunity to participate in supervised recreational games and activities.*

*The kind of behavior ripping and running out of control for me was out of my league but often seemed to be the only thing to do. Peer pressure is a bitch...*

*After stealing from Mayfair we would then ride back to the neighborhood on our bikes laughing and throwing donuts at each other.*

*Living in Sunnydale offered so many improvisational games especially with McLaren Park serving as an opportunistic background.*

*We played impromptu games, 1,2,3 heats, a hide and seek chase game, hide and go get 'em, a chase the girls and kiss them game, nic knock, knocking on a residents door real loud and running away before the person could answer their door.*

*We explored San Bruno Mountain behind the Cow Palace, stole sodas from the motel vending machines on Geneva Avenue, swam in the muddy toxic waters behind PGE on Old Bayshore, and caught lizards on KYA Hill.*

*Building wooden soap box derby style coasters with two-by-fours, and planks of wood we stole from construction sites nearby was a Sunnydale tradition as was flying dime store kites from the Dale to the San Francisco Bay.*

*We got our wheels from old grocery store shopping carts or barbarians from the railroad cars down by the S&W factory and Schlage Locks.*

*In the summer when we would race recklessly down Blythedale, Brookdale and the top of Sunnydale Avenue way past John McLaren Elementary School.*

*Some of the coasters rivaled the soap box derby cars we saw on TV.*

*The brotha's would freshly spray paint their coasters, outfit them with transistor radios and bicycle horns.*

*A few guys found steering wheels from abandoned junked cars, and used rubber bottoms of old shoes for breaks, they made back seats out of wooden fruit crates, then flew down the hills throwing caution to the wind.*

*Many broken bones and facial scares remain from these suicidal reckless escapades.*

*Mikey T' rode down Brookdale on a coaster, lost control, went under a parked car, got hung up on a loose muffler and was pinned beneath the car until a tow truck and the paramedics rescued his dumb ass.*

*In the summer months you could always find Sunnydale children swimming at John McLaren Swimming Pool right next to Hertz Playground at the corner of Visitation and Hahn Street.*

*Whoever said black folks couldn't swim because we had no buoyancy was crazy.*

*The pool even had two black lifeguards, the Scott Brothers.*

*Sunnydale mother's wore many hats. I can remember Gregory's mom, playing tackle football with us.*

*Ms Griffin was fine, she looked alot like Dionne Warwick.*

*We had no idea she played basketball and ran track in college.*

*Ms Griffin, Gregory's mom, worked at Candlestick Park for the San Francisco Giants as an usherette in the VIP private suite*

*I guess that's why from her job at Candlestick Park, Willie Mays, Jim Ray Hart and Willie McCovey weren't ashamed to give her a ride home from the ballpark, stop over and play cards and dominoes.*

*Jim Ray Hart would get toasted then walk to the Little Village Market buy us kids whatever we desired, himself, more than a couple of shortnecks then be outside playing strikeout with us youngstas.*

*Renee, the oldest daughter, could flat out outrun a lot of brothers in her house slippers and nightgown.*

*Sunnydale mothers had their hands full trying to maintain households and raise enthusiastic youngsters but they performed these unselfish tasks magnificently.*

*The role of the single mother and women in The DALE took on many non traditional roles.*

*The daughters in the community played significant surrogate mother roles at a very young age helping to raise their younger siblings, many sacrificing their own childhoods for the sake and responsibility of family.*

*Sunnydale was a resourceful supportive community where everyone pitched in to raise the children of The Dale*

*It would be unprecedentedly a downright shame not to mention some of the young Sisters of Sunnydale who sacrificed so much of their lives contributing to the wellbeing of their families.*

*Through it all, these Sisters of Sunnydale made it through the mud, crap and bullshit overcoming enormous odds to become beautiful butterflies.*

*"We had some some Bold Black Beautiful Women back in the day"*
*Coyle Jefferson*

*Sista's like Brenda Thomas became a dentist.*

*Debra Sharpe is a doctor.*

*TC Caracter, had a long successful career working for the DMV as a State Employee.*

*Lucille Henderson, became a private business owner.*

*Velma Jones and her sister Helen Bailey became successful business entrepreneurs.*

*Helen's daughter Tracy Vaughn would later reach national acclaim co-starring as Levita with Cedrick The Entertainer on the Steve Harvey Show.*

*Women young and old contributed to the well being of the family.*

*My sister Theresa taught me how to ride a 3 speed bike, Momma ordered from a mailhouse catalog.*

*She was always reading and encouraged me to read books and write.*

*I wrote my first two act stage play "The Hat" before entering Jr High School. A storyline about stereotypes and two young secret lovers.*

*Theresa, like me, found escapism in books, storytelling and creative writing.*

*Without any doubt the escapist self isolation characteristics, fear and untold sexual abuse I experienced were major contributers to my long time history of alcohol and drug addiction.*

*My first ghostwriting job, for a nickel I wrote corny ass poetry for the brotha's tryn' to get bonus points from the young girls in the hood.*

*"Twit was the night when I looked into your eyes so sunny and bright" silly stupid stuff that sometimes worked...*

*Funny how these cats would stumble and stutter over the words.*

*Ms Caracter, in her kitchen apron with a pot of red beans cooking on the stove came outside to play fast pitch strikeout with us, going deep off of Rich, a pretty good picture and one of the older white kids who lived on Sunnydale Avenue.*

*Sunnydale was a made to order children's playground that so many of the brotha' and sista's because of adult responsibilities being reared in a single parented home forfeited the opportunity of a normal childhood.*

*The school of life caught them early.*

*During the mid 60's riots the bus stop on Sunnydale and Hahn was where the brotha's congregated, ringing fire alarms yellen' "Burn Baby Burn" throwing rocks bottles and molotov cocktails at the police from behind the bushes then disappearing into the night.*

*This was a difficult time for me living in a Black community and attending a White school.*

*Today what stands out in my mind about the mid 60's riots was at the time my mother was in Waco Texas tending to my grandmother and my sister and brothers were left to care for me.*

*Being the responsible siblings that they were, my sister took me over to Ms Griffin's house smack dab right on the corner of Sunnydale and Hahn to spend the night with Gregory and Yolanda while Theresa and Renee left us alone in the house and went outside to show their solidarity.*

*Ms Griffin was at work. I don't think Cedelle ever had a day off from work. My brotha's were long gone into the night.*

*Gregory and Yolanda and I watched the chaos from the upstairs bedroom.*

*Theresa ' and Renee were out in front protesting, fist held high yelling at the police "Burn Baby Burn" Power to the People, Black Power...*

*The Revolution Won't Be Televised*
*That's What Gil Scott Heron Wrote*

*Unfortunately for Renee and Theresa The Revolution Was Televised*

*Momma in Texas saw Sunnydale on a live television news broadcast showing Renee and Theresa protesting and immediately telephoned home.*

*"If y'all don't get yo' black ass home in that house right now' and take care of my baby" to say that was the end of my sista' and Renee's Afro wearn' revolutionary Free Huey, Power to the People careers is an understatement.*

*Our adventures took us far and beyond Sunnydale and traveled with us throughout our youth.*

*Some of us were addicted to impromptu fun and games behavior much like those dependent on fixing their drug addictions.*

## *The Cake*

*Going dressed to kill at weekend parties in the Lakeview neighborhood was the Sunnydale thing to do. It seemed like every girl in the neighborhood was fine as all outdoors. At a garage party in Lakeview celebrating Balboa High School's Turkey Day football Championship victory with everyone having a good time dancing and drinking Annie Greens Spring, Spanada and Akadama Plum wine in a huge punch bowl, that's is before Big Doug tossed his Tijuana Smalls Cigar and poured a pint of 90 proof Bourbon Delux into the punch bowl.*

*Folks were having the time of their lives slow dancing rubbing up on each other trying to get their bump and grind grooves on.*

*Without my eyeglasses on drunk as can be I stumbled over to the table to check it out a.huge Congradulation's Bucs' Cake.*

*This dude from Lakeview, Randy, dressed in an all white two piece suit was slowly dancing next to me with a girl of my dreams, but I was drunk and she didn't want anything to do with me.*

*Sunnydale dudes had a huge dislike for Lakeview brotha's and many of those cats in Lakeview looked down on us because we were from the projects.*

*Dude pushed me and I fell face first in the cake, and all hell broke out. Chop laughed his ass off, knew I didn't like this dude, and told me "Jeff, Randy pushed you in the cake".*

*To make matters worse I went over to ask the girl for a dance. Need not tell y'all she turned me down and ran away from me.*

*The brawl was Sunnydale vs Lakeview all over again.*

*Big Doug picked up the punch bowl and dumped it over Randy's all white suit with Chop going about his business whuppin' some Lakeview ass.*

*The cake fight was on and that night I was the only one who got to eat a piece of a cake.*

## Six Seaburgers Bitch!

*Lunchtime at Balboa High School after we had spent up our money buying and smoking weed, the munchies took over.*

*There were two legendary fast food outlets near our school campus that everyone went to.*

*Tick Tock was famous for its Seaburgers and french fries, as was H&S Fish and Chips.*

*Big Doug had an old ride we called the Blue Baron, we used to park nearby and this day it was my turn to go up to the window and order, snatching the food and run,*

*Keep in mind we ain't got a dime to our names. We had pulled this lunchtime caper off many times at other fast food places.*

*But our snatching the food and run caper wasn't authentic unless it ended with "thank you bitch"*

*I went to the window with the car running and ordered Six Seaburgers!*

*When the cashier, this lady who knew my momma, handed me the order I snatched it but not forgetting "thanks bitch" laughing and forgetting that next to the restaurant was a building front that you had to duck under, when running.*

*Laughing without looking ahead in front of the entire student body I ran smack dab into the building and staggered out cold to the parking lot with french fries and seaburgers all over me, my partner's high and laughing their asses off not to mention that woman, the cashier, momma's friend beating the hell outta me with a broomstick.*

*We pulled this stunt so many times that a H&S staff employee took a picture of me and circulated photos of me around the school.*

## The Wig

*One night at the end of a Lakeview garage party, people began making their exit down a dark alleyway.*

*Chop and I were walking behind a Lakeview wanna b pimp and his woman with a huge wig on her head.*

*Al and Roc were still dancing, trying to get their last freaky deaky' bump and grind roll on.*

*The wanna-b pimp dressed in a $50 dolla' passionate pink Sears Sucka suit he must have brought on Market Street walked in front of the woman with the wig followed by Chop and me.*

*To this day I don't know what got into me, I'm sure the 40 ounce of Colt 45 had something to do with it but for some odd reason I reached over Chop grabbed ahold of the wig and dropped it right in the unsuspecting hands of Chop' the woman screamed to her man,* **"he took my wig off"**

*The wanna b pimp threatened to kick Chop's ass, well he should not outta' said that' Chop handed me his dixie cup then beat the rhinestones off the wanna b's $50 Sears Sucka suit.* **I drank the rest of Chop's wine and enjoyed the laugh of a lifetime...**

## Chop's Rap

*Whenever the fella's went out to a red light garage party, Roc, Al and I made it a point to grab a girl and slow dance right next to Chop to hear his wacky make no sense at all soap opera come on mac' lines.*

*To get into the party it cost one dollar and you were entitled to a drink or a joint, or the two of your choice. We had a system of who would buy the joints or drinks, but the end result we were gonna be high and full of that courageous or outrageous oil.*

*We'd be slow dancing to the Dells Stay In My Corner, the Friends of Distinction Going in Circles, the Originals Baby I'm For Real, and Chop would start his "Mac A Thon", like this...check out this Ghetto Rap!*

*"Ya know baby you're so fine with you **I Only Have One Life To Live**, my hearts beat' so fast after this dance you gonna have to take me to **General Hospital**, cause you and me gal' are **Young and Restless**, baby you're my **Guiding Light**, while the two of us **Search for Tomorrow** at the **Edge Of the Night**, in the **Dark Shadows** in **Another World** cause baby we only have **One Life to Live**...blah blah blah...sometime his rap and mac lines BS, got him to first base. Sometimes...*

## The GardenHose

*Steven C was up to his old tricks again when he funneled a water hose into the mailbox of light skin Ricky B's living room for no reason at all while Ricky B was upstairs doing the nasty with Maxine W.*

*We stood outside watching yet another one of Steven's dastardly deeds flooding a house with a waterhose.*

*Ricky looked out his bedroom window and saw the fellas laughing thinking we were high from smoking some tea that Rick told us was weed, but he sensed something was right in the neighborhood. He couldn't have been more right,*

*Water was coming underneath the front door. Steven took off running, we continued to laugh and Rick came outside with some raw eggs and threw an egg right on the mark bullseye bam!*

*The egg landed right on Steven's eyelid, busted on impact and dripped down his face like those sunny side up eggs momma used to make.*

*The point to all this madness was that we never compromised on our outrageous behaviors and certainly upon arriving home would we tell our mothers anything about our ghetto escapades.*

*They had far too much on their plates trying to put plates with food on our tables.*

*Little did we know that much of what we did even though harmless was for many us behaviors from not having a fatherly influence in our homes upon returning home from days and nights of what we thought was Ghetto Fun.*

*Those with fathers did their thing but made a point of cutting the nights and days short because this was something their fathers would not tolerate.*

*A lot of us from single parent homes were blamed for things we did not do by the parents of the kids that hung out with us who ratted on us.*

*There were many knocks at our door from parents wanting to see my mother about her children hanging out with Coyle and Victor. They said my brothers were being bad or negative influences on their children.*

*Needless to say Momma answered our door with her rolling pin and many parents went away with "that woman's crazy look in their eyes". Some of the neighborhood's outrageous kids came from some of those so-called functional two parent families in a Po' Kids Paradise full of impromptu games.*

# CHAPTER 33

# COLOR THEM FATHA'

*With all the fun and games so many of the young brothers and sisters going everywhere doing their own thing treading on borderlines of getting into trouble succumbing to peer pressure the pressure to curtail reckless abandonment fell on the shoulders of the mothers and young sisters of Sunnydale.*

*There were Black Men around but they were spread thin. It was difficult enough trying to raise their own families while taking on the task of looking out for the children without a father in the household.*

*Surely their absence from the Black Family in our communities have contributed greatly to family dysfunction and our communities decline.*

*The incarceration rate of Black men in prison is substantial.*

*The murder rate of young Black men killing one another is incredibly significant with the prison population housing black men young and old who have grown up fatherless.*

*The absence of the black men in the household along with the number of other infestations in our communities are well documented.*

*Children growing up without a strong father figure are at risk to succumb to negative influences, peer pressures, poor education, and family core values.*

*"A Black Man who has time to invest in his fellow Man is a Man who cares about the well being of his community" C Jefferson*

*"Not only is a Man someone others can depend on but he is a Man with the commitment and strength to have an impact in the lives of the people who need him most" M Pitre*

*"Tributes aren't enough for these unsung heroes.*

*They go about their work expecting nothing in return, just the satisfaction of seeing young Black Men living productive lives. They ask for nothing in return" L Bryant*

**The late poet, songwriter and musician Gil Scott Heron in his debut album composed this masterful composition describing the pain and hardship the Black Man has endured when he sang.**

*Pieces of a Man*
*Gil Scott Heron*

*Jagged jigsaw pieces*
*Tossed about the room*
*I saw my grandma sweeping*
*With her old straw broom*
*She didn't know what she was doing*
*She could hardly understand*
*That she was really sweeping up..*
*Pieces of a man*

*I saw my daddy greet the mailman*
*And I heard the mailman say*
*"Now don't you take this letter to her now Jimmy*
*Cause they've laid off nine others today"*
*He didn't know what he was saying*
*He could hardly understand*
*That he was only talking to*

*Pieces of a man*

*I saw the thunder and heard the lightning!*
*And felt the burden of his shame*
*And for some unknown reason*
*He never turned my way*

*Pieces of that letter*
*Were tossed about that room*
*And now I hear the sound of sirens*
*Come knifing through the gloom*
*They don't know what they are doing*
*They could hardly understand*
*That they're only arresting*
*Pieces of a man*

*I saw him go to pieces*
*I saw him go to pieces*
*He was always such a good man*
*He was always such a strong man*
*Yeah, I saw him go to pieces*
*I saw him go to pieces*

*Regardless of their whereabouts we salute our Black Fathers and*
*Color Them Fathers...as song by: The Winstons*

# Color Him Father

## The Winstons

### About Color Him Father

*"Color Him Father" is a song released by funk and soul group The Winstons. It was released in 1969, and reached number 2 on the R&B charts and number 7 on the Billboard Hot 100 that same year. Its composer, Richard Lewis Spencer, won a Grammy Award for Best R&B song in 1970. "Color Him Father" is one of the best known songs by The Winstons*

*Without hesitation we celebrate and pay homage to the Black Fathers and Black Men in Sunnydale. Their Brotherhood.*

*Statistics show that close to 70 percent of all births to black mothers are nonmarital, giving rise to the stereotype that black fathers are largely absent.*

*However, while black fathers are less likely than white and Hispanic fathers to marry their child's mother, many black fathers continue to parent through cohabitation and visitation, providing caretaking, financial, and in-kind support.*

*Black men have for too long been labeled trifling, lazy and countless other derogatory demeaning things and not involved in raising their children.*

*Black men have been said to be irresponsible, dependent on the strength of strong Black women to raise the family.*

*There are those who say the Black Woman has more strength than that of the Black Man, but renowned Civil Activist the late Dick Gregory offers this analogy of those beliefs.*

*Gregory and his wife Lilian* had *11 children and had* this to say to those who offer opinions about *Black Men and Black Women and their roles in the Black Family.*

*Gregory* speaking before a church congregation in the south made these comments.

*"The Black Woman will never be stronger than the Black Man"*

*Gregory went on to say that Black Women have been and are more responsible than the Black Man, but they are not stronger".*

*Mr Gibbs, my Bayview nextdoor neighbor, was notorious for leaving home, going to the grocery store to buy a quart of buttermilk, be gone for days, then call home from Mississippi.*

*He used to tell me this while drinking his downhome moonshine from a mayonnaise jar, "boy no matter what you do, you are still a man and the Man of the House '' echoing Gregory's statement.*

*The gist of what he was saying was that all of what the Black Men has endured, there are but a few women who could withstand what society has dished out to the Black Man.*

*In Sunnydale these black men contributed equally to the well being of the community. They were not Sunnydale's Papa Was A Rollin' Stone Fathers.*

## These Are Black Fathers Who Were involved!

*Mr Williams,* this hard working black man and his wife raised 8? 9? 10? wonderful children and operated a candy store at the top of Brookdale

*Mr, Porter,* Chop's dad would ride the bus downtown everyday to check on the brotha's shining shoes in Union Square

*Mr Pietre,* Baby Ray's dad who coached baseball at Hertz Playground and bought tickets for kids to see the Giants play at Candlestick Park

*Mr Peters,* started the Sunnydale Boys Scout Troop

*"Mr Peters got me my first job as a custodian with the school district. From him I learned that it the responsibility of a man to look out and help others"* Leon Booker

*Mr Nevels,* formed the Sunnydale Jets semi pro baseball team, gave discounts on haircuts when he wasn't drinking with the fellas

*Mr Latham,* Douglas' dad worked for the US Postal Service he tried his best to help a few brothers get jobs with USPS

*Mr, Bruce,* Sunnydale do it all maintenance man, if ya' dropped a bag of potato chips on the ground he'd picked them up before they hit the sidewalk

*Grandpa Scales,* raised his grand daughter and kept his front yard and garden immaculate

*Howard, Ola Mae's Man,* this brotha' was a Black Man who made a tremendous impact on *Roc and Chop,* wit' his good domino playn' self

*Robert "Lil Mo" Mae Burleson's bow,* the same can be said about *"Lil Mo"* treated the Burleson children like his own flesh and blood

*LC,* owned the record store and bought groceries for families without food

*Obie,* his wise crack'n business partner always willing to give you a ride to the doctor or grocery store if ya' were willing to listen to his Marcus Garvey Back to Africa Pan African beliefs

*Mr LaBlanc,* worked on cars in his spare time lent his tools and helped folks keep their cars running

*Mr, Jackson,* Ricky's father, played semi pro football and coached Pop Warner teams at Crocker Amazon Park

*George Davis,* went above and beyond to engage the neighborhood in positive activities

*Tony Harrison,* Sunnydale's door-to-door outreach worker

*Booker,* worked for Muni, always came to the Dale with a positive attitude just don't sit on his GTO

*Mr Qualls,* the neighborhoods unofficial school crossing guard, who had trouble crossing the street by his damn self

*Mr Hughes,* tough love Dad, a good listener, had time for everybody, some of the time

*Big Black,* store owner gave credit and would deliver the groceries to your house, especially the younger single women

*Uncle Ike,* hardest working man in Sunnydale, worked at the store, was always walking through the neighborhood delivering bags of groceries for Big Black, swept up the Front, do anything for everybody anytime

*Mr Caracter,* mister fix it man had a tool in one hand a short neck drink in the other

**Mr Pitre,** John, Melvin and Pete's dad, together with his wife they raised three adventurous boys with a stern hand

**Mr Odoms,** talk about you like a dog, a dog' then buy you a drink, and tell ya what you didn't wanna hear. Then talk about you like a dogg'

*"It didn't make us youngsters who had a father feel like we were better than those kids who didn't have one because the Black men who were in Sunnydale did their best to provide guidance and support to those without a father, that's what made growing up in Sunnydale special. We had Black men willing to help out when needed"* Melvin Pitre

**We pay tribute and acknowledge those Sunnydale Community Brothers, Black Men, Black Fathers and Color Them Fatha'**

# CHAPTER 34

# PLEASE DON'T WEEP FOR ME

*An Excerpt From The Author's Book Nora's Song*
Written through the Heart and Soul of Henrietta Harris

*Nora sat there in her 4ᵗʰ story apartment looking out the window at the afternoon rain rocking back and forth in the old family chair listening to the somber music of Lady Day.*

*Nora was not unique, but to most that crazy woman in the window, who seldom was seen outdoors but from the street level she could be seen gazing out of her apartment window minding her own.*

*She resented the sunshine, worshiped the rain. Too many unpleasant traumatic experiences under the sunlight had happened to her in her younger life. The broad daylight rapes and lynching forever tormented her.*

*The chair she had brought with her from down south on the Greyhound bus many years ago had been passed down from generation to generation and was Nora's last remaining physical connection to her southern past.*

*With the rain pounding down on the neglected deteriorating wooden windowsill rinsing the dirt and smut away Nora knew the little sparrows she loved to feed would not come today.*

*Down below across the street people gathered standing in front of Gibson's Mortuary to pay their respects to another family whose lives had been shattered by a barrage of bullets that ricocheted through the neighborhood only a week ago.*

*The faces below were the same ones she knew very well, even the downpour could not wash away the sorrow and the tears, it was to Nora a very common sight.*

*She shook her head in disgust and counted on her feeble fingers the number of funerals that took place over the last few days.*

*Her bedside window was her salvation from the shame and sorrows below, damn! She thought to herself, clutching her faithful Bible, Five funerals in five days! Funeral after funeral the loss of life was everywhere-all around her.*

*Nora had lived in the 12 story roach infested building from the time the Palace was first constructed.*

*Shrugging her head more, she gazed down on the gathering crowd and thought out loud "the Pink Palace! Wasn't nothing pink and it sure as hell wasn't no palace"*

*There was no sunshine-shining on Sunnyside Elementary School down at the end of the block.*

*The schoolyard was a dumping ground for bodies being tossed there, accumulating faster than the garbage at the junkyards,*

*Nora knew all the families, shared in their grief and could only offer unspoken condolences from her bedside window.*

255

*She remembered the one day it seemed as if there were back-to-back-to-back funerals all day long for young men in the community.*

*Nora had wondered who some of them were and where were the funeral people taking them, the death tolls were adding up and the graveyards were filling up. four, maybe five funerals in one afternoon, a dying shame.*

*Out there on the streets were many of her long time friends, somebody's mother, grandmother, parents to the deceased.*

*Like Nora many were widows themselves faced with the hardships of raising their children on their own.*

*Nora recalled attending the services of a young man, Grandma Gabby's great grandson who was cut down by a hail of bullets right outside her building.*

*The two women were long time friends and had come north together years past*

*At the services friends and family of the deceased gave testimonies and paid homage to the young man.*

*But when a very frail Grandma Gabby stood before them the crowd grew silent. She delivered a heartfelt plea to stop the senseless killings, with the entire congregation weeping, barely able to hear her trembling voice.*

*Her testimony touched many a heart that day but before the ushers escorted her back to her seat she told the entire congregation "Life is much too precious and my time may be growing near, but when it comes please don't weep for me. When my time comes my life on this earth will not have been cut short, Please don't weep for me".*

# CHAPTER 35

## THE CONVERSATION

### Leaning on the Lord

*God's Calling in All of Our Lives is a tremendous feeling of Spiritual Freedom.*

### God's Sits High and Looks Low

Laying down your burdens on *Him* is what *He* wants from *All of Us*.

There is no doubt *He* shared a *Precious Moment* like this with *Ms Henrietta*.

Throughout the *Good Book, the Scriptures* reveal countless stories of *His Chosen Ones*.

With her relentless community service, a *Scared Boomstick, Bible in Hand* and *Her* unconditional devoted *Love for Her beloved Sunnydale Community, Ms Henrietta* more than fulfilled the *Lord's* plan for *Her* meeting his acceptance into the *Gates of Heaven*.

There were many days she could barely muster up the strength to perform her *God Given* responsibilities, to comfort those in need.

Oftentimes burdens get heavy sometimes and we can't find peace of mind, but all that we have to do is fall down on our knees and thank the *Lord* for hearing our pleas.

One day there had to be a tranquil solitary moment when the *Good Lord and Ms Henrietta shared this Conversation and Words between them.*

*Before she was called Home.*

*The Lord:* Ya know Henrietta your work down here is done, I have greater plans for you in my Kingdom.

*Ms Henrietta:* These old' bones of mine ache all the time

*The Lord:* Let not your Heart be troubled, for thee who believe in me shall indeed be set free.

*Ms Henrietta:* My Father I just wanna please you and help those in need.

*The Lord:* There are many who have been called.

*Ms Henrietta:* And few who have answered my Father.

*The Lord:* Put down your broomstick my child, toss that walking cane and worn out house robe aside for I have replaced them with a pair of Golden Slippers and a long White Robe.

*Ms Henrietta:* I place my Life in Your Hands my Father

***The Lord:*** You have my Word Dear Child your work down here is done, there will be a better day in the neighborhood for I my child am in the business of making beauty from ashes.

Imagine and visualize in the ***Gates of Heaven, Ms Henrietta*** and ***Sam Cooke*** both looking down on ***Her*** beloved ***Sunnydale Community, smiling and singing together A Change Is Gonna Come.***

### Sometimes Helping Hands

### Need
### A Helping Hand

*Few in the community knew their constant calls for Help was taking an enormous toll on Ms Henrietta's health when she without hesitation responded to their pleas for Help.*

*Having to raise five children on her own was a tremendous task, there was always bad news waiting for when she returned home from helping others in the neighborhood. Her family life was no walk in the park by any means.*

*The compassion and commitment she had for others was her Achilles Heel.*

*Many knew of her physical limitations but kept her emotional vulnerability hidden relying on strong Faith to provide her the strength to Lend a Helping Hand to others.*

*She and women like her never wavered on their will, the desire, the need to help others, but Life's demands on them were enormous, each day they are confronted by insurmountable odds, carrying the woes and needs of the people in their communities on feeble shoulders, barely having the strength to rise each morning but knowing that so many lives were dependant on them.*

# CHAPTER 36

# SUNNYDALE'S "ROC"

## A CALM IN THE STORM KINDA' BROTHER

Randy Ray Minix
*"Trouble will find you, especially if you're
looking for it" Randy Roc Minix*

Al Burleson and Randy Ray Minix

*"Roc was one of those brothers young in age but thought like an old wise man or someone who had been on this earth before"* Glen GT Taylor

The Minix family lived on Santos Street near the Rec Center across from the bus stops where all of the Jr High and High School kids gathered catching the buses to Luther Burbank or Balboa High School.

It was also a place where the parents boarded the 30 Express or 15 Third buses going to work downtown.

*"You won't find brothers and sisters, school kids parents going to and from work standing on bus stops and street corners nowadays times have changed but that's what we did back in the day"*

Roc lives now in Leland Mississippi with his wife Mary, their children and grandchildren and from time to time returns to visit his childhood friends and take a drive thru the old neighborhood.

*"Man time has changed a lot of things in Sunnydale, I just pray the old street stuff, crime and all that comes with it in all of our communities finds another place to lay its ugly head"*

Ola Mae Minix was a kind hearted jovial hard working woman.

She was always who loved to cook and didn't mind her children having company over.

On any day while she was cooking the clatter and slamming of dominoes at the kitchen table didn't disturb her, except for maybe a few choice excitable words, slips of the mouth from the brothers being too serious about their dominology playing.

Randy's grandmother, Sister Minix and my mother were close friends in the Truth.

His sisters Diane, Dolores, Elmira and Noreen were joys to be around. Undoubtedly this joyfulness was part of their DNA, all except Noreen who looked you over from head to toe trying her best to insult you, in good fun but she was quick to pin on you one of her silly names for everyone who stepped inside the front door.

The sisters could play the dozens with the best of them. But they kept a watchful eye out on their little brother and his choice of side kicks. Al Chop and I were always welcomed in the Minix household.

*"Randy moved at a slower pace in his thoughts. I just wished he was a little faster in the 440 relay" Glen Chop Porter*

*"We were always told bad news will beat you home. Mom wasn't lying about that. Many of time us kids playing doing something stupid, ole man trouble beat us home knocking at the front door waiting in the living room with our Mothers eating our dinner before we got home"*

His thoughts of the new changes going on in Sunnydale run parallel with his childhood experiences.

He was one of the early members of the Sons Of Sunnydale.

*"I am all in for the new development and what the changes can bring to the neighborhood, but my hope is that a little of the old remains there, for the people and families who still have ties to the neighborhood it's important that Sunnydale's history of neighbors helping neighbors remain intact. Sunnydale has a rich history like many of our communities"*

Roc was a calming influence in the neighborhood, well liked and a deep thinker.

He would look at a brother contemplating mayhem straight in the eye then calmly tell the brother *"something just ain't right about what*

263

*you're planning on doing"* A remarkable characteristic for a young brother.

*"I truly think when we were growing up in Sunnydale, the four of Alvin, Lil Jeff, Chop and me were allergic to the police, until we started playing Pop Warner sports with the Police Athletic League. That's what kept the four of us out of trouble"*

Roc possessed the characteristics of an old gray headed bearded biblical wise man.

*"I just wasn't raised that way, it didn't make no sense at all getting into real trouble, Ola Mae wasn't having none of that stuff from me. So I gave that crazy criminal stupid behavioral shit second, third and fourth thought. Believe me bruh, moms wasn't having it"*

His calming influence made a tremendous impact on Al, Chop and me.

*"You know most of the things we did ripping and running through the neighborhood, we never gave it a second thought. We weren't into doing dumb things, had no desire to run the streets and follow in the footsteps of some dudes that got caught up in the streets. Hell we were goofing off being silly but not stupid. A lot of the brothers were out to prove themselves, make a name for themselves and all they did was end up in the criminal justice system or on drugs. Our pockets might have been empty but we were not stuck on stupid"* the four of us had our minds on nothing but getting into ghetto mischief"

He was so right in his determination to *steer us away* from following in the footsteps of the brotha's who took to the streets *snatching purses, bugarizing* leading lives of *criminal intent.*

No matter how hard we tried, the four of us fell drastically short of coming in contact with the law.

*"The things we did playing ripping and running through the neighborhood we never gave it a second thought. We never got into any real trouble either. Ghetto games are not in any school yard activity program playbook. Hell I cannot remember all the things we did, we was having too much fun to remember it all"*

We were cut out for *ghetto mischief,* our *forte* was limited to *stealing salami and cheese* from *Mayfair Market,* then riding' off into the sunset on our bicycles.

*"I cannot to recall any brotha's doing 5-to10 years for stealn' cheese and crackers".*

The four of us were a click, and have enjoyed a *lifetime camaraderie* that other brotha's our age and some even older yearned to be a part of our crew.

There was always a new candidate being interviewed to join in our *ghetto goof off club.*

Douglas L, Darnell H, Rick B, James "Shorty" H, and 14 year old Hayakafa Tony, who could out drink most of us put together ran the streets with us including the outrageous Steven C whose ghetto escapades and corky behavior more than met the standards we were looking for.

We were the *Temptations,* the *Mimptones* of comedy, always recruiting our version of *Dennis Edwards, Richard Street, Ali Ollie Woodson* to join in the festivities.

*"Chop Steven Al, Lil Jeff and me, started a singing group, called the **Fabulous Antiques, singing oldies but goodies** and at one time called ourselves the **Intelligents,** a name **Chop** bestowed on us, even though he had to repeat kindergarten"*

*"We stuck with the original name not really knowing what an **Antique** was but the name sounded good".*

*"All the young brothers hanging out together were part of a singing group" K Burleson*

**The Bounce** made popular by the **Olympics** was a 2 maybe 3 minute song, **maybe** but with **Al** singing lead and always singing **"one mo' time"** our version was more like 10 minutes long. It was our signature song.

*"We wasn't the best of the groups but we never got booed at the talent shows" Al Burleson*

`Man, we would practice at my house, in the Caracter's living room, the bus stop anywhere but especially in front of **Ms Henrietta house, that woman resting her soul musta** been seriously deaf in one ear because we were terrible".*

The only words to describe our singing were we sounded worse than four screeching tires, or that eerie sound of schoolteachers scraping chalk over a chalkboard and that's not even an adequate description.

**Ms Henrietta** always came to her back window, looked out, smiled and went back to baking us her famous homemade cookies.

*"One of the many perks **we** knew came from hanging outside her door, sitting on those cement parking lot stairs was a magnet for catching some of Sunnydale's finest PYT's".*

Can't help but make you remember every time you hear young street corner groups harmonizing, flashbacks of inner city youngsta's singing their hearts out **growing up with big dreams of becoming recording stars.**

*"I remembered in the beginning the four of us sang so off key the* **black birds and crows** *would come out of the trees, diving at our heads and trying to get us to move on ".*

Sometimes we sang until the neighbors complained, **"go home to ya' momma's house and let me get some sleep**

***Noreen, Roc's*** hyperactive sister called us ***"The Funny Company"***

*"We practiced all night long until our harmony in our own minds we thought was tight, even though The Bounce was now* **15 minutes long***. We used to leave Al on stage by himself singn'* **one mo' time"***.

We kept at it and the results were always a customary thanks for your participation close but no cigar ***third place finish in the Sunnydale Annual talent.***

We were youngsta's who created mischievous ghetto games and played from sunup to sundown or until we got hungry for something to eat.

*"I can't ever remember* **going hungry or being without,** *that's the way it was back in the day".*

Back then in Sunnydale front and back doors were seldom locked, women hung clothes outside and children played without incident, people looked out for one another.

Not a day went by that the four of us, ***Al, Roc, Chop and me*** were not together, the four of us to this day remain inseparable.

*"Back in the day it didn't make no sense at all getting into real trouble, Ola Mae wasn't having none of that stuff from me".*

# CHAPTER 37

## TIGHTER THAN TEN TOES IN A SOCK

*Economic Social and Racial disparities led more than just to finger pointing between Viz Valley the Eichler Homes the Geneva Towers The DALE.*

*Tensions mounted and there were no mediators to broker a peace offering between the neighborhoods, yet there were community leaders like the Geneva Towers Vernon Long, the Eichler Homes Mr Smith who was a homeowner and San Francisco Probation Officer and Sunnydale's Geogre Davis and Tony Harrison who met to address problems and concerns the division was causing.*

*What had been a tolerable unofficial treaty between the neighborhoods was now a bad sign of the times, attitudes were quickly changing, even token relationships soured and pressures were mounting as the communities disassociated themselves from one another and tried to take on their own separate community identities.*

*Sunnydale at the very bottom of the economic/social totem pole, had fewer resources.*

*It was now quite apparent that the people in Viz Valley, the Eichler Homes and Geneva Towers didn't want Sunnydale around.*

*At the **bottom of the totem pole stood Sunnydale with the least and most to lose.***

*Sunnydale had little choice but to stand its ground countering the publicized and physical attacks with slip and move jabs, nothing less.*

*The Community's unpentrateable dormant Community Pride lay unearthed, it had to be resurrected and shared by everyone in the neighborhood.*

***Venturing outside of the community had always been challenging, there was never any known hostility directed at those from the neighborhood just trying to shop buy groceries quality items at Safeway, El Rancho or Mayfair Markets on the other side of Hahn Street.***

***The need to stick together was now greater than the oppressive stereotypes placed on the people and most significantly the need to be there for your neighbor.***

*It was at this the moment when community activist **Tony Harrison, George Davis** and **Ms Frierson, Ms Hopkins** of the EOC and **Ms Rose** at the Sunnydale Community Center and **many others took the bull by the horns, took on the challenges among themselves with help from community** residents to develop a true sense of communityship encouraging residents to look/reach deep within themselves and discover new found **community prideship and joy** "**a Sunnydale against the world attitude**"*

***The people of Sunnydale became "Tighter Than Ten Toes In A Sock"***

269

*"What took place was the separation in those other neighborhoods, a few blocks away. Sunnydale took the brunt of the criticism and blame for something we had little or nothing to do with. This was really the basis for getting the Sons of Sunnydale organized. It was people from Viz Valley, the Eichler Homes and Geneva Towers that started destroying their communities but Sunnydale took the rap. Our needs were basic: just putting food on our tables and the safety of our seniors and children"* **Glen Chop Porter.**

Sunnydale was going to have its own identity, kinship, a prideful walk wherever residents traveled in the city.

*"People could drive and walk through our neighborhood but we had no right being in theirs"* **Robert Butchie Freeman**

When, if someone asked you where you're from, the answer was now a resonating *"We're from Sunnydale! With Pride and Joy!"*

*"In terms of community pride. We were ten times better off than the people of Viz Valley, the Eichler Homes and Geneva Towers, but some of us didn't know that"* **Glen Chop Porter**

Because of this newfound identity, backs started to straighten up, heads were lifted high, there was a new walk in the neighborhood and we could hear people shouting *"We're From Sunnydale"* With Pride and Joy!

*"When the homes in Viz Valley started to look run down and the original people, from the Eichler Homes and Geneva Towers, moved out they were replaced by people from the projects just like us from across town and from different neighborhoods something bad had to happen but we had in Sunnydale longevity and stabilization. Our transitions from wherever we came happened a long time ago"* **Robert Butchie Freeman**

*This was Ms Henrietta's vision not of new buildings but new hearts and communityship, neighborhood pride is what she dreamed of.*

**Davis and Harrison** *took to the streets standing in front of the EOC building, walking through the neighborhood often going door-to-door encouraging brothers to go to school, furthering their educational pursuits.*

*It was Davis who encouraged Victor to enroll in San Francisco State College.*

*He would visit school campuses and talk with the school counselors about tutorial assistance programs and help those residents that were eligible to fill out applications for civil service jobs.*

**Mr Davis** *realized that joblessness triggers decline, depression violence and drug usage so he sought to negotiate with local contractors to hire Sunnydale residents.*

**Ms Frierson, Ms Hopkins and Ms Rose** *started developing community based and family activities, such as field trips, campus visits, youth and young adult groups, talent shows, recreational indoor and outdoor activities, and the Summer Youth Employment Program.*

**Davis and Harrison** *made their daily rounds to Hertz Playground or other areas where the brothers socialized.*

*The mental stigma of being less than quickly evaporated.*

*The physical challenges from neighborhood hoodrats outsiders from other communities, Davis convinced the brothers to not go looking for trouble but to stand up in what they believed in.* **Pride, Family and Communityship.**

*"Sunnydale was always picking itself off the deck and it was Geogre Davis that showed us how" Skip Roberts.*

*Ms Rose extended the hours of the community center and added women groups, art classes, cooking and sewing classes, gardening groups, and black history classes that gave our sisters a sense of strong Sisterhood.*

***Each of these unsung heroes understood the power of community involvement.***

*Ms Rose hired long time resident **Leo Toastie Nelson** as her Recreational Director.*

***Nelson** immediately began organizing ping pong and pool tournaments, talent shows, domino tournaments, and Friday/ Saturday night dances.*

*Entertainment shows featured local bands like **Granny Goose and The Soul Chips, Captain Crunch and The Soul Bunch, Sisters of the Ghetto, Sunnydale's own Levi Bryant and The Riveras, the Promatics** with Sunnydale's own **Warren Wilson** riding high on their R&B hit single **"I Can't Stop You"** and of course one of the most underrated singing groups in the Bay Area. **Sunnydale's pride and joy, The Emotions!***

*Five sharp dressing brothers who could sing their asses off, two of them **Otis" Wiggie' Stroman Smith and Ronald Brown** were from Sunnydale, but the quintette ran into licensing issues with those sisters from Chicago with the same name and **Soul Train's Don Cornilious** in their corner.*

*They were **that close** to making it to the top! But had to change the name of the group.*

***Bernard S, Wiggie's younger brother, Damu and Michael C** formed a younger version of the group and continued the tradition.*

*The Stroman Smith Family* could all sing their sista' **Martha's** voice could put Aretha on notice. I'm serious...

**Damu** went on to fame and to this day is the base singer for **Talk of Da Town** a soulful harmonizing group that has toured the world over singing Doo Wop.

**Although our Emotions** scored a few hits as the **Windjammers and Master Plan,** unfortunately they never garnered the same audiences and musical support to help them reach the top.

I'd place them right up there with Bay Area legendary groups, **The Ballads and the Natural Four** from Oakland, **the Performers, out of Bayview Hunters Point.**

Street Corner singing groups in Sunnydale and throughout the Bay Area were as popular as those trying to make it in Detroit.

Sunnydale's talent shows brought out the best.

Folks came to talent night suited and booted. It was a **"make it or break it"** night in the hood.

Man! The audiences at the Rec Center could be harsh! Boo acts right off the stage! Even with yo' momma in attendance...

The TV Gong Show could not compete with the audiences at the Rec Center.

At **Talent Night**. there wasn't an ounce of pity for those who were shown the door, and most definitely lacking skills to showcase their skill sets.

It didn't take the Rec crowd long to show those without talent needing to polish up their acts on the way out the door.

*Getting booed off the stage was one thing but the embarrassment didn't stop there because if you were booed off the stage, instantly you became the bulk of jokes and a legendary life long neighborhood clown unable to live your dreadful performance down.*

*Lightskinned **Ooh Baby Baby look alike** singing' Smokey Robinson, **Vernon D** always stole the show, walked away every show with the first prize.*

*He had the women squirming in their seats along with a few of those not to mention Sammy sensitive kind of guys, dudes crying out for' mo'.*

*Some people thought **Vernon** was better' looking than his sister' **Daralynn** and bruh that's saying' a helluva lot. A helluva lot!*

***Daralynn** may have been the finest PYT in the Dale, certainly among the top 10 of all-time.*

*Sunnydale had some of the finest if you weren't looking straight ahead walk right into a **telephone pole** looking women in the city,*

***Jimmy and Cindy N, Jackie R, Cheryl P, Cathay S, Anna G, Annette H, Ann P, Reggie B, Marva and Debra T, Patricia H, Jackie F, Sandra F, Darlene B, the Ewing girls, the Minix Sista's, just to name a few.***

*Both **George and Tony** loved sports, they had decent hoop games and athletic abilities and were instrumental in helping to organize Sunnydale football games at Hertz Playground, **the Ole' Young Bowl aka The Needle Bowl which ultimately became Sunnydale's Ghetto Super Bowl.***

***Sunnydale had found its new identity "Tighter Than Ten Toes In A Sock"***

# CHAPTER 38

## SUNNYDALE'S GHETTO SUPER BOWL

*"The only thing missing' was John Madden" Levi Bryant*

*Man **Bowl Day** for years became a Sunnydale tradition and the people in the neighborhood came out in droves to this epic neighborhood gathering. It was inspired by Geogre Davis*

*"If you didn't play in Sunnydale's Ghetto Super Bowl the whole neighborhood talked about **yo' momma' yo' ugly sista' and yo lil' brotha wit' the wooden leg**" Glen Chop Porter*

***"I was playing football at the University of Washington. As soon as I arrived home for the holidays, the fellas was at my house recruiting me for the Big Game" Al Burleson***

*Entire families came to Hertz Park the day of the game.*

*People brought picnic baskets, shared their food and wine, partied hard, played dominoes and music, set up tables and lounge chairs, and sold plates of soul food. It was **Ghetto Fabulous**!*

*It was an honor to play in this game and bragging rights were extremely high.*

*The game always coincided with the climax of the NFL playoffs or Super Bowl so football was definitely in the atmosphere.*

*Oh what a thrill it was seeing **the people dancing to the music,** enjoying themselves, cheering the players on and having the time of their lives.*

*It was a day when Sunnydale was as they say **"able to lay our burdens down"***

***The Ghetto Ole' Young Bowl** pitted a group of shit talkn' street corner White Port and Lemon Juice drink' chain smokin' hangn' on the Front all day ova' the hill way pass their athletic prime brotha's and their I couldn't give a damn attitude about sports in the first place against us youngsters who lived every minute of our days playing street or organized ball.*

*"The older cats I remember would come to the game on full tilt reeking of alcohol, they had been out all night carousing and was in no condition to play tackle football, but the Ghetto Bowl was big time fun" Randy Roc Minix*

*The **Ghetto Bowl** game was all about communityship and brotherhood or for some time to get higher than a kite.*

*One of the legendary statements came from **Levi B "I got the right corner"** he proudly proclaimed trying to play cornerback with a bottle of **White Port** in his hip pocket.*

***"I got the right corner" "I got the right corner"** became his signature statement.*

*After giving up touchdown after touchdown feeling no pain he retired to the sidelines joined in the festivities started playing his congos and felt no shame.*

*To this day we still tease him about that.* **"I got the right corner"**

*The score never mattered but the old cats finally one game got their glory when* **Darrell C ran back an 80 yard kickoff return untouched for a touchdown** *after our entire team collided trying to knock the living hell outta' this always talking' mess Son Of Sunnydale.*

*Anybody but Him,* **DC** *never let us youngsta's forget his one time Ghetto Bowl claim to fame.*

*What he did forget was the score. It must have been* **100 to zilch** *all in the name of* **ghetto fun.** *Ask* **"I got the right corner"** *Levi B, he'll tell ya' bout' it.*

**The Ghetto Ole' Young Bowl** *was all about a wonderful time and a community celebration.*

# CHAPTER 39

# CHOP'S COMMUNITY BLUES

## Down on Hahn Street

## with

## Glen "Chop" Porter Son of Sunnydale

### *It was Chop who coined the phrase "Tighter Than Ten Toes In A Sock"*

*"He was always coming up with those Ghetto Phrases. It was like he woke up in the morning and came outside and had a new Phase for the Day" Glen GT Taylor*

*"At the domino table, anywhere just chopping it up with the fellas, Chop was likely to say anything that sometimes didn't make no sense at all, but when we thought about it later, you know what? What he said did make sense" Al Burleson*

*"Glen had a poetic side about him. Maybe not in the traditional sense but in an off the wall creative street corner spoken word way of expressing his thoughts" Randy Roc Minix*

*"Glen was one step ahead of his thoughts and two steps behind what came out of his mouth" Eric Peters*

*"Brainstorming was by far not Chop's forte. He came up with some out of this world capers like when he tied a chain to the back of his sidekick's truck, then they wrapped it around a phone booth to get the coins out. They revved up the truck drove off dragging only the phone booth with broken glass falling everywhere. Damn fools didn't realize the phone itself was not connected to the phone booth" Glen GT Taylor*

*It was at Olivet Baptist Church before a packed house during the funeral services for Sunnydale's Danny Danko Doyle he delivered the phrase **Tighter Than Ten Toes In A Sock.***

*The two of them were long time friends and their relationship grew tighter with Sunnydale's decline and adaptation of its notorious nickname the Swampe' D*

*Chop loved to listen to message songs in particular one of his favorites Donny Hathaway's The Ghetto and Curtis Mayfield's We People Who Are Darker Than Blue.*

*"He would walk around Sunnydale with an address book full of girls phone numbers he got outta the phone book, call them up and practice his lines on them" Randy Roc Minix*

*"Chop had some poetic thoughts that Jeff used to write down on paper and we would go out to these red light garage house parties and use these corny lines. It was funny when two of us were slow dancing with a girl close to each other or danced with the same girl who had just heard the same doo funny rap a few minutes ago" Al Burleson*

**When he heard that we were writing *A Song For Ms Henrietta*, he asked if I could help him with some thoughts he told me were circulating in his head.**

**"I just keep getting these deep thoughts about Sunnydale the people and the Community Blues Down on Hahn Street" he said, and I'd like to bounce this idea across your head" Those were his exact words.**

**Over the telephone the two of us created Chop's Community Blues Down on Hahn Street**

### Chop's Community Blues
### Down on Hahn Street

Nothing but the Blues Down on Hahn Street.

I stood on the corner where the brothers played congas and drank their wine. I looked out for my brothers but couldn't recognize any friends of mine.

I passed through the DALE just the other day and everything was long gone including the green lawns.

Grassy green lawns that felt like new carpet the only thing that remained was the Little Village Market.

Standing on the corner where we use to hang out

Nothing but prideless faces, a community in doubt

A place where people don't seem to care what Life's all about

I stood on the corner where we use to hang out.
Prideless faces, a community in doubt.

Makes me wonder why Life can be so cruel. No children at the bus stop waiting to go to school.

Remembering the days we swam at John McLaren Pool

Sunnydale and Hahn, where we hung out. Now just a place for those who are strung out

A place where people don't seem to care what Life's all about

Prideless faces, a community in doubt.

Circumstance and hardship outsiders say may be the blame. Living in Sunnydale, there is no need to be ashamed.

I stood on the corner where the brothers played congas and drank their wine. I looked out for my brothers but couldn't find any friends of mine.

Gone were days when we didn't have to lock our doors.

The only thing the same is Sunnydale is still poor.

Times have changed, it's not like it used to be sadly anymore. Where the brothers played congoes, drank wine in front of Black's Store

A community devastated lying down, damn near drowning in a Swamp, a land so dense with attitudes as tense everything old worn out like a rusty barbed wire fence. Life at the Bottom makes no sense.

An atmosphere that breeds nothing just self defeat nothing but the Blues Down on Hahn Street

The Blues is something we all know about it. Been here forever. Years before Covid.

Not even a protective mask can save us from the pandemic, Community Blues is here to stay, it's in the game to win it.

Ghetto Blues. The bearer of bad news. Nothn' but the Blues Down on Hahn Street, like wearn' shoes too small, guaranteed to hurt your feet. Nothn' but the Blues Down on Hahn Street.

A giver of nothn' a taker of all hope. Have ya' head spinin' like the Devil on dope. Offer you the world on a bogus promissory note.

Nothn' but the Blues Down on Hahn Street. Nothing to do, but groove' to a ghetto beat, nothing, all around just self defeat nothing but the Blues Down on Hahn Street

An unwanted guest is Community Blues, it comes into your house without invitation, stays through the night without a reservation.

Laughing in the faces of those down on their knees who can only Pray, Lord have Mercy Please. Be better off standing in line for some government cheese.

Suck the Life right outta you. no need to fight. The Blues is everywhere all through the night.

No food to eat so you put ya' children to sleep. Mothers too sad to cry, all they do is weep. Daddy's out in the night, making babies they won't keep.

Awful stench fumigates the air, feeding a baby spoiled milk left from a broken down frigidaire. Community Blues seldom sleeps and never cares.

Never is He Community Blues, the bearer of good news, even on the first of the month He'll bring ya the Blues.

Like a fly on the wall, Community Blues knows it all, like the stories of those who died without writing their Life Scriptures on the wall. If Hahn Street could talk, Community Blues would tell it all.

Of wanna b pimps, coulda' been playaz' to drop a dime on their brotha's, nothn' but haters, to hungry kids with no food in the refrigerator, to the hot lil' hoochie momma' and the guys who laid her, to false prophets claimn' it will be greata' lata.

Nothn' but Community Blues, bad news down on Hahn Street.

Shoeless souls groovn' to the beat, nothn' but Community Blues Down on Hahn Street.

Ghetto street corna' romance in times of despair, while time stands still, Community Blues doesn't care.

Troubles and hardships have nothn' to reveal, like a grand jury indictment the contents are sealed, like the brotha' on death roll praying' for an appeal, to Community Blues it's no big deal.

I stood on the corner where the brothers played congas and drank their wine. I looked out for my brothers but couldn't recognize any friends of mine.

For day to day survival the people in the Swamp compete, nothn' but Community Blues Down on Hahn Street.

*Glen "Chop" Porter*

# CHAPTER 40

# POCKETS FILLED WITH POVERTY
## A Poverty Poem

In a darkened place you'll find no applause.

Thinking Ghetto Live is Living Large Ain't Nothn' But a Ghetto Facade

Dig deep down in your pockets like a gravedigger searchn' for gold and you'll find nothn' but balls of lent.

Frantically searchn' through crevices in an old worn out couch, you'll find nothn', not even a red cent.

Landlord three days from wanting his rent.

Waiting for another check welfare hasn't been sent.

Pockets turned inside out not even a ball of lent.

In three days the man's gonna want his rent,

Nothin' in yo' pockets, not even a red cent.

Open up the icebox, a stale piece of cold baloney says close the refrigerator door I'm here all alone, nothing' to eat in here not even a bone.

Might be better off boiling a pot of water and filling it with stones.

So hungry are you, your stomach just wants to be left alone.

Dreams of eating a bowl of cereal are only dreams of defeat, no such thing as a Breakfast of Champion out there on the streets.

We send our children to school hungry expecting them to learn.

Nothing in their stomachs it's food that they yearn

empty stomachs heard from miles away, the free lunch at school their only meal today.

Times between meals are not often great. I can't help but feel their hunger, stomachs growling, moaning, grumbling, rumbling worse than the Loma Prieta Quake.

A bowl of Furina to greet you when you wake. no such thang as Shake N Bake. A Happy Birthday without a cake

A darkened place with no applause.

Yet there are those who claim they are living large. Ain't Nothn' But a Ghetto Facade.

Frantically searchn' through crevices, you'll find nothn', not even a red cent.

Dig deep down in your pockets nothn' just balls of lent.

Better hurry, find yet another excuse, tell the Man you can't pay the rent.

# CHAPTER 41

## SUNNYDALE'S LIFE CHANGING DIAGNOSIS

Poverty has been around for ages, our Lord and Savior himself was born in a manger.

The effects of poverty look very much like the symptoms of a disease, physical health conditions and societal conditions associated are believed to be important risk factors.

Childhood poverty is associated with low self esteem and development delays.

Without a doubt there are many contributing factors to the widespread of the disease, and its impact on our neighborhoods.

Its related symptoms are however preventable and treatable.

There is a huge difference between being poor and being temporary without.

Like those with money who are spiritually poor and those without money who are gratefully rich.

The effects of the disease have reached epidemic proportions throughout the inner city communities.

The disease has no remorse, does not discriminate, and leaves an indelible mark on generations upon generations.

Doctor's have no prescribed medications to rid our communities of the disease.

Visiting the community health center will not eradicate the problem, nor its symptoms of despair and hopelessness.

The San Francisco Mayor's Office of Housing and Community Development and its supporters recognized that Poverty being Poor is not a fatal disease, and began developing a Life Changing Diagnosis to address the problem in Sunnydale.

The developers have sought out second opinions, a Plan B approach to develop effective strategies to implement a comprehensive gameplan addressing the needs of those in the community, a door-to-door street advocacy approach to spread the word encouraging residents to become involved in the recovery of their community.

With residential involvement the chances for recovery are promising as expressed by the residents of the community themselves.

If the people's voices remain silent the opportunities for complete Revitalization are nil.

Too many community developments have failed miserably in this respect by not valuing the concerns of the people.

Putting in place shiny new things without the community's input, values and visions rapidly become broken, worn down objects of decline in a short period of time.

Our communities are fragile and require careful care and handling like most fragile things.

The people in the communities need to be fed sustainable nourishment and not given promissory notes of false hope and far fetched dreams.

The values of the community must come first and foremost, the voices of the people must be heard.

The need to put food on the table, clothes on our backs, a roof over our heads, a safe neighborhood to live in, is paramount to the well being of the community.

Try explaining the cause and effect of Poverty versus Being Poor, the differences to a household of hungry mouths, a slum landlord, bill collectors and a child on the verge of going down life's wrong path.

I am sure you will agree, by far this is not, and will not be the topic of discussion around dinner tables in the inner city communities.

Some claim poverty is inherent others say poverty is conditional, but all would agree that it is in one way or another a dreadful disease.

The Life Changing antidote has to come from within our communities.

Their solution is to empower people, help residents develop a sustainable sense of purpose, a sense of community, a sense of ownership.

There are countless philosophical differences, controversies, opinions that Poverty and being Poor are not one in the same and in some instances are as different as night and day.

Scholars argue that Poverty is a psychological state of mine.

Being Poor living in Poverty are intertwined, however where the family and community's basic needs are concerned the only real things that matter is the basic need to meet their essential needs.

Our Family's, Our Community's do not survive on philosophical differences, they have never eaten Opinionated Poverty Poor Sandwiches...

It does not matter to the Family where the Bread comes from but only that it reaches the table.

As far as the people are concerned, it doesn't matter who builds the house, upgrades the buildings around them, just as long as the house gets built without collapsible materials.

Undoubtedly there is a huge difference between being poor and being temporary without.

Living in the Ghetto does not make you Ghetto.

More importantly Poverty and its related symptoms are however preventable and treatable.

# CHAPTER 42

## DOWN BUT NOT OUT

Hard times, neglect and hopelessness had Sunnydale on the robes gasping for air, clenching, holding on for dear life, about to lose its communityship, pride and will to fight back.

Like a fighter's corner man. Many begged Life's referee to stop the onslaught, the devastation. throw in the towel, accept defeat.

Take it like a Man, take it like a Woman, take it like a Community.

There were those who refused to cash in on their doubts that Sunnydale could withstand the brutality of its oppressive, life threatening opponents.

Don't let go was the motto of San Francisco's Mayor's Office and the Drive that motivated Ms Henrietta to help her community get up off the deck.

The exteriors of Community's can fall down but The People who reside in them can Get Up as long as there is something or someone there to Catch Them When They Fall-Encourage Them To Get Back Up.

Within all of us there are unquestionable remarkable qualities of unconditional compassion to help others-a deep desire to survive against all odds.

Ms Henrietta was that courageous community street fighter, the epitome of a champion being Down But Not Out.

She was a proponent of looking up in times of despair.

She bore the tears of troubled times; she wore the skirts of a woman so meek in stature but so big in pride and love for her beloved Sunnydale Community.

Ms Henrietta was Sunnydale's campsite light, a tough critic of herself in a world of shadows and dimly lit streets.

There are many people who have succumbed to we deserve less than attitudes, lost hope and seem not to care-but often these are the same individuals underneath their faceless surface exteriors are the very people who really do care.

They possess a deep rooted self centeredness for their fellow man. These are the very people who are the first to respond during times of need

We all have the rugged strength to endure despair and overcome adversity and the God Given Ability To Fight Back and get up off the deck.

The Man-The Woman who is temporary without is not poor.

Being poor is a Spiritual Deficiency - a self inflicted condition of defeat.

We do not have to live in a world where we are limited because of our circumstances.

It's not a physical condition but a mental one to keep going when the odds are against you.

# CHAPTER 43

## NOT THE LAST LAP

*Harold Williams, "Sunnydale now has the chance going from last place to first place"*

**In 1960, 28 year old Abebe Bikila amazed the world when, unknown and unheralded, he won the Olympic marathon.**

**He attracted the world's attention not only being the first East African to win a medal, but also because he ran the event barefoot.**

*His decision to run in the race bare feet, he said: "I wanted the world to know that my country Ethiopia, has always won with determination and heroism."*

This kind of *"against all odds' courageousness* is what **Ms Henrietta's** devoted unconditional spirit and dreams inspired the writer and contributors of this composition.

The beneficiaries of this creation we hope will be those marginalized communities across this nation and a prelude to community development marathons necessary for the revitalization and empowerment of the people from these neglected, isolated and often forgotten neighborhoods.

Revitalization in Sunnydale can serve as a blueprint for developers, and have a long lasting marathon impact on community based residents and at-risk communities.

By far this kind of vigorous community activism and development is *Not The Last Lap.*

The **Sons of Sunnydale** congratulate and acknowledge the efforts of the unsung *trailblazers for their commitment to implement change in the Sunnydale community.*

*The contributions of all those responsible for the making and development of a revised Sunnydale Community will be treasured and respected by those who share in this magnificent undertaking.*

*Along the way there is no doubt the San Francisco Mayor's Office of Housing and Community Development, the vast developers and organizers were met with insurmountable odds and challenges throughout the project and process.*

*Change is often hard to embrace and by far too many community development promises have fallen way short of providing proposed beneficial economic and social changes.*

*At long last, thanks to San Francisco Mayor's Office of Housing and Community Development, and Mercy Housing, change is in the air in Sunnydale.*

*We encourage the readers of this composition to step forward and be willing to share in the vision and the dreams of Ms Henrietta.*

# CHAPTER 44

# MANY RIVERS TO CROSS

*MLK once said "Our basic mobility should not be from a smaller ghetto to a larger one"*

Dr. King's prolific statement exemplifies that the people who face the greatest obstacles to live in communities that are safe and provided with vast opportunities for self sufficiency and equality have no place to go but up.

We must understand and believe in ourselves that the deck is only stacked against us when we let circumstance dictate our well being.

The road to economic independence has many detours, but can be successfully navigated if we know the destination we are headed in.

We must embrace the true meaning of the protest songs in the south when freedom marchers were hosed down, beaten attacked by vicious police dogs but kept on marching, singing *"I ain't gonna let nobody turn me around"*

It's not how fast we get to our destinations just as long as we get there. No doubt we have *Many Rivers To Cross.*

We must rely thoroughly on sensible decisions, planning and realistic approaches turning our failures inside out realizing that success is just failure turned inside out.

The signs of hope are all around us. We got no place to go but upward bound, and if we keep on moving in the right direction there will not be many more of the *Many Rivers To Cross.*

## No More Backwards Thinking
## Time For Moving Ahead

Politicians and greedy developers have dramatically defaulted on bogus proposed revitalization proposals in our inner city communities.

*THE SF HOPE REBUILDING PROJECT IS IMPROVING THE LIVES IN PUBLIC HOUSING COMMUNITIES BY RELYING ON RESIDENT VOICES TO BE HEARD AND THE PEOPLE NEEDS VALUED.*

*THIS INVESTMENT IN THE PEOPLE BUILDS TRUST AND HAS A SIGNIFICANT IMPACT ON THE RESIDENTS AND THE COMMUNITY AT LARGE.*

Historically, in many of our communities new development has fallen way short of proposed plans and developers have been exposed through lies and repeated promises that have produced little or nothing.

*That almost prehistoric and general philosophy does not exist in the Sunnydale Revitalization Project.*

*Fear of outside influence mismanagement and mainly trust is not evident in Sunnydale, where developers have taken the necessary steps to collaborate with the community respecting the needs and concerns of the people, sharing with them the value of community input and collaboration that are essential to the well being, safety and economic development of their community.*

It's a difficult task. For years, proposed outcomes of new opportunities have been tossed around, goals have fallen way short and communities have been left without explanation.

Developers who have committed these falsehoods are undeniably responsible for making amends.

Their anticipation, their aspirations have produced nothing but apprehension. Politicians and pocket hungry developers are humanely in debt to our communities.

They have created a mistrust among residents, bitter feelings towards outsiders that will not go away too soon.

Our communities have long been inundated with drugs and sedated by development, so much that community leaders in low income communities are no longer overly enthusiastic about revitalization projects.

Our community leaders through trial and error have embraced tangible well defined sound mental approaches to what needs to be done in our communities,

We no longer trust or are willing to invest the future of our children and our communities in the hands of get rich quick fix development.

Our motto is simply *"No More Backwards Thinking Time For Moving Ahead"*

No longer will we rely on, invest or place our dreams, visions and futures in the scheming hands of development who have turned our hopes and dreams into nightmares.

*The Sunnydale Revitalization Project has more than embraced the communities dire concerns that there is no longer the need for them to be looking backwards through the rear view windows and therefore the developers share in the belief there is "No More Backwards Thinking Time For Moving Ahead"*

*Together Towards*
*A New Day A New Sunnydale*

# CHAPTER 45

## OH HAPPY DAY

From inside the walls of *Sto' Front Churches, the voices of Sto' Front Preachers* across this country and their pleas for community engagement are being heard.

The words of the Sunnydale *Sto' Front Preacher on Sunnydale and Hahn Streets* pleas for change resonate through the community and are alive with significance today.

There's a meeting way over there of *Sunnydale Brothers and Sisters* in the *Heavens* above with *Ms Henrietta* leading the *Heavenly Choir Singing and Praising The Lord's Name.*

Change had made its way to Sunnydale.

*There's a New Day-A New Community in a New Sunnydale.*

No doubt *Ms Henrietta* is smiling down leading the cheers and joyful tears on her beloved *Sunnydale Community.*

*Kudo's* to *the San Francisco's Mayor's Office* and the courageous community development soldiers of good fortune for their relentless humanitarian efforts to bring revitalization to the people living in the Sunnydale community.

Their task building new housing was *not an easy one* and their work to engage a diverse population of community residents still requires a *stick-to-ice-tive door-to-door campaign* designed to foster community pride and resident participation but they are proving worthy of the task..

Let those who have posted countless videos on *YOUTube* depicting the community as a crisis and unsaintly place - replace that negative energy with creative juices - proudly telling people of *A New Day-A New Sunnydale*

*The Praises have gone up The Blessings have come Down*

In order to help the residents grasp the magnitude of these new changes they must see more than new buildings and construction going on around them.

The community must embrace a true feeling of fellowship and trust to share in the dreams, plans and visions proposed.

**The San Francisco Mayor's Office** has thrown out a **Life Preserver** to those on board a sinking Communityship-that all the people of **Sunnydale** have to do is reach out and grab ahold of this merciful **Lifeline...**

*A Prayer for all of Sunnydale*
**Heavenly Father We Come Before You This Day**

*Heavenly Father,* May resistance, leadership, community involvement and concern sit high atop the mantles in each and every home in the community.

Let the people resuscitate themselves with unconditional love and support for their neighbors and help breathe life back into their own community.

May the residents develop insatiable appetites, an unquenchable thirst to take pride in the **Newness** around them and share in the core values of **Revitalization in Our Community.**

Let the efforts of communityship not be spontaneous but employ dedicated individuals who care deeply about the people, the families in our community.

May the people accept the courage to change the things they can., and strive for a better day then shout with joy and embrace *A New Day in their Community and sing along with Ms Henrietta OH HAPPY DAY... Amen*

# CHAPTER 46

# WE ARE FAMILY

## By

## Otis "Bubba" Hughes

*It's A Family Affair*

Pleased am I too share these words of inspiration to all:

First and foremost people need to realize all of our communities and families are linked together. *We Are Family.*

We moved from Crocker Amazon over the hill to Sunnydale in 1955 and our relationship with the Harris Family is long standing.

*My Mother and Ms Henrietta* were true friends.

That's why the two of them made a sacred bond to *Sing* at the funeral services of one another, whoever would depart this *ole' earth first.*

As youngsters our families grew up together, sharing in the good times and comforting one another in the sad times.

Ms Henrietta lived a long life. There was a lot of *Life in that Woman. A Community Saint dressed in a thick wrap around robe, nightgown and house slippers.*

*If our journey has touched your heart then all of who contributed to our story we say to each of you there is no need to shed any tears of sadness because that's not Ms Henrietta what she would have wanted us to do.*

Her compassion was *God Given* and *His Will* was to look after others.

So many of our brothers, sisters have been called and made their way to the *Heavens Above they are truly missed.*

Hard times and circumstances have led to downfalls and demise, taking with it *Many of a Good Man, Many of a Good Woman, Many from a Good Family.*

Too many of our brothers and sisters got caught up in the fast life traveling down the wrong roads, and are not here to share in this glorious moment, but they are *Here in the Spirit a*nd shall not be *Forgotten.*

Sometimes it is so hard to let go of our past, but it is so necessary for us that are here to reserve a *Special Place* in our *Hearts for those Special Memories and those Special People.*

Every community can benefit from our story and those people who now reside in Sunnydale can share in the *Sunnydale Family tradition of neighbors helping neighbors.*

It is so very important that we link *the Old with the New for* all of our communities and families are linked together. *We Are Family.*

I encourage you all to stop, look, listen and embrace this untold story of *A Community Saint Ms Henrietta, dressed in a thick wrap around robe, nightgown and house slippers.*

Pleased I am to share with you and be a part of this wonderful journey back to the place where I grew up. *It's A Family Affair*

*Otis Bubba Hughes*

# CHAPTER 47

# SUNNYDALE'S REUNION

## Hope That We Can Be Together Soon

*Family reunions date back to emancipation when formerly enslaved people sought out family they were separated from while enslaved.*
A Continuous Celebration

GETTING TOGETHER AGAIN AT THE
SUNNYDALE REUNION

The emergence of the Sunnydale Reunion according to organizers long-time and former residents *Ann Pietre and Debra LaBlanc* was first designed to help reunite, restore and develop healthy community partnerships with the neighborhood's past residents, new families and organizers to build strong relationships and viable foundations for future generations.

Countless others have made it their mission to reunite their community by bringing together those residents from the past with those individuals who reside in Sunnydale today.

The two women and others began to host Sunnydale Reunion at the Rec Center and other venues depending on their availability.

No matter where the reunion was held the organizers placed emphasis on developing a *continuous celebration of communityship.*

*We encourage you all to come to our next reunion and celebrate Sunnydale's rich history, and pay homage to those who have passed away while we unconditionally welcome those that are new to the Sunnydale community.*

*The DJ'S will blast music from the past bringing back golden, funky chicken, popcorn, the skate, the swim, the mash potatoes, the four corners and always entertaining the electric slide dancing memories for community folk on the dance floor dancing their assess' off. Twistin' the night away. What a beautiful sight.*

On the day of the reunion, excitement and community pride runs deep.

The gathering is filled with balloons and monogrammed T-shirts.

The culinary highlight of the event is men, women and children sitting around banquet tables holding hands as the oldest man at the reunion is called upon to Bless the food. *What a delight!* ...

Reunions have now been identified as effective ways to engage and communicate valuable information critical to the survival of low

***The Sons and Sisters, the organizers of Sunnydale Reunion*** undoubtedly has become an indispensable resource for empowerment and guidance, and in turn, recognized the event to help fosterhope, empowerment, community awareness, strength, leadership and stability.

*A shout out to all.* ***Come to our next reunion and celebrate Sunnydale's rich history.***

# CHAPTER 48

# WORDS OF INSPIRATION

*Harold Williams, Sunnydale now has the chance going from last place to first place*

*Kathy Frierson, We only hope our story finds a soft place in the hearts of communities like our Sunnydale was*

*Coyle Jefferson, Without struggle there is no change. Changes are happening in Sunnydale*

*Skip Roberts, The organizers deserve a high five the people deserve a badge of honor, they both deserve each other*

*Gloria Ann Pitre, People have a right to embrace their history. Ours was a Magical Place in Time*

*Thomas Warren, Pride in our community has been restored*

*Melvin Pitre, The new neighborhood was not built with a deck of playing cards. I don't think the walls now will come tumbling down*

*James Nelson, Every community has the ability to come together and be a system of support for the people who live there*

*Annette Hughes, Things haven't changed overnight but I am sure the people there now are waking up feeling much better about themselves and their community*

*Otis "Bubba" Hughes, Hopefully drive by's are being replaced with scenic and safe drive throughs*

*Leon Booker, Not only is the smell of fresh paint in the air, but there is a fragrance of hope and change in the community*

*LaFrance Graves, Look at Sunnydale now on the way up. Way up*

*Eric Peters, Let the children be the beneficiaries of Sunnydale's revitalization*

*Glen "Chop" Porter, The community never got the credit it deserved now Sunnydale can be the talk of the town*

*Kermit, Al, Val and Lisa Burleson, So long and goodbye to the old, and we welcome the new. How proud we are, today there's hope in our beloved community*

*Randy 'Roc' Minix, It's been a long time coming people from the past are just as proud and happy for the community*

*Levi Bryant, My folks are still out there I can feel more relaxed knowing that things are getting better for them*

*Robert Taylor, Gotta keep praying, gotta keep moving on ahead, no more backward thinking, time for moving ahead*

*Tyrone Ferguson, Alot remains to be seen but the community, the people are off to a good start getting back on their feet again*

*Robert "Buchie" Freeman, I am proud to be apart of the old, grateful to witness the new*

*Glen GT Taylor, Love what their doing out there makes me proud to tell people I grew up in Sunnydale*

*Randy Campbell, This is why our story is well worth being told*

*Walk With Me*

*Towards a dream to bring our community together. May the dark clouds darkened days give way to brighter days.*

*Change cannot happen without struggle and sacrifice. We don't have to do it alone. The seeds of change have been planted.*

*Soon we will see them blossom and spread beautiful fragrances of joyfulness, giving us a new identity, and a new way of life.*

*There's a difference maker in all of us worth being excited about.*

*Walk With Me Towards This Dream*

# Don't Let Go Of Your Dreams

*Realists* are those who don't give up. *Dreamers* sometimes just need a little encouragement to believe. *Realists* are not *Dreamers*

While dreamers are more on the impulsive side, ***realists*** are more stubborn to see things out.

***Ms Henrietta*** was not only both, but a true visionary dedicated to shaping the future of her community.

More than anything ***Ms Henrietta*** was a ***Humble Servant.***

Her dreams of Sunnydale being a community that refused to survive on bread crumbs, accept handouts and do without their basic needs was evident in the groceries she took to families needing help putting food on the table.

She never complained about her life and her environment, she had a cheesy grin and encouraged the people to Dream big, to look beyond the obvious to reach for the moon and if they fell short of their goals, they'd land among the stars.

Dreams are very important in Life.

Sunnydale's well being meant the world to ***Ms Henrietta.***

She believed our future would not be decided behind closed doors or in a conference board room but through neighbors helping neighbors.

That was the driving force behind her door to door street advocacy.

She was a fierce fighter, no ordinary woman, no ordinary trailblazer, bold and beautiful, softer than Charman.

Because of her and so many others and their unconditional compassion, diehard efforts many individuals in the community reached their potential.

**"Don't Let Go Of Your Dreams"** she used to say walking through the neighborhood.

She went to troubled spots, hangouts and hidden cuts in the Dale, places where the brothers and sisters felt scared of the cutts hideouts, places they thought no one could find them, but **Ms Henrietta** had that intuitive old school motherly **GPS** and knew just where to find them.

The Lord, they say, moves in mysterious ways. Her Unshakeable Faith was her Guiding Light

She was often in pursuit of the brothers, the sisters hiding out in cuts, the ones who needed her the most, the ones on the verge of slipping through the cracks.

She held court in some of the most unsavory places a person could imagine.

You always knew when she had penetrated the perimeter because the brothers and sisters would end up taking their embarrassment out on one another venting and arguing like two dogs behind a picket fence with no passerby to bark at.

**Ms Henrietta** without scolding them, with her wildly grin would simply walk away smiling knowing she had touched them with her healing hands.

She had an amazing ability to fit in where she could get in,

Her sense of community was not flawed. A firm believer in her people, her community, her family and her dreams that Sunnydale could be a better place to live for all of its beautiful children.

Until her final breath she never *"Let Go Of Her Dreams"*

## FROM HEAVENS WAY

*When Henrietta, Her Royal Court, the Sons and Sista's of Sunnydale smiled down from Heavenly Way on their Beloved Community they saw Revitalization, New Faces and an Oasis in the Swampe D, a Glorious Garden Paradise with the people of Sunnydale Embracing All of God's Glory and all that God has to offer them*

## The End

## Every Kid In Sunnydale Played Outside The Recreation Center Sitting Atop Benny "The Bear" Bufano

*Not a day went by that I didn't spend time riding on the Bear in front of the Recreation Center. I think I still have a few of the bumps and bruises to remind me"* **Kathy Stewart**

### *Parting Comments From*
### *The Sons and Sista's of Sunnydale*

**Coyle J,** *I think our story is no less than a masterpiece*

**Melvin P,** *The playground, the pride and the people that's what it was about.*

**Ann P,** *Sunnydale a place so magical*

**Leon B,** *People pitched in, that's how I remember growing up in the neighborhood. It was community first.*

**Bubba H,** *We had some damn good times*

**Thomas W,** *Delighted am I to share these priceless reflections*

**Al B,** *Love it OG, make Sunnydale great again*

**T Ferguson,** *Man you delivered the word*

**Butchie F,** *Damn forgot about some of those things we use to do*

**Eddrenna P,** *Now I realize how special a place was Sunnydale*

**Burl G,** *It feels good to go back and I am so proud of the community where we grew up, ain't nothing' like back in the day.*

**Bubba H,** *May cruise through the Dale this weekend*

**Maxine H,** *Hard to hold back the tears, feels like yesterday today*

**Levi B,** *Thanks bruh for taking us back to the Dale*

**Lafrance G,** *Sunnydale is always welcome in my house*

**Roc,** *Feels like going home Jeff*

**Fred C,** *Man I remember when Sunnydale had two churches*

**Wille F,** *Wow! We had some crazy ass times back in the day*

**Robert T,** *Ms Henrietta was Sunnydale's very own Sadie*

**Brian T,** *I didn't grow up in the hood, but now I wished I would have*

**Al B.** *Jeff the Guru*

**TC,** *Makes me wonder if the Little Village is open right now*

**Thomas W,** *Brother brother brother my hats off to you Darro*

**Ann P,** *Ms Henrietta cared for all of us. She was our Heart and Soul*

**Robert T,** *Like that part about the school of life bruh*

**Fred C,** *Still got the scabs and scars on my knees from sliding down them hills*

**Annette H,** *Beautiful brotha' beautiful*

**Coyle J,** *Can't tell you how proud I am of you lil' brotha'*

**Butchie F,** *Y'all ain't never gonna let me forget that bull....t Are you?*

**T Ferguson,** *Forgot about them dogs that use to chase us*

**Roc,** *Feels great to go back to Sunnydale*

**Chop,** *Man is that you outside my house asking Pops can I come outside and play?*

**Bubba H,** *The Hot Tamale Man, I can hear him now yellen' Hot Tamale Hot! Tamale!*

**Skip R,** *Wow! From the top on the hill to the Front, I remember the neighborhood*

**Brian T,** *Y'all never paid to get into the Cow Palace*

**Levi B,** *I still got the right corner!*

**Lafrance G,** *Haven't been back to Sunnydale til' right now.*

**Roc,** *Brother Jeff you went door to door inside the houses and sat down in the living rooms to write this piece*

**Kermit B,** *Grandma's Hands bruh*

**Al B,** *Bruh I've read a lot of your stuff, but this my brotha' speaks for itself, great job Jeff all my hard work being ya' friend teaching you how to write has paid off*

**Rafiki Webster,** *Through all that, most of us did ok, I thank the mothers who supported and disciplined us, they taught us to respect our elders, community and each other, which gave us our sense of value. The Sunnydale Housing Projects had lifelong generational families, but many young families came to Sunnydale with the goals of eventually buying a home and making the transition to home ownership. The families who stayed and the kids of the Sunnydale Housing Projects became my lifelong friends, even today, though some have passed. We were fortunate enough to have a community center in the projects that provided a meeting place for activities, talent shows, community meetings, and cultural events and most importantly a place which helped us develop pride in our community. We had childhood heroes, the older brothers and sisters in the neighborhood who we would emulate because they were cool, suave, but we knew not to embark on the types and the paths, activities unfortunately some of them were involved in. Though we had our ups and downs in the community, residents that lived in your building or the building across from you were family. Too many on the outside we were no more than a dislocated isolated struggling neighborhood but to those of us who lived in the Sunnydale Public Housing Projects on the inside we were a Prideful Resilient Community"*

*Sherman Phillips, Ann Pitre, Randy Campbell, Kerm Burleson*

# Many Thanks

## From the Writer

*To all who contributed their invaluable time and input to our composition of A Song for Ms Henrietta you deserve a hug for humanity along with a high five, powerful fist bump and a huge pat on the back - words cannot express my sincere appreciation to each of you. Many Thanks is what you deserve.*

*To Sisters of Sunnydale Maxine Hughes who kept discovering our past by combing through arcades of photos blowing up our text line day and night. Thank you Sisters*

*Special Thanks to Ms Vanessa Wagner SF Homerise, and the incredible Ms Sharon Hurt for all her technical support and encouragement.*

*The Tech Staff of the Daly City Westlake Public Library for being supportive and technically sound.*

*Henrieeta Harris was an absolute unsung community legend who lived a remarkable, amazing, inspiring life.*

*Thanks to all of you for joining me on this wonderful journey.*

*Ms Henrietta saw more in her lifetime than most of us could ever imagine or think of.*

*My hope is that her story and the stories of those from our beloved Sunnydale community will serve as an antidote for communities throughout, helping people to take pride in their neighborhoods, and live better fulfilled happier lives.*

*Ms Henrietta was an incredible woman from an incredible community of incredible people.*

*Without reservation let me thank you all with the utmost of respect and appreciation. So grateful am I to have you along on this journey with the Sons of Sunnydale.*

**"Now we no longer have to wait until we see each other during trying times. We can simply turn through the pages of our stories and struggles and reach out to all of our Sunnydale, Sons and Sista's." Randy Campbell**

# About the Author

**DARRO VAN JEFFERSON**, *has been writing since his early days growing up in the Sunnydale Housing Projects.*

*Darro credits his creative inspiration to his mother Victoria and sister Theresa who encouraged him to explore the world outside of his community, refusing to let his creative energy lay dormant and express himself through creative writing.*

*He is a Playwright/Dramatist for his San Francisco based production company DooFunny Studios*

*Some of his early influences were James Baldwin, Nikky Giovanni, Ron Sellers, Sonja Sanchez, Burial Clay, Ed Bullins, Amiri Baraka and Lorraine Hansberry.*

*In 1969, he was introduced to Program Director T R Samuel and Station Manager Leon Del Grande of KALW Radio, the school district radio station and NPR affiliate who offered him the opportunity to produce his stage play The Hat, a inter racial love story about a troubled young man dating outside of his race and venturing outside of his community.*

*The play was shipped out to various drama programs in the school district and also used by remedial learning classroom teachers as a learning instrument for engaging struggling students.*

*That summer Del Grande and Samuel, brought Jefferson on board to write, produce and host various public affairs programs.*

*He further studied under radio personality producer and renowned engineer, Mean Jim Green, on-air celebrities KDIA Bob Jones, KSOL Herman Henry and the legendary founder of KPOO Radio Joe Rudolph, and many others who contributed greatly to Darro's broadcasting approach, technique and development.*

*With sister Theresa in his early broadcasting days who encouraged him to express himself through creative writing.*

*He would stay with KALW for nearly 10 years perfecting his craft before embarking on a professional career in news, sports, music, print media, broadcast journalism and other entities where his writing skills contributed greatly.*

*Darro was further inspired by Jack L Cooper, the first African American radio disc jockey, vaudevillian and who in 2012 was inducted into the National Radio Hall of Fame.*

*Cooper's original materials and on air performances were literally stolen from him right over the airwaves, and he was never given credit for their creation.*

*The culprits were white stage, radio vaudeville performers depicting Black actors changing their names, behavior and the materials in the scripts entirety, case and point Amos N Andy.*

*In 1972, Jefferson teamed with renowned actor Barry Shabaka Henley and Blues Historian Neal Hatten and created the NEA Award winning radio theater drama program Here Comes The Sun that showcased performing local artists, musicians and playwrights.*

*Aspiring young talents, Danny Glover, singer actor Cindy Heron of En Vogue' comedian D Alan Moss, renowned acapella stars Talk of Da Town, up and coming blues songstress Barbara Gainer, playwright Robert Alexander, children's story teller and educator Carolyn Alexander were only a very few artist and theater production companies throughout the Bay Area who performed over the airwaves on Here Comes The Sun.*

*Playwright Arnie Passman brought Cooper's journey back to life in his radio drama production "If We Told'em You Sold'em" that Henley Hatten and Jefferson recorded and produced on KALW Radio.*

*The author of A Song For Ms Henrietta is pleased to inform the reader that there are several original completed stage plays yet to be produced are in the process of being converted to book publications including, Daffodil, Nora's Song, Curves Balls in the Dirt, I Ain't Always Been Blind, A Dolla' in My Pocket, Chocolatiers, The Resuscitator, Burleson, Jill's Journey and Bubbledelious' that we hope to share with you soon.*